(continued from front flap)

perspective and subject matter: with allusions to ancient mythology and folklore, Welty creates an incisive, comic-realistic portrait of the South's oral culture. Though transcending them herself, Welty responds to the usual preoccupations of the South, deftly casting humor and critical insights on the region's unique mythology. Finally, Manning compares Welty to other Southern writers and seeks to define her position among them.

This volume is a demonstration that Eudora Welty does indeed possess a profound and imaginative social vision of the South. It should be of great interest to anyone interested in the life and works of Eudora Welty. The book is also suitable for courses on Southern literature, American literature, Southern culture, or women's studies.

ABOUT THE AUTHOR

CAROL S. MANNING is Assistant Professor of English at Mary Washington College, Fredericksburg, Virginia.

With Ears Opening Like Morning Glories

EUDORA WELTY AND THE LOVE OF STORYTELLING

Carol S. Manning

CONTRIBUTIONS IN WOMEN'S STUDIES, NUMBER 58

Greenwood Press

WESTPORT, CONNECTICUT • LONDON, ENGLAND

Library of Congress Cataloging in Publication Data

Manning, Carol S.
  With ears opening like morning glories.

  (Contributions in women's studies, ISSN 0147-104X;
no. 58)
  Bibliography: p.
  Includes index.
  1. Welty, Eudora, 1909–   —Criticism and inter-
pretation.   2. Southern States in literature.
3. Story-telling—Southern States.   I. Title.
II. Series.
PS3545.E6Z76   1985   813'.52   85-921
ISBN 0-313-24776-5

Library of Congress Catalog Card Number: 85-921
ISBN: 0-313-24776-5
ISSN: 0147-104X

First published in 1985

Greenwood Press
A division of Congressional Information Service, Inc.
88 Post Road West, Westport, Connecticut 06881

Printed in the United States of America

10 9 8 7 6 5 4 3 2 1

Copyright Acknowledgments
The author and the publisher are grateful to the following publishers for generously giv-
ing permission to use extended quotations from copyrighted works of Eudora Welty:
Losing Battles and *The Optimist's Daughter,* copyright © 1970, 1972 by Eudora Welty.
Reprinted by permission of Random House, Inc.
Excerpts from *A Curtain of Green and Other Stories, The Wide Net and Other Stories,
Delta Wedding,* and *The Golden Apples,* copyright © 1941, 1943, 1946, 1949, 1969,
1970, 1974, 1977 by Eudora Welty. Reprinted by permission of Harcourt Brace Jovan-
ovich, Inc., and Russell & Volkening, Inc. as agents for the author.
Excerpts from *The Ponder Heart* and *The Bride of the Innisfallen and Other Stories,*
copyright © 1954, 1955 by Eudora Welty. Reprinted by permission of Harcourt Brace
Jovanovich, Inc., and Russell & Volkening, Inc. as agents for the author.
Photograph of Benvenuto Cellini's Perseus reprinted with permission of Alinari/Art Resource of New York City.

To my parents, Virginia and Farno Clark Manning,
for all the stories they've told

"I was probably a troublesome child with my curiosity, because I asked a lot of questions and I loved to just sit in a room with grown people talking, anyone talking. My mother has told me how I would sit between two people, setting off for a ride in the car, as we used to do on Sunday, and say, 'Now start talking!' My ears would just open like morning glories."

—EUDORA WELTY (Interview with Jean Todd Freeman)

"The truth is, fiction depends for its life on place."

—EUDORA WELTY ("Place in Fiction")

CONTENTS

PREFACE

> But the total tone of the criticism to date is faintly apologetic. One may
> speak of Faulkner's Southern world without fear that he will be charged
> with regionalism, but Welty's stories continue to be discussed as "tran-
> scending locale." Surely her reputation is firmly enough established that
> there is no need to assert the universality of her themes by virtually ig-
> noring the significance of her Southern setting.[1]

In the passage above, from an essay published in 1975, Charles E.
Davis identifies a curious phenomenon in the study of Eudora Welty's
fiction. Despite readers' agreement that her settings and the dialogue
of her characters are unmistakably Southern, despite reviewers' responses to hers as a Southern world, despite Welty's own repeated testimony to the importance of place to fiction, only in the last few years
has her portrayal of the South become a major theme of Welty scholarship. The orthodox view has held that Welty is a versatile writer who
renders Southern dialogue with precision and humor but whose concerns are not regional but universal, her varied fiction speaking not of
history and social conditions but of the lives of individuals. Even reviewers' occasional criticisms of her vision of the South have seldom
stimulated study of her South. On the contrary, to the charge, for example, that her vision is nostalgic and uncritical, her defenders have
often answered by turning the argument aside: her subject, some insist, is not the South and her kinships are not Southern in particular.[2]

This defense may contribute to the apologetic tone which Davis
senses in Welty scholarship, but critics' wariness of the term "regional-

ism'' cannot alone explain the scant attention which, until recently, Welty's South has received. In 1979, in an essay in which he dared to suggest that Welty may have a social vision after all, Albert J. Devlin offered another explanation: "In Welty's case, . . . acute emphasis upon the distinctiveness of each story has obscured from critical view the formation of a larger social vision."[3] The observation is perceptive. For until the popular and critical successes of *Losing Battles* and *The Optimist's Daughter* in the early 1970's, Welty was known chiefly through her short stories, and these were generally treated as little literary gems so varied that—unlike the stories of, say, Peter Taylor or Ernest Hemingway—no sense of a vision of a culture emerged from them. Even when scholars identified themes or motifs linking some of the works, as Robert Penn Warren did in an essay on her first two volumes of short stories, they rarely saw the Southern settings of the works as significant to those links. And with these intriguing and now much-anthologized early stories, long-enduring critical approaches to Welty's fiction were established: favorite topics of study have been the works individually, the author's style and especially her allusions to myth, her interest in the mystery of the inner life, and the universality of her themes. Although these lines of inquiry might be sufficient (though not exhaustive) with regard to the early fiction, they ignore the social and artistic vision which crystallizes with *Delta Wedding*.

And, indeed, since the publications of *Losing Battles* and *The Optimist's Daughter*, the Southernness of Welty's fiction has necessarily won more attention. These two novels draw profusely and imaginatively not only on Southern settings and Southern dialogue but also on familiar concerns and conventions of Southern literature, and they are forcing us to recognize similar concerns and conventions, usually more subtly treated, in much of the preceding fiction as well. While the author's universality is still the dominant theme of Welty scholarship, Devlin and others have turned to the importance of her Southern roots.[4]

In this book, I am interested in what Welty's fiction has to say about a place and a people, but I want to demonstrate that her vision of the South is part and parcel of a broad unifying thread underlying her seemingly disparate works. I was brought to study of her fiction some twelve years ago by a fascination with how extensively and comically she depicts the South's oral culture. Over the last few years, I have come to see her portrayal of the oral culture, which has received little study, as related revealingly to her much-discussed uses of ancient mythology and fairy tales: both are clues that virtually every aspect of Welty's art—content and theme, form and technique—has been shaped by a love affair with storytelling that began for her in childhood. This study will suggest that, first of all, young Eudora Alice's enthusiasm for hearing and reading stories has made Welty herself a storyteller. Whereas much modern fiction seems almost storyless, story and traditional methods of storytelling are central to Welty's art. Second, not only might the love of storytelling explain the author's universality, but also it has provided her a specific subject in, and a particular perspective on, the Southern culture. Her portrayal of a society of talkers and storytellers links her to a tradition of Southern literature, but the nature of her portrayal is distinct in that literature. And, third, through continued pursuit of the love of storytelling Welty has developed a ready familiarity with many traditions of oral and written narrative, from ancient mythology to the Southern literary tradition, and these she draws on freely both for technique and for implication about a place and a people. Though not herself prone to the usual Southern preoccupations with certain themes or issues, Welty has in effect responded to these preoccupations, deftly casting humor and critical insight on the myth of the South.

ACKNOWLEDGMENTS

In the years of preparation of this book, I have had the counsel and encouragement of a number of people. Chief among these is Bob Fullinwider, my husband, who has supported me with patience, faith, and sound advice. I benefited early in work on the study from critiques by Fred Silva, Ed Sklepowich, and especially Joan Schulz, and more recently from critiques generously provided by Virginia Fowler and Thomas Daniel Young.

I am grateful to Mary Washington College for grants which supported final preparation of the manuscript.

ACKNOWLEDGMENTS

NOTE ON CITING WELTY'S WORKS

The following abbreviations are used, and page references to the listed works are given in the text.

BI   *The Bride of the Innisfallen and Other Stories*. Harvest Book. New York: Harcourt Brace Jovanovich, 1955.

CG   *A Curtain of Green and Other Stories*. 1941; rpt. in *Selected Stories of Eudora Welty*. New York: Modern Library, 1954.

DW   *Delta Wedding*. New York: Harcourt, Brace, 1946.

GA   *The Golden Apples*. New York: Harcourt, Brace, 1949.

LB   *Losing Battles*. New York: Random House, 1970.

OWB   *One Writer's Beginnings*. Cambridge, Mass.: Harvard University Press, 1984.

OD   *The Optimist's Daughter*. New York: Random House, 1972.

PH   *The Ponder Heart*. New York: Harcourt, Brace, 1954.

RB   *The Robber Bridegroom*. 1942; rpt. New York: Atheneum, 1963.

WN   *The Wide Net and Other Stories*. 1943; rpt. in *Selected Stories of Eudora Welty*. New York: Modern Library, 1954.

*With Ears Opening
Like Morning
Glories*

1
INTRODUCTION: FROM APPRENTICESHIP TO VISION

In "The Corner Store" (1975), an essay about her childhood, Eudora Welty remembers people she saw and adventures she had as she ran to and from the corner grocery on errands for her mother. Generalizing about this experience, she writes, "Setting out in this world, a child feels so indelible. He only comes to find out later that it's all the others along his way who are making themselves indelible to him." [1] A sensitive comment on the forming of a child's consciousness, the remark also seems suggestive about the making of an artist. Surely Welty's own art has been influenced by all that she has met along her way. A keen observer and listener with a prodigious memory, she has a vast store of things seen and things heard on which she draws. She said as much in an interview when asked the source of the dialogue of her characters: "Once you have heard certain expressions, sentences, you almost never forget them. It's like sending a bucket down the well and it always comes up full. . . . And you listen for the right word, in the present. . . . [W]hat you overhear on a city bus is exactly what your character would say on the page you're writing." [2] In "The Corner Store" itself the author uncovers, perhaps unconsciously, one example of this use of memory. The song she remembers a farmer chanting as he peddled his wares on her street when she was a child is, the reader will find, the original to the chant that Fate Rainey, "the buttermilk man," sings as he hawks his wares in *The Golden Apples* (1949).

Without writing a confessional literature or disguised autobiography, Welty borrows directly from life. That we can trace the actual origins of certain details of her works, however, is not the point. The point is, rather, that most of her works are characterized by an appreciation of the ordinary happenings of everyday life, an appreciation apparently born of a lifelong receptivity to the life around her.

But obviously ordinary life alone does not define her fiction, or the author would not have been called a romantic as well as a realist or have been said to write such varied fiction that it defies generalization. There is a second crucial influence on her fiction, one that might seem to run counter to the first. It is a love of stories and storytelling. Katherine Anne Porter recognized this influence very early in Welty's career, though she could not have foreseen at the time how significant the influence would prove. In her introduction to Welty's first book, Porter wrote, "[A]lways, from the beginning until now, she loved folk tales, fairy tales, old legends, and she likes to listen to the songs and stories of people who live in old communities whose culture is recollected and bequeathed orally."[3] In another essay about her childhood, in interviews, and in *One Writer's Beginnings* (1984), the autobiography about her early years published shortly before her seventy-fifth birthday, Welty has documented this love of storytelling and revealed its birth in her early exposure to oral and written narrative.

In the essay "A Sweet Devouring" (1957), Welty describes the pleasures of her childhood reading as "like those of a Christmas cake, a sweet devouring." As soon as she devoured one book she was ready for another; "selection was no object."[4] In *One Writer's Beginnings*, she recalls that she read through her family's library book by book, shelf by shelf. She devoured encyclopedias, Stoddard's Lectures, the Victrola Book of Opera, Mark Twain, Ring Lardner, and, when she received it for her birthday, a ten-volume set called Our Wonder World. Her favorite volume contained all the traditional children's stories: fairy tales, myths, fables, legends, a history of Joan of Arc, a bite of *Pilgrim's Progress*, a large slice of *Gulliver* (*OWB*, 6–8). In an interview, she describes herself as "a ferocious, voracious reader" who as a child read "lots of fairy tales and all the childhood books" and who continues to read "practically everything."[5] Her eclectic reading in recent years has ranged from the latest children's books to the mysteries of Ross MacDonald and the subtleties of Elizabeth Bowen.

Just as Welty has been, since earliest childhood, registering the life around her, so has she been, since earliest childhood, absorbing all that she reads. Much from her reading has become as indelible to her as the farmer's chant which she heard as a child. In "A Sweet Devouring,'' she recalls the villains and victims of specific childhood books (*Five Little Peppers, The Tales from Maria Edgeworth*, ''the false and true'' Campfire Series) as vividly as if she had read the books the week before. And anyone familiar with even a few of Welty's own stories or with the scholarship on her work is aware that she draws as freely on the stories she has consumed over a lifetime as she does on the life she has absorbed. About her use of mythology in *The Golden Apples* Welty has said, ''I just used [myths] as freely as I would the salt and pepper. They were part of my life, like poetry, and I would take something from Yeats here and something from a myth there.''[6] Without imitating what she has read, Welty dips here and there into her storehouse of memories.

The love of storytelling has given her more than a repertoire of story traditions on which to draw; it has, in the first place, given her the motivation to write. Not always sympathetically, critics distinguish Welty's fiction from that fiction which seems motivated by the authors' personal traumas or by concern with social and political issues. Welty herself insists—and the tone and character of her fiction suggest—that her motivation is a purer interest in storytelling. This motivation grows not only from her voracious love of reading stories but equally from her voracious love of hearing stories. Born in Jackson, Mississippi, in 1909, she grew up in the South where, she has said, ''storytelling is a way of life.''[7] Conversation there ''is of a narrative and dramatic structure and so when you listen to it, you're following a story. You're listening for how something is going to come out and that . . . has something to do with the desire to write later.'' Whereas Northerners ''don't want to hear . . . in the starting-at-the-beginning-going-all-the-way-through style,'' Southerners, Welty says, ''would listen to talk forever.''[8]

In the South that Welty knows, storytelling is a part of everyday life, and its subjects arise from the life of the community. Storytelling is not, however, mere imitation of life. Indeed, its major attraction might be the divergence of the story told *from* everyday life. Oral or written, storytelling appeals to and draws on the imagination. Whereas everyday life may seem dull and shapeless, storytelling brings structure to happenings (''you're following a story''), prunes away some things and emphasizes or exaggerates others to provide drama (''of a narrative and dramatic structure''), creates suspense and promises resolution (''[y]ou're listening for how something is going to come out''). In *One Writer's*

Beginnings, Welty describes her childhood fascination with a neighbor's tale-telling: "What I loved about her stories was that everything happened in *scenes*. I might not catch on to the root of the trouble in all that happened, but my ear told me it was dramatic. Often she said, 'The crisis had come!' " (p. 13).

Welty's fiction combines a realist's sensitivity to everyday life, a storyteller's imagination and pleasure in entertaining, and a story lover's familiarity with many traditions of written and oral narrative. But the combination and its effects vary from one work to the next and, moreover, produce notable differences between her early fiction and her subsequent works. In fact, although they include details from everyday life, many of Welty's early stories may not leave the impression of ordinary experience. A reviewer of her first book, *A Curtain of Green* (1941), thought that only two of its seventeen stories "report states of experience that could be called normal," and Robert Penn Warren has said that her second story collection, *The Wide Net* (1943), immerses us in a special world: "The logic of things here is not quite the logic by which we live, or think we live, our ordinary daylight lives." [9] Despite the justifiable admiration they elicit, Welty's frequently anthologized early stories are, I think, works of apprenticeship. They anticipate in important ways the works that were to follow, but their author had not yet settled on the artistic vision and the focus on the character and ways of a people apparent in the larger body of her fiction.

What she had settled on was a love of storytelling. And though its influence would grow more complex and its effects more varied over the years, this love is as important to her latest novel as to her earliest short story. In this study, I undertake to demonstrate how extensively this love has molded Welty's art and especially how it soon converges with her interest in the ordinary people of her region. This chapter introduces its influences by suggesting that the love of storytelling both explains the variety and novelty of the early fiction and, conversely, is central to the realistic vision and the narrative voice of the subsequent fiction.

Welty's early writing, represented in three books published in rapid succession—*A Curtain of Green* (1941), *The Robber Bridegroom* (1942), and *The Wide Net* (1943)—served her, it seems, as an apprenticeship: an apprenticeship in the art of storytelling. In these works the young author introduced themes and tried out methods that she would expand, contract, refine, remold, or dispense with in the subsequent fiction. She seems to have been energetically learning her craft, stretching herself, experimenting. She varied technique and context in the seventeen stories of *A Curtain of Green*, so much so that, despite their Southern settings and their implications about place, no unifying vision emerges from the whole. The variety is such that, for Robert Penn Warren, "It is almost as if the author had gone at each story as a fresh start in the business of writing fiction," and for Robert Van Gelder, "[I]t is as though there were no brand of one mind upon the stories." [10] Her next collection, *The Wide Net*, containing stories written within roughly a year's time, does give evidence of the "brand of one mind," but though seven of the eight stories are set along the Old Natchez Trace, the volume's unity does not derive from a shared image or theme related to a culture but, as critics regularly note, from a shared dreamlike quality. The legend and romance associated with the Natchez Trace and reflected in several of these stories seem to have inspired the author to experiment with various ways of evoking the suggestiveness of dreams. *The Robber Bridegroom*, also set along the Old Natchez Trace, was a different experiment. Several times longer than any of the early stories, it is recognized as an exuberant mixture of motifs from fairy tales and American folklore, uniquely adapted to a Southern frontier setting.

The young author who as a child had spent hours engrossed in the reading of "fairy tales and all the childhood books" and raptly listening to stories being told was now herself delighting in the act of storytelling. Drawing on her long acquaintance with narrative traditions, she tried her hand at several kinds of stories. She wrote an allegorical story, the sparsely narrated "A Still Moment," in which three driven men whose paths cross coincidentally deep in the wilderness respond individually to the beauty of a white heron; a ghost story, "The Purple Hat," in which a woman allegedly is repeatedly murdered but never dies; and a "Southern Gothic" story, "Clytie," in which an old aristocratic family is seen degenerating within a decaying house. [11] For "Asphodel" she borrowed tempestuous, aristocratic lovers and a destroyed Southern mansion from Southern romance; and, as previous critics have observed, she may have modeled the obsessive storyteller of "Keela, the Outcast Indian Maiden" on the one in "The Rime of the Ancient Mariner." In these or other stories, she alluded to or borrowed from myth, folklore, historical legend, fairy tale, and the folk humor tradition, all simple story traditions she had known and loved since childhood. She cast Mike Fink in *The Robber Bridegroom*, Aaron Burr in "First Love," the naturalist Audubon, the outlaw James Murrell, and the evangelist Lorenzo Dow all in "A Still Moment." About *The Robber Bridegroom* she said shortly before its publication, " 'It is about the Natchez Trace, and planters' beautiful daughters and Indians and bayonets and so on are in it—and a lifetime of fairy-tale reading. Everything in it is something I've liked as long as I can remember and have just now put down.' " In the same interview she remarked that since she had begun to write stories she no longer had time to meet many people, " 'but that [did]n't seem to matter much' " since she could rely on her imagination.[12]

Evidently, in these early works Welty did not set out to mimic life— though that might be included, and certainly, as she has said, the story had to be "true to life"[13]—but to tell a good story. In fact, some of the stories were inspired by stories she had heard others tell. Her very first published story, "Death of a Traveling Salesman," had such an origin. A neighbor in Jackson, Mr. Johnson, told a tale about going to a farmer's house on business and being informed by the farmer's wife that her husband had " 'gone to borry some fire.' " That remark stuck with Welty: "I could not have made up 'He's gone to borry some fire,' but, beginner though I was as a writer, I think now I began truly, for *I knew that for a story when I heard it*" (emphasis added). Similarly, "Keela, the Outcast Indian Maiden" was inspired by a tale about a bizarre incident that someone told her.[14]

Still other stories followed from momentary glimpses of people unlike herself or a few words heard from them. She was not drawing on familiarity but on a curiosity about the world and a spontaneous recognition of the potential of a story in a person or incident. On a day's excursion in the country, she saw such a potential in an old Negro woman who walked slowly but purposely by; "A Worn Path" was the result.[15] Fats Waller came to town and played at a club, and she was so moved by the performance that she "tried to write my idea of the life of the traveling artist and performer," thus creating "Powerhouse."[16] Another story, "Acrobats in the Park,"[17] about a family of circus acrobats, seems a painting, a tableau, as though the people are seen hazily in the distance as they sit under a tree sharing a lunch. For Welty, there was a mystery to such people—where was that old woman going? and why?—and, like a detective, she set out to solve the mystery or, more often, to create a sense of the mystery. People and settings different from those of her comfortable home environment intrigued her; they stirred her imagination and became the stuff of her fiction.

Not only are these characters not of her everyday world; several are in some way abnormal and others have experiences which are novel if not bizarre. Innocent Jenny Lockhart seeks love but receives multiple rapes ("At the Landing"). Joel Mayes, a twelve-year-old deaf mute, awakens one night to find Aaron Burr scheming schemes in his room ("First Love"). Keela, a dwarfish, club-footed Negro man, has been imprisoned by a circus, disguised as an Indian maid, and forced to eat live chickens as a circus stunt ("Keela, the Outcast Indian Maiden"). Still other characters have mental, emotional, and physical abnormalities; or, like Sister of "Why I Live at the P. O." and William Wallace of "The Wide Net," they behave in comically extreme ways.

These stories reflect the author's storytelling imagination, an imagination stirred by things heard and people observed, but an imagination formed from her reading of "all the childhood books" and from her absorption in the dramatic talk-tales of adults. The stories seem designed to entertain an audience, to amuse, surprise, or even shock. Though they treat ordinary human emotions—loneliness, boredom with the routine of life—the specific experience chosen to depict these emotions often seems exaggerated or even extraordinary. In several interviews Welty has recalled that as a teenager she began a story set not in her native South but in faraway Paris with the sentence, "Monsieur Boule inserted a delicate dagger in Mademoiselle's left side and departed with a poised immediacy." She laughs about her youthful attraction to the exotic and her deliberate avoidance of the local and ordinary: "Oh, you know, I was writing about the great world, of which I only knew Jackson, Mississippi." [18] Though in her earliest published stories she generally relies on regional settings, she often is still portraying the exotic in character or action. In fact, in "Flowers for Marjorie" she includes an action reminiscent of that of Monsieur Boule, though now the setting is not faraway Paris but faraway New York City. While his pregnant wife talks calmly to him, Howard suddenly thrusts a kitchen knife into her side and then departs, leaving her sitting at the window, her arm propped casually on its ledge.

Critics have tended to see Welty's use of such extraordinary actions and abnormal characters as reflective of a contemporary interest in the theme of alienation, a theme frequently appearing in twentieth-century fiction as criticism of a modern impersonal world and promoted through creation of a sense of the grotesque. Robert Penn Warren finds this theme recurring in the stories, and Alfred Appel, Jr., generalizes that in portraying "individuals who are alienated and isolated from the world" Welty is "the quintessential modern short story writer." [19] I suspect, however, that this popular modern theme is not a deliberated, personal one for Welty but something else she takes from her voracious reading, for the tone of the stories counteracts the direness of the theme and thus undercuts the theme's seriousness, hinting that the author's own emphasis is elsewhere. Warren has noted that despite the "sad, or violent, or warped" substance of the stories of *A Curtain of Green*, the book is "exhilarating, even gay, as though the author were innocently delighted . . . with . . . the variety of things that stories could be and still be stories." [20] That is, the stories exude the innocent delight a storyteller takes in the act of storytelling. This discrepancy between tone and content is very like that encountered in children's stories such as "Hansel and Gretel" and "Little Red Riding Hood"— and in Welty's own folk–fairy tale *The Robber Bridegroom*. And as with fairy tales, the discrepancy encourages our detachment from the characters, for it discourages suspension of disbelief. Thus, while "Flowers for Marjorie" does concern Howard's mental imbalance caused by his fear and helplessness in the alien big city, Howard's inner life is overshadowed by bizarre actions reported by the author with a tone of exuberance. Rather than being much disturbed by Howard's or other characters' predicaments—most of the characters are, after all, only sketchily depicted—we applaud the author's clever imagination and enjoy the stories as stories, just as we do in reading *The Robber Bridegroom*, which, with its mean stepmother, its talking, severed head hidden in a trunk, its "bandit of the woods" who has a secret identity, and its tongue-in-cheek tone, is an obvious case of storytelling.

And right away, the opening passages of these stories set a mood for storytelling. Whereas the later short stories tend to begin without introductory exposition and with the action already in progress—that is, with the slice-of-life approach common to realism—the early stories typically begin in traditional storybook fashion. The stage is set and the major character simply introduced: "It was December—a bright frozen day in the early morning. Far out in the country there was an old Negro woman with her head tied in a rag, coming along a pine-woods. Her name was Phoenix Jackson" ("A Worn Path," *CG*, 275). With bare facts stated cryptically and enigmatically, Welty's ghost story begins with a suspenseful style characteristic of mystery and detective stories: "It was in a bar, a quiet little hole in the wall. It was four o'clock in the afternoon. Beyond the open door the rain fell, the heavy color of the sea. . . . It was in New Orleans" ("The Purple Hat," *WN*, 141). Other stories open with a fairy tale tone of wonder. Though Welty never uses the phrase "once upon a time"—fiction rules this phrase out, she says, because it would immediately advertise a story as mere pretense[21]—she does evoke "once upon a time" by adopting the simple language and the tone of innocence and amazement a sto-ryteller uses in telling or reading stories to children: "One morning in summertime, when all his sons and daughters were off picking plums and Little Lee Roy was all alone, sitting on the porch and only listen-ing to the screech owls away down in the woods, he had a surprise" ("Keela, the Outcast Indian Maiden," *CG*, 74). This opening is as appropriate to a children's story as is that of *The Robber Bridegroom*, which clearly borrows fairy tale conventions: "It was the close of day when a boat touched Rodney's Landing on the Mississippi River and Clement Musgrove, an innocent planter, with a bag of gold and many presents, disembarked" (p. 1).

In these stories and others, Welty proves her talent as a storyteller. In "Keela," after disarming us with a childlike tone of innocence, she shocks us with the substance of the story. In "The Wide Net" she mystifies us, as a storyteller likes to do, by tingeing the bare facts with allusions that hint at something more. Her reading of mythology, fa-ble, and fairy tale lies behind the more mysterious stories; her famil-iarity with the frontier humor tradition is evident in the concrete and chatty ones. "Petrified Man" magnifies the vulgarity of a beauty shop setting and the shallowness of the characters to the edge of caricature and then ends in the way folk humor tales often end, with the comic triumph of an underdog. Little Billy Boy, after being spanked by a throng of bitter beauty shop women, yells at them as he struts off, " 'If you're so smart, why ain't you rich?' " (*CG*, 55).

The early stories are beautiful examples of storytelling that make provocative use of conventions from a number of narrative traditions, yet even the best of critics has on occasion spoken of them in terms which ill fit their simplicity. (Welty is, one says, making a "frontal attack on the enigma of the universe.''[22]) I do not mean to suggest that these works are superficial or without subtlety. They do indeed intrigue and mystify, and much has been written informatively about meanings lying beneath their surfaces. However, efforts to wring deep meaning from them frequently do injustice to the basic source of their mystery. "Every good story," says Welty, "has mystery—not the puzzle kind, but the mystery of allurement."[23] A fan of detective stories, she has insisted that her story "The Purple Hat," which critics have seen as a mystifying symbolic story, is no more than a playful ghost story; and when told that someone had written an article about the meaning of a mule's face appearing at a window in the story "Death of a Traveling Salesman," she responded, "It meant a mule was looking in the window."[24]

The mystery and novelty of Welty's early stories need not be products of a modern sophisticated, highly symbolic and allusive literary style; they more likely belong to the ancient art of storytelling. Welty's is the mystery of allurement, the storyteller's enticement to the reader. "Whatever happened, it happened in extraordinary times, in a season of dreams, and in Natchez it was the bitterest winter of them all"—thus begins "First Love" (*WN*,3), a story which happens along the Old Natchez Trace during the early nineteenth century, borrows directly from historical legend, and has the soft focus and slow motion of historical romance.

With *Delta Wedding* (1946), her fourth book, a significant development takes place in the author's art. Whereas the early fiction exhibits strong doses of the exceptional and unreal—fantasy in *The Robber Bridegroom*, the abnormal and "the highly spiced"[25] in *A Curtain of Green*, the suggestiveness of dreams in *The Wide Net*—*Delta Wedding* and most of the subsequent works are infused with the quotidian and normal. In this the larger body of her fiction, Welty characterizes concretely the day-to-day lives and special events of some quite ordinary people. And she makes us care for them. Portraying them in depth, she attaches them firmly to time and place, reveals their pasts, leads us to wonder about their futures, and shows us the social and cultural milieus which have formed them. Whereas uppermost in her mind in the early fiction seems to have been the desire to tell a good story, and a variety of types of stories, in the subsequent fiction she seems interested equally in the character and customs of a people.

People scurrying around fiercely but not going anywhere, just getting married, getting home, burying loved ones, working, playing, visiting, fussing, loving, talking, telling tales—this is the world of most of Eudora Welty's fiction. Evidence of this realism of everyday life appears, side by side with the exaggerated and bizarre, in the early fiction as well, and with implications about the Southern culture, but the dominant impression there is of sketchily depicted characters performing parts in delightful, in some cases satirical, well-rounded stories. Apprenticeship works, the early fiction anticipates the later in many ways—all the later features are there, in bits and pieces—but it is with *Delta Wedding* that a vision centered on a culture clearly crystallizes. With *Delta Wedding*, the Southern family and community replace the isolated individual and the abnormal one as Welty's favorite focus.

But Welty does not now ignore the lonely individual and the mentally or physically crippled one. She includes these but treats them differently. In *Delta Wedding*, for example, the retarded child Maureen and her insane mother Virgie Lee move around on the periphery of the action but are not its axle—in contrast to the major role such characters have in the early fiction. Welty presents Maureen and Virgie Lee as only part of the extended Fairchild family. Similarly, in "Kin" (*The Bride of the Innisfallen*, 1955), rather than focusing on Uncle Felix, a paralyzed old man shunted away in a back room of his own house, or on Sister Anne, a lonely old maid without a place of her own, Welty reveals the present and the past of a large, old family and makes her central character Dicey Hastings, a happy, healthy young woman enjoying a rare summer visit down home. Moreover, though a few distraught, alienated characters appear in the later fiction, their suffering generally is not itself the central fact of the relevant works, unfurled through comically grotesque incidents, but instead contributes to a subtle and realistic portrayal of family or community. This contrast is illustrated in the difference between the author's treatment of Clytie in the early story "Clytie" (*CG*) and her treatment of Miss Eckhart in "June Recital" (*GA*).

In the early story, she presents Clytie Farr's isolation and desperate need for love head-on and joltingly. Clytie is seen hurrying like a frantic chicken through the streets of the small town of Farr's Gin, frightened of people yet driven by a need for human contact. At the end of the story, Clytie drowns in a rain barrel, her suicide occurring as she dementedly seeks companionship with her own human face which she sees reflected in the barrel's water. The extremity of her despair is epitomized in the grotesqueness of her death, "her poor ladylike black-stockinged legs up-ended" from the barrel and hanging "apart like a pair of tongs" (*CG*, 178). In the later story, Miss Eckhart, a piano teacher, experiences a comparable acute sense of isolation and desper-ate need for love, but the portrayal of these this time is indirect rather than stark: Miss Eckhart is seen largely through the meandering mem-ories of a former pupil and the uncomprehending eyes of a young boy who spies on her.

Nonetheless, Miss Eckhart's suffering is more moving and mean-ingful than Clytie's, and this despite the absence of any such bizarre image to reflect it as Clytie's death in a rain barrel. For not only is the pretense of realism in "Clytie" belied by the storyteller's tone of mock innocence, but also Clytie's suffering derives from an unusual situa-tion whereas Miss Eckhart's derives from an all-too-recognizable cir-cumstance having both regional and universal relevance. Clytie's al-ienation and helplessness result from the prolonged crippling of her life by her family, an old aristocratic family now vegetating inside their decaying house—an extraordinary family in real life but one not atyp-ical of melodramatic Southern literature of the period (a literature with which Welty the avid reader would have been familiar). With the father now a blind, paralyzed invalid, one brother a whining drunkard, and the other brother dead of a shotgun wound, the overly proud oldest sister Octavia has become the head of the family. To hide the Farrs' declining fortunes, she has tyrannically cut the family off from the community—" 'Go away! Go away! What the devil have you come *here* for?' " (*CG*, 164)—and forced Clytie to assume the role of household servant. No such eccentric behavior accounts for Miss Eck-hart's similar plight. A timid person considered an outsider by the small Southern community to which she has moved, Miss Eckhart does not easily make friends. She is rejected by her neighbors because her cus-toms are not theirs—a rejection commonplace in closely knit commu-nities like Morgana, Mississippi:

Missie Spights said that if Miss Eckhart had allowed herself to be called by her first name, then she would have been like other ladies. Or if Miss Eckhart had belonged to a church that had ever been heard of, then the ladies would have had something to invite her to belong to. . . . Or if she had been mar-ried to anybody at all, just the awfullest man—like Miss Snowdie MacLain, that everybody could feel sorry for. (*GA*, 58)

Near the end of this story, as Miss Eckhart, now a deranged old woman, is led off by the town marshal after she has in her despair attempted to set fire to her former piano studio, she is deliberately ignored by both her once-favorite pupil and a group of neighborhood ladies who meet her on the sidewalk as they return to their homes from an afternoon rook party. Familiar though it is, their casual and self-protective unconcern is more jolting than is Clytie's fantastic drowning in a rain barrel.

Through her treatment of the family and community in the larger body of her fiction, then, Welty has created works which are subtly but significantly revealing about traditional society in general and the South in particular. According to many writers and much Southern fiction, the family is in fact the defining characteristic of the Southern culture; it is, Andrew Lytle has said, "*the* institution of Southern life."[26] Welty vividly characterizes the Southern family through its rituals and conventions—not, however, with the reverence one might suppose due an institution. Her portrayal of the wedding festivities in *Delta Wedding* is a case in point.

From the novel's first pages, the action revolves around the approaching wedding. All the Fairchilds' hectic preparations for and apprehensions about the wedding are portrayed: the cake-baking, the ordering of dresses, the arrival of presents and flowers and guests, the knitting of bridesmaids' mitts, the worries about whether the altar can be built in time and about Troy the overseer as bridegroom, the rehearsal supper and dancing. Hence, the reader anticipates that the wedding itself will be the climactic moment. But surprisingly, Welty passes the ceremony off with a half dozen sentences, chiefly these two: "Then the women put their handkerchiefs to their eyes. Mr. Rondo married Dabney and Troy" (p. 214). This unexpectedly concise treatment of the wedding is surely anticlimactic.

And purposely so. For the real subject of the novel is not the long awaited wedding after all, nor specifically the preparations for it, but the Fairchilds and a way of life. The understated account of the wedding plants ironical implications about society and traditional rituals. Maybe, realistically, the wedding *ought* to be reported briefly and tersely. For aren't the preparations for a wedding (Delta-style, anyway) more time-consuming, more engaging, more nerve-wracking than the event itself? Isn't the wedding in fact anticlimactic? And then there are those few details which Welty does select to represent the occasion. Tongue

in cheek, she epitomizes the wedding through an incident which reputedly is typical of all weddings, the crying of the women. She thereby
suggests that all the apprehensions were for naught, for this wedding,
which set the Fairchilds all aflutter, turned out to be just like any other.
But she does not say "Then the women cried"; her sentence is itself
comic, for by recording only what an observer would see the women
do—"Then the women put their handkerchiefs to their eyes"—she in-
timates that many of the women may not actually cry but that the important thing anyway is a display of emotion. Just as the bride must
wear white and the bridesmaids' mitts must be knitted and the altar
must be garlanded with flowers, so is female emotion a traditional element in the ritual of any successful wedding. The ironic statement gently
mocks the Fairchild women and the larger society for their social for-
mulas.

   It is tempting to explain the greater depth of characterization of people and place in these later works as an unsurprising consequence of
what seems a shift in Welty's primary fictive mode, a shift from the
short story to the novel. Yet Welty insists that she is a short story writer
by nature who writes novels only by accident. The lengths of her works
have "accidentally" grown with her interest in the family and community. Whereas most of her early characters exist to perform their
parts and they stay subservient to their functions, many of her subsequent characters take on lives of their own that influence the very shapes
of the works they appear in. The vitality of the characters of *The Golden
Apples*, for example, spurred the author to change stories begun as un-
related pieces into a series about the same characters as she suddenly
realized that "this story's people were that story's people at a different
time in their lives." And *Losing Battles* (1970), which she had intended as a long short story climaxing with Jack's arrival home, grew
to over 400 pages as the author became "hooked" on the family.[27]
Indeed, the Vaughn clan took on such lives of their own that they
threatened to write *Losing Battles* themselves. Welty recalls,

I could hear someone saying—and I had to cut this out—"What, you never
ate goat?" And someone answering, "Goat! Please don't say you serve *goat*
at this reunion. I wasn't told it was *goat* I was served. I thought—" and so
on. . . . Well, all these things I would just laugh about and think about for
so long and put them in. And then I'd think, that's just plain indulgence. Take
it out! And I'd take it out.[28]

Although the dialogue about eating goat did not get into *Losing Battles*, Welty's comment reveals and reflects a lot about her art. A family's conversation about the food served—or not served—at a family reunion reflects her realism of the ordinary, and the tone of the passage mirrors the tone of her realism. Her families and communities, including a few who appear prominently in the early stories, display an exuberance in living that vibrates through the fiction. The children are in perpetual motion; the adults, indefatigable talkers, enjoy all-day visiting, though they are equally happy when busily preparing for the arrival of company; and community events—be they weddings, funerals, reunions, piano recitals, a trial for murder, a river-dragging for a missing wife, a good-bye send-off for a retarded citizen—are noisy occasions for excited participants (in *Delta Wedding*, such happy worry over whether the shepherdess's crooks for the bridesmaids to carry will arrive in time!). We can say of Welty's characters, as she herself says of Jane Austen's, "Through all the mufflings of time we can feel the charge of their vitality, their happiness in doing, dancing, laughing, in being alive. . . . The clamorous griefs and joys are all giving voice to the tireless relish of life."[29]

In these works, there is no discrepancy between tone and content. The spirit inherent in them is the same as that which Welty describes and expresses in the "Foreword" to *One Time, One Place* (1971), a collection of photographs she took during the Depression: "If I took picture after picture out of simple high spirits and the joy of being alive, . . . I can add that in my subjects I met often with the same high spirits, the same joy. Trouble, even to the point of disaster, has its pale, and these defiant things of the spirit repeatedly go beyond it, joy the same as courage."[30] From *Delta Wedding* on, this attitude toward life pervades the fiction through the characters and the author's tone. That this view of life is present in a number of her early stories but not evident in many others—present, for example, in "A Worn Path," in which an old black woman overcomes obstacles to fulfill her duty to her sick grandson, but not in the previously mentioned "Flowers for Marjorie" and "Clytie," in which the main characters give in to their despair—suggests that, in the early fiction, this vision had not yet fully formed.

Typified by her zest for living and her careful observation of life, Welty's vision matures as both comic and realistic, or comic-realistic. The author has acknowledged the affirmative quality of her fiction,

saying, "it does lie in my nature to praise and to celebrate things."
Yet though she affirms and relishes life, she portrays human flaws and
incongruities of the Southern culture unflinchingly. Comedy's "methods, its boundaries, its *point*, all belong to the familiar," she says.[31]

But what accounts for her movement from the writing of separate,
individually fascinating stories to a unifying vision with the Southern
family and community at its center? The answer might very well lie in
her love of storytelling in general and her attentiveness to her region's
oral tradition in particular. Whereas early in her career the love of storytelling had led her to delight in the act itself of telling a story, eventually it would lead her to the oral culture of her region for subject and
theme. For from *Delta Wedding* to *The Optimist's Daughter* (1972),
Welty's portrayal of the family and community is, in large measure, a
portrayal of a talkative, storytelling people. This development had been
anticipated by a handful of early stories, stories such as "Why I Live
at the P. O.," "Petrified Man," and "Lily Daw and the Three Ladies." Welty has said that "P. O.," a dramatic monologue narrated
by a gregarious post mistress, "grew out of . . . a lifelong listening
to talk on my block where I grew up as a child,"[32] and clearly "Petrified Man," "Lily Daw," *Delta Wedding*, and most of the subsequent fiction are also dependent on the author's lifelong interest in the
South's oral tradition.

The Southern family depicted in *Delta Wedding*, *Losing Battles*, and
"Kin" (*BI*) is a clan of inveterate tellers of family tales. So were Welty's Andrews kin. In *One Writer's Beginnings*, Welty indicates that
her mother, Chestina Andrews Welty, was herself a storyteller. She
entertained young Eudora Alice with tales about Chestina's own childhood in West Virginia; and on summer visits to the Andrews homeplace, while little Eudora listened, captivated, Chestina "talked family" with her mother and five adoring brothers. This family storytelling
would stay with Welty. It was for her a source of knowledge as well
as a source of entertainment. In reconstructing her family's past for
One Writer's Beginnings, she relies heavily on tales her mother told
her. She narrates her Grandfather Andrews's life in considerable detail, but points out that everything she knows of him she had learned
from her mother, for her grandfather had died before she was born.
She would come to know of her grandfather only "what the stories tell
about him" (*OWB*, 53).

Welty's father and her father's family would not directly contribute to her fascination with Southern talk and hence to her portrayal of the oral culture, but they may have done so indirectly. Unlike the Andrewses, the Weltys were not storytellers. At one point in *One Writer's Beginnings*, Welty observes, "My father is not the one who told me this: he never happened to tell us a single family story" (p. 63). And about her family's annual visit to the Welty homeplace in Ohio, immediately following their annual visit to the Andrews home in West Virginia, she remarks, "At the end of the day at Grandpa [Welty's] house, there wasn't much talking and no tales were told, even for the first time" (p. 66). The contrast between the gay, talkative Andrewses and the silent, self-contained Weltys emphasized for Welty the distinctiveness of each, and perhaps intensified her fascination with the former's vocalness. Moreover, as an artist who frequently sets chatty characters off against silent ones, and vice versa, she shows her appreciation of the literary value of the contrast itself.

Like other parts of life that Welty has observed and experienced, and like the literature she has read over a lifetime, the oral culture she has been immersed in since childhood is a resource she draws on for her fiction, but a resource that is more important than most. Just as little Eudora Alice, on summer visits to her mother's home in West Virginia, is charmed and excited by the storytelling of the Andrews family, so in *Delta Wedding* is nine-year-old Laura McRaven, on a summer visit to her mother's home in the Mississippi Delta, charmed and excited by the storytelling of the vivacious Fairchild family. Just as Chestina Andrews Welty and her five brothers "talked family" endlessly every summer when they reunited at the homeplace on a mountain top in West Virginia, so in *Losing Battles* do Beulah Beecham Renfro and her five living brothers "talk family" endlessly during their annual August reunion at the homeplace on a hill top in northeast Mississippi. Furthermore, since the publication of *One Writer's Beginnings* in 1984, it has become evident that Welty has borrowed for her fiction, and especially for *Losing Battles* and *The Optimist's Daughter*, various specific incidents and details not only from her own observations of her family but also from the family stories she was treated to by her mother. Literary sleuths will be tracking these connections for years to come.

Given Welty's long fascination with family storytelling and Southern talk, it is not surprising that the oral culture should come to be

represented prominently in her fiction. What may be surprising is not
the frequency of her portrayal of the oral culture but the complexity
and incisiveness of the resulting portrait. Despite her immersion in the
oral culture, she is able to see it with objectivity. She exploits the realism and inherent comedy of ordinary speech, but not merely for the
picturesqueness of such speech. She exposes the roles the oral tradition plays for the Southerner and hence its importance to the culture.
She shows it to be ritual and mask, diversion, and sustainer of the past.
It is at one and the same time a social art, entertaining the family and
community, and a social menace, boring strangers and serving to vil-
lainize and to exclude persons deemed outsiders. Perhaps most cru-
cially, through it the society makes heroes of ordinary men. In *Delta
Wedding, The Golden Apples, The Ponder Heart* (1954), *Losing Battles, The Optimist's Daughter*, and several separate stories, Welty
characterizes, and undercuts, the Southerner's propensity for romanticizing.

Her revealing comic-realistic portrait of this Southern world is ex-
amined in the next several chapters. Later chapters will show that, in
depicting this world, Welty borrows significantly from the vast acquaintance with narrative traditions which she has acquired through her
long love of storytelling. Underlying her portrayal of the Southern
community and commenting on the society are conventions and motifs
from many narrative traditions, from ancient mythology to the Southern literary tradition itself. It remains for the rest of this chapter to
demonstrate that in moving from apprenticeship to vision the author
does not reject one role or purpose for another. Though she becomes
a comic-realist who chronicles a storytelling people, she never ceases
being an enthusiastic storyteller as well.

In fact, her delight in the imaginative tale and her familiarity with
story traditions are evident outright in two exceptions to the realism of
her later fiction. "Circe" (*BI*) is her clever rewriting, from Circe's point
of view, of one episode of *The Odyssey*; and *The Shoe Bird* (1964),
featuring talking, thinking birds, is a children's book which, according
to Alfred Griffith, makes use of the Henny Penny motif in this genre.[33]
In her comic-realistic works, her storytelling continues but her narrative voice is appropriately more subtle and, moreover, is well suited
to the subject of her comic-realism. As heard in her prose style, this
storytelling voice owes much to her long exposure to the oral tradition
of her region.

Welty's prose style has frequently been described as puzzling, imprecise, dreamy, allusive, and remote.[34] This adjective-laden, impressionistic style (most apparent in some of the stories of *The Wide Net*), however, is by no means her only style. Generally, her prose has qualities of ordinary speech. Welty favors precise, concrete language and creates vivid word pictures. Her preference for the concrete over the abstract is indicated in her criticism of a passage from *Pilgrim at Tinker Creek* by Annie Dillard, which she reviewed for *The New York Times Book Review* (March 24, 1974). In regard to Dillard's philosophizing, which she quoted ('' 'The world has signed a pact with the devil; it had to. . . . The terms are clear: if you want to live, you have to die; you cannot have mountains and creeks without space, and space is a beauty married to a blind man' ''), Welty wrote, "I honestly do not know what she is talking about at such times. The only thing I could swear to is that the writing here leaves something to be desired." But Dillard's imaginative and visual description of an action, the stalking of a muskrat ('' 'Stalking is a pure form of skill, like pitching or playing chess. Rarely is luck involved. I do it right or I do it wrong; the muskrat will tell me, and that right early' ''), earned Welty's praise: "This is admirable writing" (p. 5).

By joining dialogue and simple, precise language with irony and implication in characterization, Welty has fashioned a prose style distinguished by an unusual economy of words packed with meaning, a style she uses frequently in her comic-realistic works. It is illustrated in the sentence below from "Sir Rabbit." One day while out hunting in the woods, Junior Holifield, his wife Mattie Lou, and Blackstone, a Negro hired hand, come across the glamorous, womanizing King MacLain. Junior repeats a question from King and then answers it: '' 'Sighted e'er bird? Just one cuckoo,' Junior said now, with his babymouth drawn down as if he would cry, which meant he was being funny, and so Blackstone . . . hopped on one foot for Junior, but Junior said, 'Be still, Blackstone, no call for you to start cutting up yet' '' (*GA*, 90). Very concisely, Welty has drawn a detailed picture. Feeling threatened by King's charm and legend, Junior tries to gain the upper hand by making King an object of derision. He puts on a great show of wit and nonchalance, and Blackstone responds as he assumes his white boss expects, with an exaggerated act of appreciative, knee-slapping amusement: "*and so* Blackstone . . . hopped on one foot *for* Junior" (emphasis added). But Junior's efforts were for the benefit of his wife; he wanted Mattie Lou to join in his ridicule of the glamorous King, and because she does not, Blackstone's laughter seems obviously exaggerated and Junior thus feels rather ridiculous. Hence, he calls Blackstone down. In one sentence, Welty communicates all this, and she does so using simple language, predominantly monosyllabic nouns and verbs.

This passage demonstrates the conversational nature of Welty's style. Clauses are strung together with "and so," and the narrator's word choice is as informal and colloquial as is Junior Holifield's. Welty tends to use adjectives sparsely, to avoid long series and combinations of modifiers, and to favor concrete nouns and strong, imaginative verbs— a style characteristic of oral tale-telling about comic incidents.[35] In the Weltian world, whether the narrator is a character or an authorial voice, seldom do people run or stroll or walk; instead they trot:

So Mama trots in. . . . I says, "Well, Stella-Rondo had better thank her lucky stars it was her instead of me came trotting in with that very peculiar looking child." ("Why I Live at the P. O.," *CG*, 97)

I hate this little parade of us girls, Nina thought, trotting fiercely in the center of it. ("Moon Lake," *GA*, 101)

Elvie trotted inside. (*Losing Battles*, 327)

And where but in oral tale-telling would we likely meet the splendid verb which appears in the last line of the following excerpt from "Sir Rabbit":

"What you doing here, girl?" Mr. MacLain beat his snowy arms up and down. "Go on! Go on off! Go to Guinea!"
She got up and skedaddled. (*GA*, 97)

The oral nature of Welty's style is demonstrated by syntax as well as by specific word choice. The use of "came" or "went" as a linking verb followed by a present participle, as in the sentence "Jack . . . went leaping into the reunion" (*LB*, 188), is rare in written discourse but common to the oral narration of comic happenings. Welty uses such phrases frequently in telling her stories: "Out there in the country they had undone their knee buckles and came jingling . . . " ("Sir Rabbit," *GA*, 87); "In a little while here came bumping a wagon" (*DW*, 200). Because in oral narration the storytellers aim for a sense of action and immediacy, they often choose the "came jingling" and "went leaping" structures, which give the impression of on-going action. And by postponing the subject through use of an inverted sentence pattern and at the same time creating anticipation with a slow, monosyllabic opening—"*Just then here came Roy*, riding on his billy goat . . . " (*DW*, 68, emphasis added)—Welty the tale-teller seems to be setting the listener up for a surprise.

The oral tradition has shaped Welty's narrative voice extensively and deliciously. In the attitude she sometimes takes toward her characters, the way she describes their actions, the insight she brings to such descriptions, we can recognize a local tale-teller amusingly narrating a tale about a local event or a town character. In "June Recital" (*GA*), the author smoothly and convincingly falls into the tone and style of oral narration when Old Man Moody and Mr. Fatty Bowles appear on the scene. In this story, which combines tragedy with comedy, the portrayal of Moody and Bowles provides a moment of bold comedy that relieves the tension created by the subtle portrayal of Miss Eckhart's unhappiness and isolation and that contrasts with the ironic but sympathetic portrayals of little Loch Morrison and his sister Cassie, through whose eyes much of the action is seen. As Miss Eckhart, now senile and more alone than ever, begins a fire in her former piano studio, town marshal Old Man Moody and Mr. Fatty Bowles arrive at the house on an errand. Peering through a porch window and discovering Miss Eckhart's arson, they turn brave crime-stoppers.

They lifted the screen out, and Mr. Fatty accidentally stepped through it. They inched the sash up with a sound that made them draw high their muck-coated heels. They could go in now: they opened their mouths and guffawed silently. They were so used to showing off, they almost called up Morgana then and there.

Mr. Fatty Bowles started to squeeze himself over the sill into the room, but Old Man Moody was ready for that, pulled him back by the suspenders, and went first. He leap-frogged it. Inside, they both let go a holler.

"Look out! You're caught in the act!" (*GA*, 71)

This portrayal of Old Man Moody and Mr. Fatty Bowles reveals Welty the storyteller at work—and play. The passage has all the marks of oral tale-telling. Its direct focus is actions; its sentence structure is simple; its language concrete, largely monosyllabic, and frequently colloquial; and its verbs in particular strong and colorful. Like many folk humor tales, it makes a recent happening seem absurd by reducing the people involved to stick figures or buffoons.

But the men look foolish not only because of their actions but especially because of the attitudes giving rise to the actions, which are the real point of the tale. Although young Loch Morrison observes the two men from his perch in a tree nearby, it is clearly not his view but Welty's—or a raconteur's—ironic view that is given, for it is an amused storyteller, not little Loch, who would be able to recognize, and likely to exaggerate, the men's feelings of self-importance: "They were so used to showing off, they almost called up Morgana then and there." Neither man wants the other to be more of a hero than is he, as is effectively intimated in the second paragraph quoted. Moreover, their yell " 'Look out! You're caught in the act!' " is a bit of swaggering, an excessive display of authority and courage, given that the villain is obviously weak and disoriented and the danger only the struggling flickerings of an unprofessionally set fire. And in the paragraph which follows those quoted, the storytelling voice is heard in simple diction and images which implicitly ridicule the men's grasping at the heroic and their attempt to prolong and intensify their little adventure. Rather than reporting flatly that the men ran around the table and into the parlor, Welty, the raconteur, adopts language appropriate to a description of the football players they might like to be: they "made a preliminary run around the table to warm up" and then "charged the parlor." Like explorers making their way through a dense jungle, they "trod down the barrier of sparky matting and stomped in"; heavyweights that they imagine themselves, "they boxed at the smoke" but only succeeded in hitting each other. Thus does the storyteller depict, and mock, the men's bravado. Yet while she reduces the men to buffoons for the sake of amusing her audience, they seem real nonetheless. They are local folk known to the tale-teller and to everyone else as "Old Man Moody" and "Mr. Fatty," and their desire to be heroic, to shine for a moment, is very human indeed.

The tone of delight which seems inherent in Welty's fiction and which we have observed previously has, then, still another chord. The characters' "tireless relish of life" is frequently enhanced by a tone suggesting the delight a small-town raconteur takes in regaling an audience with tales about local folk whom she expects the audience to recognize. This storyteller may embroider or color the facts and paint characters with irony, but she nonetheless views the characters with a mixture of love, penetrating insight, and tolerant amusement.

To return for a moment to the contrast between the early stories and the mature fiction, the elements of love and tolerant amusement are what are often missing in Welty's treatment of the early characters. Typically, the narrative voice of the early stories invites the reader to delight in the characters *as characters*, not as breathing, feeling, ordinary human beings. Does Old Mr. Marblehall of the story by that name really lead a secret double life with nearly identical wives and sons at opposite ends of the same town? Or does he only imagine that he does?[36] But does the reader care whether he does or not, except as the ambiguity creates a literary puzzle to solve? In this story, in fact, Welty increases the reader's detachment from the main character by unsubtly employing an omniscient narrator or storyteller who, directly addressing her audience as "you," in effect invites the audience to join her in viewing Mr. Marblehall as a figure in a tale. Unlike the implicit raconteur of the Old Man Moody–Mr. Fatty Bowles passage, who gives the impression of reporting (and making understandable) the actions of a couple of local fellows who are very much a part of a community, this omniscient storyteller seems to be pulling the strings of a puppet:

Old Mr. Marblehall never did anything, never got married until he was sixty. You can see him out taking a walk. Watch and you'll see how preciously old people come to think they are made. . . . They stand long on the corners but more impatiently than anyone, as if they expect traffic to take notice of them, rear up the horses and throw on the brakes, so they can get where they want to go. That's Mr. Marblehall. He has short white bangs, and a bit of snapdragon in his lapel. He walks with a big polished stick, a present. . . . He has on his thick, beautiful, glowing coat—tweed, but he looks as gratified as an animal in its own tingling fur. You see, even in summer he wears it, because he is cold all the time. (*CG*, 179)

But though her stance as storyteller grows more subtle and tolerant as her vision matures, Welty is, early and late, a storyteller. She is also—but late more consistently than early—the poet and historian of a storytelling people. As we shall see in the next several chapters, she has progressively painted a revealing picture of the Southern oral tradition ("a treasure I helped myself to"[37]) and the families and communities who share it. Writing in a conversational style born itself of the region's active oral tradition, Welty proves herself the oral culture's most discriminating admirer and its most incisive critic.

2
WHERE THE HUMAN VOICE IS SELDOM STILL

> And it seemed we were always listening to older people telling stories, their voices blending into the nights, about the Great Flood of '27, or about the owner of the funeral parlor who walked down main street and killed one of the newspaper editors with a pistol, then came back to his funeral parlor and lay down in a coffin and shot himself through the head. Always the stories being told![1]

> Conversation in the South is different. It is not hurled stones, as in New York, but moonshine passed slowly to all who care to lift the bottle. It takes humor and meaning not from one-line jabs but from stories. A story does not have to be long; the merest anecdote will do.[2]

There is no question that an oral culture has thrived in the American South. It has encompassed lively conversations, yarn-swapping, reminiscences of families and old friends, gossip, superstitions, the oratory of politicians and the parables of preachers, and, if interpreted broadly, country music, spirituals, and the blues. Literary and sociological discussions frequently refer to "the conversational arts," literature draws on them, and television has popularized country musicians and Southern storytellers. While the South has no exclusive claim to an oral tradition, nor to the characteristics of this one, it does have an oral culture that has attracted much attention. Southerners are storytellers, people say.

This oral culture is often seen as one explanation for the South's having produced many fine writers. It has, surely, contributed to the large love of storytelling that has made Eudora Welty the writer that

she is. But the oral tradition not only has been important to the creation of a literature but presumably has also been reflected in that literature. For if an active oral tradition has indeed been prevalent in the
South, then many literary portraits of Southern families and communities must include it. Although close examination of the oral tradition
itself is beyond the scope of the present study, the picture of the oral
culture presented by Southern literature is relevant to the study. A
comparison of Welty's treatment of the oral culture with the treatment
of it characteristic of many other writers of this century reveals both
her kinships to others and her individual vision. In certain ways, Welty's portrayal of the oral culture contrasts tellingly with the usual portrayal.

The contrast appears in substance and method and seems to reflect
different motivations behind the portrayals. Welty's portrayal seems an
extension of her broad and acute interest in oral and written storytelling. She portrays a diverse oral culture, and portrays it as fully as she
does her characters. Other writers tend to represent the oral culture more
selectively, their interests apparently being not in the oral tradition per
se but in one or another branch of it or in a theme or characterization
which the use of a certain branch serves. The dominant image in these
more selective portraits is linked to the thematic interest in the past
which many Southern writers have shared since the Civil War. The
first pages of this chapter briefly describe a pattern in portrayal of the
oral culture which developed after the Civil War. This pattern will serve
in the rest of this chapter and in subsequent chapters as a backdrop for
illuminating Welty's distinctive treatment of the oral culture as well as
her relation to other Southern writers.

With writers as different as Charles W. Chesnutt and William Faulkner
having drawn on different aspects of it, the oral culture is reflected
variously in the literature which has come out of the South. Its influence also seems possible, however, in at least two literary patterns.
Internal evidence and scholarly studies suggest that the tall tales and
humorous sketches carefully crafted by the Southwest frontier humorists, such as *Georgia Scenes* (1835) by A. B. Longstreet and *The Flush
Times of Alabama and Mississippi* (1853) by Joseph G. Baldwin, may
have been inspired in part by an actual folk humor tradition current
then and surviving today in the folksy yarn-spinning of many rural
Southerners. In his study of the humor of the Old Southwest, Walter

Blair has linked the written tradition to an oral inspiration, reporting that folk humor tales were popular entertainment among saloon patrons and stagecoach travelers in rural America of the nineteenth century.[3] Like the written tales of the humorists of the Old Southwest, folk humor tales tend to rely on hyberbole, to spoof their major figures, and to be designed primarily to amuse and entertain.[4] But if the humor of the Old Southwest owes something to an oral tradition of conscious comic exaggeration, the second and, for this chapter, more significant literary pattern owes much to an oral tradition of largely unconscious nostalgic exaggeration. This latter pattern emerged after the Civil War and relates to attitudes and concerns which followed that war.

The late nineteenth century was a time when, as Louis D. Rubin, Jr., has said, "the old Confederates were being so assiduously mythologized and the Lost Cause was transformed into a legendary struggle of heroes."[5] James Branch Cabell was a witness to that mythmaking:

They [your elders] spoke . . . as to a paradise in which they had lived once upon a time, and in which there had been no imperfection, but only beauty and chivalry and contentment. They spoke of womanhood, and of the brightness of hope's rainbow, and of the tomb. . . . But above all did they speak of a thin line of heroes who had warred for righteousness' sake in vain, and of four years' intrepid battling. . . . [6]

Just as a native folk humor tradition may have bred a mode of fiction, so does this nostalgic storytelling tradition seem to have done so, for many works of the late nineteenth and early twentieth centuries are themselves such romantic tales about stainless Confederate heroes. But the fiction also began to portray families and communities engaged in nostalgic storytelling, and this motif would become common to the literature of the Southern Renaissance. In fact, storytelling about the past, and not just the Civil War past, probably represents the dominant image of the oral culture in twentieth-century Southern literature. In many works, it is the only kind of storytelling the characters engage in—and the only evidence that these characters have an oral tradition.

As tales told as true about incidents in an individual's or group's past, the oral reminiscences of a family or community would seem naturally to comprise a loose or flexible mode of storytelling.[7] As depicted in Southern fiction, however, oral reminiscences are more cut

to a pattern. For not only do many Southern characters show a propensity for tales about the past; they show a propensity for similar
tales. Their reminiscences exhibit conventions as distinct and recognizable as those of the contrived tall tale—and conventions very different from those of the tall tale. Whereas the tall tale is likely to spoof
its major figure even as it exaggerates his abilities, the reminiscence
depicted in Southern fiction tends to honor or to enlarge its major figure. Whereas the major figure of the former is likely to be a rambunc-
tious, spitting, bragging commoner, the major figure of the latter is
likely to be a member of the aristocratic or plantation South, or someone who aspires to be, for generally it is this group that is shown to
narrate tales of family or community heritage. Typically, such tales
depict the heroics, adventurousness, passions, sacrifices, strong wills,
accomplishments, tragedies, and eccentricities of neighbors and family
members. Often about war—the Civil War, World War I, and, more
recently, World War II—the tales may be tragically heroic or comically romantic and subtly heroic, perhaps depicting deaths of loved ones
who served in the war. But not uncommon are tales about relatives
and neighbors who displayed determination, daring, and courage during the war or self-sacrifice and family devotion through incidents at
this or other times. Tales about mysterious outsiders whose behavior
scandalizes but also titillates are also included. Whatever the content
of the individual tale, the major figure is likely to exhibit a sense of
humor, spiritedness, loyalty, bravery, and daring, or he (she) has a
romantic and tragic obsession. The tale is narrated by an adult who
knew the person personally—a neighbor, an elderly friend, an aunt or
grandparent, a servant.

    While there are naturally exceptions to and modifications on this
pattern, illustrations supporting it abound. They range from ex-slaves'
narrations about the war deaths of heroic, angelic young masters in
Thomas Nelson Page's *In Ole Virginia* stories (1887)[8] to Emily Cutrer's tales about several generations of handsome, charming young
Bolling men in Walker Percy's *The Moviegoer* (1961). The prototype
of the pattern is Jenny Du Pre's tale about her brother Carolina Bayard
Sartoris in William Faulkner's *Sartoris* (1929). According to this tale,
Bayard, a Confederate soldier, was killed when he gallantly but reck-
lessly returned to a Yankee camp to steal anchovies to go with the coffee he and other Confederate cavaliers had previously stolen. The tale,
which Miss Jenny has repeated periodically for fifty years, implicitly

glorifies Bayard for his spirit of fun, his recklessness, and his bravery, qualities which the children who hear the tale feel called upon to emulate. The tale exemplifies purposes very like those of the classic folk epic: while its ostensible purpose is to entertain, it is also a means through which the family preserves tribal history, glorifies a tribal hero, and reinforces approved values.

Even comic and seemingly incidental tales belong to the pattern. In Stark Young's *So Red the Rose* (1934), the Bedford children love Mammy's tale about the time Duncan Bedford as a young boy smashed a hot potato on Mammy's neck when she tried to hug him. As in Page's Negro dialect stories where a slave's fear contrasts humorously with a young master's bravery, the black narrator here is a comic figure, but, again as in Page's stories, her foolishness only serves to enhance the spiritedness and independence of the young hero of the tale. In the same novel, Mrs. McGehee makes a humorous anecdote of her husband's daringly standing up to an unscrupulous Senate colleague, but her husband's nobility and the values the tale teaches are unmistakable to any who hear it. By treating the incident lightly, Mrs. McGehee has decorously protected the modesty of her husband, who is right there when she tells the tale to their nephew.

This pattern in portrayal of family storytelling is not evident in literature which pre-dates the Civil War. Its absence is not remarkable in the period's adventure novels about the Revolutionary War and combat with Indians. In the domestic literature of the period, families are shown to engage in storytelling now and then, but no special emphasis is given to the storytelling, nor is it represented primarily by the reminiscence. The Meriwethers of John Pendleton Kennedy's *Swallow Barn* (1832), a fictionalized social study of a plantation family, are illustrative. If we were to say the Meriwethers have an oral tradition, we would have to say it is a versatile one, including not only conversations and occasional reminiscences but also ghost stories and simple anecdotes about family members and friends. In the chapter actually entitled "Storytelling," the reference is to a local character's stories about Goblin Swamp, such as one about a daredevil ruffian who is repeatedly tricked by the devil—a tale combining the ghost story and Southwest humor modes. And a favorite family tale is about a trick one of the Meriwether slaves played on a family friend, Mr. Chub, the local parson and school teacher. According to the tale, one night after Mr. Chub had become a little drunk and had fallen asleep while smoking, "a

saucy chamber-maid'' had the audacity to set his collar on fire, causing the parson to jump up and begin stripping off his clothes, to the
amusement of several observers.[9] This tale pokes fun at its main character, as do many tales in the folk humor tradition. It seems designed
largely to entertain those who hear and tell (and read) it and to express
affection indirectly for the parson whom it good-naturedly mocks.

The pattern in portrayal of the oral culture which develops after the
Civil War parallels and echoes the much-discussed interest in the past
which grew after that war. Generally, the purpose of the portrayal seems
primarily thematic. In Page's stories, for example, the use of an ex-
slave as narrator of a reminiscence about his former master and the
good old days '' 'fore de war' '' seems a means adopted by the author
to defend the old way of life rather than necessarily a reflection of a
pervasive oral tradition among ex-slaves. Page's short stories express
the author's own nostalgia for a lost past; they are written extensions
of the oral romanticizing of the past then common in the author's society. Similarly, in works of writers after Page, a character's reminiscence frequently serves to promote a theme critical of the present age:
the reminiscence introduces a more attractive period which contrasts
with the materialistic and mechanized present. But some authors of the
Southern Renaissance portray the custom of nostalgic tale-telling in order to comment indirectly upon it. In *Sartoris*, Faulkner employs Miss
Jenny's narrations of the Civil War adventures of her dead brothers not
only to introduce background about the family and thus a context against
which to see present action, but also to represent the family as tellers
of romantic tales about the past. For *Sartoris* is not about the Civil
War but about the makers of myths about that war: "She had told the
story many times . . . and as she grew older the tale itself grew richer
and richer, . . . until what had been a harebrained prank of two heed-
less and reckless boys" is transformed into a tragedy about two valiant
angels.[10] Indeed, though not considered one of Faulkner's best works,
Sartoris is significant as one of the earliest works in which a Southern
author consciously makes examination of the family–community saga
tradition a major concern—and significant too for the comparative
broadness of its portrait of the oral culture, a portrait dominated by the
nostalgic reminiscence but, in this case, including much more.

While Faulkner's fiction is not consistently critical of the romantic
view of olden times, he, Katherine Anne Porter, Walker Percy, and
others have often questioned this view promulgated by some of their

elders and predecessors as writers. Through their characters' sentimental storytelling, they expose the romanticizing of the past. Faulkner does so with Aunt Jenny's storytelling; Porter does so with the older generation's tales about vivacious Aunt Amy in "Old Mortality" (1939); and Percy does so with Aunt Emily's tales about the past in *The Moviegoer*. At one point in *The Moviegoer*, Binx Bolling coldly assesses his aunt's romanticizations. Emily, he concludes, "transfigures everyone. . . . All the stray bits and pieces of the past, all that is feckless and gray about people, she pulls together into an unmistakable visage of the heroic or the craven, the noble or the ignoble."[11] Of special concern to these authors are the effects of such nostalgic storytelling on the listeners. The very subject of some of their works is the younger generation's reactions to the contrast they find between the past as the adults remember it (and, in Binx's case, as it is also portrayed in movies) and the present which they themselves now experience.

Like Faulkner, Porter, and Percy, Stark Young consciously portrays his characters as interested in tales about their pasts, but unlike them, he seems to endorse instead of to question the virtues of the nostalgic tradition. In *So Red the Rose*, though he records only a handful of the McGehees' tales, he has the family talk frequently about the importance of such tales and memories. One character observes that " 'a sacred memory is the most valuable thing one may have, to live by through the years.' " The novel implies that tales about the family's past give those who share them a sense of place, a feeling of belonging to a noble tradition, and values by which to live. Before Edward McGehee leaves home to enlist in the Confederate Army, his father recalls with him a long line of ancestors. The conversation illustrates the family's recognition of the interrelatedness of the past, present, and future. With roots in the past and a sense of belonging to a tradition, the family does not find death as frightening: " 'You know how 'tis in our family. It's something to know that you were loved before you were born.' " Hugh McGehee might add, "and that you will be loved after you are dead," for that is what his conversation with his son is really about. Edward is going off to war, where he may be (and, as it turns out, will be) killed, and his father is sensitive to that possibility: " [O]ur ideas and instincts work upon our memory of these people who have lived before us, and so they take on some clarity of outline. It's not to our credit to think we began today, and it's not to our glory to think we end today. . . . You stick to your blood, son; there's a certain fierceness in blood that can bind you up with a long community of life.' "[12]

Hugh McGehee expresses principles which are implicit in much other Southern literature and often explicit in social theory and literary criticism on the South. Whether the authors accept or reject the highly favorable view of the Old South, their fiction and essays frequently indicate that the Old South had, and the present-day South more so than other regions has, a sense of community with the living and the dead. As the narrator of one Southern novel says, "For it is this, not any fixation on the Civil War, but this feeling of identity with his dead (who are the past) which characterizes and explains the Southerner. . . . " And the Southern oral tradition—"that book of books, . . . that collection transmitted orally from father to son of proverbs and prophesies, legends, laws, traditions of the origins and tales of the wanderings of his own tribe"[13]—is supposed to be both evidence of that community spirit and means of sustaining it. O. B. Emerson has said, "[The oral tradition] is the key to the survival of a sense of the past. Stories are an important part of the Southerner's life—and these stories frequently revolve around events that occurred in the past. . . . "[14] Many writers of the Southern Renaissance have been interested in questions about the past and its relationship to the present or its meaning to present generations, and reminiscences of the extended family have been the authors' major means of casting a glance backward, or of allowing their characters to do so. In Porter's "The Old Order," Grandmother and Aunt Nannie "talked about the past, really— always about the past."[15] Thanks in large measure to their family saga tradition, the characters are rooted rather than rootless.

The pattern of portraying characters as absorbed by their pasts was well established by the time Eudora Welty entered the literary scene. It would become a pattern she would allude to, borrow from, and even parody elements of—much as she would allude to, borrow from, and, in some cases, parody other narrative traditions familiar to her through her voracious reading. But her major source for the portrayal of the oral culture itself has always been the life around her. In her portrayal, the oral culture is not the means to an end but the end itself.

For one thing, the noise! What a commotion comes out of their pages! (Welty, "The Radiance of Jane Austen," p. 3)

Referred to by John Crowe Ransom as possibly "one of the last novels in the tradition of the Old South," [16] *Delta Wedding* is set on a Southern cotton plantation in 1923, an idyllic rural setting in which the only concession to the twentieth century is the family automobile. Ellen Fairchild manages the household and her husband Battle the farming, but they have numerous Negro servants, young and old, to do most of the physical work. Their children, from Bluet, a toddler, to eighteen-year-old Shelley, have the leisure to pursue their interests and pleasures, aware that there is always a servant only as far away as a yell. Like the McGehees of Stark Young's *So Red the Rose*, the Fairchilds are a large, close-knit plantation family proud of their high position in the area and appreciative of family history and family values.

But despite its strong kinship to novels of the Old South tradition, *Delta Wedding* does not have the feel or sound of novels in that vein. Along with other Welty novels, it is distinguished by the author's comic-realistic vision of the South, part and parcel of which is her vision of the South's oral culture. Like the McGehees of *So Red* and the plantation families of a score or more other Southern novels, the Fairchilds of *Delta Wedding* consider visiting, entertaining, and conversation to be among life's special pleasures; however, Welty almost alone actually *shows* conversation to play a prominent role in her characters' lives. Indeed, in comparison to the gregarious Fairchilds, the Mc-Gehees seem almost stoic, and in comparison to the bustling noise of *Delta Wedding*, the echoes of war of *So Red* seem a sacred hymn. Yet the clamor and stir of a Welty work are often little more than many people talking. As Shelley Fairchild observes, the Fairchild house is "a house where, in some room at least, the human voice was never still" (*DW*, 194). And as Eudora Welty observes, "Well, in the South, everybody stays busy talking all the time—they're not sorry for you to overhear their tales. I don't feel that in helping myself [by borrowing from the oral tradition] I ever did anything underhanded. I was *helping out*." [17]

Engaged herself in the art of writing a story, Welty imaginatively and repeatedly portrays her characters in the act of telling stories. For from Leota of "Petrified Man" (*CG*) to the Mount Salus community of *The Optimist's Daughter*, her characters talk and tell tales. Whereas the quiet, sensitive, occasional conversations of Young's McGehees contribute to the portrayal of a cultured and civilized way of life, the animated talking of the Fairchilds comes across as an amusing garrulity. In works more broadly comic, Welty turns the fabled Southern "art of conversation" into the gift of gab. An exhausted listener to the one-sided conversation of Sister of "Why I Live at the P. O." or Edna Earle Ponder of *The Ponder Heart* could have originated the cliché "I couldn't get a word in edge-wise." Having just suffered a week of near-silence, Edna Earle pounces on an unexpected (and unsuspecting) guest to her boarding house and proceeds to talk nonstop for several hours. Her Uncle Daniel is another who takes nourishment from talking. Edna Earle explains, "The sight of a stranger was always meat and drink to him. The stranger don't have to open his mouth. Uncle Daniel is ready to do all the talking" (p. 17).

Not only are Welty's characters perhaps the most loquacious in Southern fiction, but they also tell more tales, and a greater range of tales, than do other characters. While Southern families in fiction often exhibit a propensity for tales about the past, Welty's characters narrate fresh experiences as often as they do distant ones. The Fairchilds repeat frequently a tale about an event which occurred only two weeks earlier; Katie Rainey of "Shower of Gold" (*GA*) and Edna Earle Ponder tell long tales spanning both the recent and the far past; and the extended Vaughn family of *Losing Battles* narrate family history ranging from two hours ago to over a hundred years ago and anticipate that the present day's activities will become another much-cherished tale. Moreover, the subjects of the tales embrace far more than the usual subjects. Uncle Daniel Ponder's favorite tale is not about exciting, heroic, or tragic figures or events. Though very much the gentleman, he enjoys telling "about the time he turned the tables on Grandpa," causing Grandpa to be mistakenly confined in the state mental asylum in place of himself—a comic tale in which innocence triumphs over experience, as happens often in tales of the folk humor tradition. These characters' very evident enjoyment of nostalgic reminiscences is only a part of their general love of narration itself. This passage about the Fairchilds would apply to many of the author's other characters as well: "For all of them told happenings like narrations, chronological and careful, as if the ear of the world listened and wished to know surely" (*DW*, 19). Such is Welty's picture of Southerners.

Just as the storytelling of Welty's characters is not focused chiefly on events from the remote past, neither are the narrators of family tales in her fiction limited to the conventional narrators of such tales in

Southern literature—blacks, fathers, elderly aunts, grandparents, and a few other adults. As the quotation says of the Fairchilds, "all of them" are tale-tellers. Children are both receivers of family stories and active participants in the oral tradition. These young narrators with their enthusiasm and natural styles contribute to the liveliness of Welty's works. On separate occasions in *Delta Wedding*, nine-year-old India, her fourteen-year-old brother Orrin, and their younger brother Roy narrate the story of the family's recent escapade with the Yellow Dog train. Similarly, the Renfro daughters in *Losing Battles* love to "hear tell" and to tell tales themselves. On the day of the family reunion, they follow their big brother Jack on his adventure and run home periodically to "tell their tale" of what has happened. And Cassie Morrison of "June Recital" hurries home from a piano lesson to tell her parents about the scandalous behavior of Mr. Voight, who exposes himself to the pupils behind the back of their teacher. Despite her father's disbelief in her tale, young Cassie understands the art of narration already. She dramatizes her tale—"She stood up at the table and waved her arms"—and she is confident that she is a better storyteller than her friend and sometimes-rival Virgie Rainey: "Virgie told on Mr. Voight too, but she had nobody to believe her. . . . Virgie did not know how to tell anything" (*GA*, 43).

We would expect that, in an actual oral culture, the subjects and moods of narrations would in fact be many and varied. Tales about the distant past and about the heroics or obsessions of family members and neighbors would, at most, be only one strong branch of the oral culture. Moreover, if the society really appreciates conversation and storytelling, children are likely to be tale-tellers as well as listeners, for they will follow the example of the adults around them, often at the encouragement of those adults. Southern writers traditionally have rarely shown the oral culture in this way, many of them being guided in their portrayals of it by themes related to the past rather than by interest in the oral tradition per se. Welty's varied and encompassing portrayal, on the other hand, suggests that she is interested in the oral culture itself, and the manner of her portrayal reflects the comic-realistic vision that guides her.

With few exceptions, she puts the tale, whatever its subject and whoever its speaker, in the natural, conversational language of its speaker or speakers. The chatter of her characters, contributing greatly to the noisy, bustling tone of her works, is a major distinction between her treatment of the oral tradition and its portrayal by many other writers, who display no preference for the oral version of the tale. In "Kin" (*BI*), in *Losing Battles*, in *Delta Wedding*, in other Welty works, the tale-telling blends into the conversation in progress; it is part of visiting and sharing and entertaining. In permitting the characters to tell their tales themselves, Welty is able not only to unfold the personalities of individuals through their speech but also to characterize the society's favorite pastime.

Her method and its effects are very well demonstrated in the following episode, which should also make clear why the domestic plantation world of *Delta Wedding* is not a world of graceful serenity. Nine-year-old India Fairchild narrates, with family guidance, the Fairchilds' favorite story currently, the one about their recent adventure on the railroad trestle as the Yellow Dog train approached. India begs to be allowed to tell the story this time.

> "Let me," cried India. "I can tell it good—make everybody cry."
>
> "All right, India."
>
> "Very simply, now, India," said Ellen calmly. . . .
>
> "It was late in the afternoon!" cried India, joining her hands. She came close to Mr. Rondo and stood in front of him. "Just before the thunderstorm!"
>
> Immediately in Shelley's delicate face Ellen could see reflected, as if she felt a physical blow now, the dark, rather brutal colors of the thunderclouded August landscape. "Simply, India."
>
> "Let her alone, Ellen."
>
> "What we'd been doing was fishing all Sunday morning in Drowning Lake. It was everybody but Papa and Mama. . . . " (pp. 58–59)

The story continues in this vein for three pages with India's family interrupting both to assist and to restrain her in her narration. Being a lively extrovert appreciative of her audience's response, India prolongs her narration with imaginative details, dramatic action, and sound effects:

> "Well, Shelley went down the bank and walked through it. I was singing a song I know. 'I'll measure my love to show you, I'll measure my love to show you—' "
>
> "That's enough of the song," said Dabney tensely.
>
> " '—For we have gained the day!' Then Shelley said, 'Look! Look! The Dog!' and she yelled like a banshee and the Yellow Dog was coming creep-creep down the track. . . . " (p. 59)

India is just now getting warmed up; the climax of her tale, her Uncle George's refusal to jump from the trestle as the train approaches because his niece Maureen's foot is caught under a tie, does not come for another half-page. If the implicit point of the tale is George's heroism, that point all but gets lost in a mass of imaginative but trivial details, dramatic effects, and interruptions, all natural characteristics of real oral tale-telling. In fact, the tale communicates more about the individuals who hear and narrate it than it does about George's heroism or about the group's view of the past. For not only is the dramatic interplay between audience and speaker inherent in oral narration; it also serves to reveal Battle's delighted absorption in the tale and his pride in his daughter's narrative talent (" 'India, you're a sight—you ought to go on the stage' "), his wife Ellen's contrasting attempt to restrain her daughter from showing off and her sensitivity to the discomfort of another daughter during the narration, eighteen-year-old Shelley's embarrassment because of her role in the tale, seventeen-year-old Dabney's enjoyment of the story itself but her older-sister attitude that India's version is too long and rather silly, and India's immense pleasure in her own performance.

The vibrancy of the narration is just what we should expect, given India's age and personality and her responsive audience. On another occasion, her brother Orrin, older and quieter and with a smaller and less enthusiastic audience, manages to tell the same story in one paragraph a half-page long. Welty's own comments about the Southern oral tradition, in an interview with William F. Buckley, Jr., are pertinent here:

Miss Welty: . . . I think the Southerner is a talker by nature, but not only a talker—we are used to an audience. We are used to a listener and that does something to our narrative style, I think. I think you could talk in the Rocky Mountains. You wouldn't get anything back but an echo. . . . Yes, we like to entertain and please, and we also rejoice in response. . . .

Mr. Buckley: . . . Well, the art of communication, therefore, gets practiced in the South, does it because people spend—

Miss Welty: From the cradle.[18]

Nine-year-old India illustrates Welty's remarks perfectly. She has been surrounded by, and practicing, the "art of communication" "from the cradle."

Except for India's copious gestures during her narration, the only definite motion in the scene is verbal. Nonetheless, the scene is full of commotion and vitality; for Welty, the telling of the tale is as significant as the tale itself, being part of the novel's action, comedy, development of character, and portrayal of the society's culture.

Unlike Welty, most other Southern writers who refer to a character's tale-telling generally are as likely to recount or summarize the tale themselves as to show the character engaged in the telling of it. Their approach, like Welty's, is in keeping with their purposes. If the tale's purpose, for author and characters, is to depict a golden past and to pay homage to its values, then it is the content of the tale alone, not the telling of it, that is relevant. Or if instead the tale, though represented as part of a reminiscing tradition, is designed largely to introduce past actions and values against which to measure current ones or to reveal the family's attitude toward its past, then again the oral quality of the tale is beside the point. The author, in any of these cases, may thus choose a rhetorical version of the reminiscence rather than a character's conversational narration.

Welty's distinctive treatment of the tale-telling becomes clearer when her method is juxtaposed to the methods of, say, Faulkner and Porter, who, with Welty, are probably the Southern writers most interested in storytelling by the extended family and community. Faulkner and Porter vary their methods with the type of tale, type of narrator, and purpose of the tale.

Faulkner presents several works as oral narrative, yet the works may not be fully convincing as oral narrative. While the story told by the narrator of "A Rose for Emily" fits exactly the tradition of community tales about local eccentrics, usually members of old families, and while "Two Soldiers" and Jason's section of *The Sound and the Fury* have the conversational styles and sense of immediacy of oral narrative, these examples are nonetheless fairly conventional uses of the first person point of view. In none of them is there a context set or listener provided to legitimatize the narrations as actual speech, the portrayal of someone talking and narrating. And though *The Reivers* (1962), subtitled "A Reminiscence," professes outright to represent oral storytelling, that of a grandfather to his grandson, the novel is not convincing as oral narrative. The vernacular is used (off and on), but there is little evidence that Grandfather is engaged in the telling of a tale to anyone. His few asides seem directed more to the reader of a memoir than to a flesh-and-blood listener; moreover, by the novel's midpoint, the pretense that the narrator is speaking to someone seems to have been forgotten. During the multi-hour (or several-hundred-page) narration, apparently both the speaker and the listener sit passively. There is no sense of motion in the telling, no sense of immediacy. And the novel ends with the last event in the narrated episode; there is no return to the present, no indication of the listener's response to the long story just heard. In this novel, the reader's interest is scarcely in a character's *telling* of a story but very much in the events of the story narrated.

In contrast, when Welty represents a short story or novel as the words of a character-storyteller, as she does several times, the telling of the tale is an event in itself. The work becomes a dramatic monologue, the speaker a garrulous Southerner entertaining herself by narrating a happening. Like Grandfather in *The Reivers*, Edna Earle Ponder of *The Ponder Heart* narrates a tale which seems several hours (and is 156 pages) long, but unlike him, she convinces the reader that she is really talking. As actively involved in her story as is India Fairchild in hers, she acknowledges her listener's presence throughout. She arrives at her narration about her uncle accidentally, through sprightly, one-sided conversation with a new guest at her boarding house: "My Uncle Daniel's just like your uncle, if you've got one—only he has one weakness. He loves society and he gets carried away. If he hears our voices, he'll come right down those stairs, supper ready or no" (p. 7). And as her digressive tale and the book draw to an end, Edna Earle returns completely to the present, still talking with full-speed ahead. Having welcomed the visitor once again, she remembers—with a yell—that it is now time for supper: *"Narciss! Put three on the table!"* (p. 155). Every word of *The Ponder Heart* is clearly oral, and clearly Edna Earle's.

Whereas Grandfather's role as narrator for *The Reivers* seems limited to that of an opening frame for the story itself, the portrayal of storytelling in *Absalom, Absalom!* is crucial to the novel. Here, Faulkner is presenting not one person's nostalgic remembrance of a past incident but at least three different interpretations of the same past, each version being determined by the personality, experience, and knowledge of its narrator. Showing the storytelling as it takes place, in the words of the individual narrators, should assist in individualizing the characters and in making the versions distinct. Faulkner chooses, however, to have an omniscient narrator share the storytelling with the character-narrators. Moreover, the narrations of the characters themselves are not always convincingly oral. The speakers are not consistently cognizant of their listeners, and their language and styles tend to be much the same and much like those of the omniscient narrator. But, then, apparently it is not the role of the narrations in an oral tradition that concerns the author but the complexity and ambiguity of truth reflected in the characters' different interpretations of the same events.

Even in *Sartoris*, where an oral tradition of family storytelling *is* a primary concern, Faulkner summarizes the storytelling as often as he portrays it. Such is true as well of Porter's treatment of a family's storytelling in "Old Mortality." The authors seem to have only incidental or sporadic interest in the oral quality of the tales; their chief interest is in the characters' romantic feelings for the past which motivate the tales. They thus are likely to choose rhetorical accounts which create the essence and the moods, rather than the words, of the tales.

For example, Faulkner chooses the heightened, poetic language of an omniscient narrator to create the mood of Aunt Jenny Du Pre's storytelling about Carolina Bayard Sartoris, Jeb Stuart, and the military maneuver for coffee and anchovies.

> Aunt Jenny, speaking always of Jeb Stuart as Mr. Stuart, told her story.
> It had to do with an April evening, and coffee. Or the lack of it, rather; and Stuart's military family sat in the scented darkness beneath a new moon, talking of ladies and dead pleasures and thinking of home. . . . Thus they sat in the poignance of spring and youth's immemorial sadness, forgetting travail and glory. . . . (pp. 11–12)

Faulkner's presentation of the romantic tale, continuing in this vein, is itself romantic and nostalgic. Had he allowed Aunt Jenny to tell the story in her own conversational words, with natural responses from her audience, he would not have achieved the same sense of the mysterious, faraway, glorious past. Thus, rather than using the language with which Aunt Jenny speaks, he uses language which captures the way she feels about the past.

Porter uses a more objective method but achieves a similar effect. She summarizes much of the family's extensive legend about Uncle

Gabriel and Aunt Amy in a cryptic style—"Uncle Gabriel had waited five years to marry Aunt Amy. She had been ill, her chest was weak; she was engaged twice to other young men and broke off engagements for no reason"[19]—thereby suggesting the family's romantic attitude toward the past through the substance of the total legend. In this case, she need not use the conversational words of a character-narrator, or even identify someone as narrator, since the summarized legend represents a group's view of the past. Porter's rhetorical method is effective for her purposes, enabling her to distinguish between two different generations' attitudes toward their family past, the attitude of the adults who pass on the tales and that of the children who listen. And Cousin Eva, the one member of the older generation whose view of the past does not coincide with that of her generation, does tell her version of the Uncle Gabriel–Aunt Amy story in her own words late in the novella.

It could be argued that the contrast between Faulkner's and Porter's techniques, on the one hand, and Welty's, on the other, results not necessarily from their different purposes but instead from their characters' dissimilar distances from the events narrated. Faulkner's characters Aunt Jenny and Grandfather, for example, are further removed from the pasts they recount than are Welty's India Fairchild and Edna Earle Ponder, and the greater distance might encourage the author to use a more somber and nostalgic approach. This explanation is inadequate, however, for Welty uses the same dramatic mode in presenting tales about the more distant past, even those told nostalgically by adults, and Faulkner frequently speaks of tales of a recent past in his same language. In *Sartoris* he presents Buddy MacCallum's narration of recent World War I experiences this way:

Buddy lay . . . talking in his slow, inarticulate idiom of the war. It was a vague, dreamy sort of tale, without beginning or end and filled with stumbling references to places wretchedly mispronounced—you got the impression of people, creatures without initiative or background or future, caught timelessly in a maze of solitary conflicting preoccupations, like bumping tops, against an imminent but incomprehensible nightmare. (p. 320)

Again, this is Faulkner's language, not Buddy's "inarticulate idiom." This time, it is not the tale itself that is important—we are not even told its details—but its vagueness, mysteriousness, the fact that even to Buddy the events described are not really comprehensible. Faulkner and Porter often use language to capture that impression—the feeling behind the tale.

Welty's differing mode of making the actual telling of the tale a significant part of her action, even when the tale seems a typical nostalgic reminiscence, is well demonstrated in *The Optimist's Daughter*. The many reminiscences about Judge McKelva, well-respected and long-time leader of Mount Salus, Mississippi, told in the days after his death, are all presented in the words of their speakers. Miss Verna Longmeier, the local seamstress, recalls the dances in the past at Clinton McKelva's house: " 'And they'd throw open those doors between these double parlors and the music would strike up! And then—' Miss Verna drew out her arm as though to measure a yard—'then Clinton and I, we'd lead out the dance' " (p. 72). Dr. Woodson recalls a boyhood adventure:

"Clint and me used to take off as shirt-tail lads with both our dogs and be gone all day up in the woods. . . . I've been his doctor for years, hell, we're the same age, but after all this time it hasn't been until now that something made me think about his foot. Clint went swinging on a vine, swinging too wide and too high, and soared off and came down on a piece of tin barefooted. He liked-to bled to death a mile from home!" (p. 74)

Miss Verna's tale about dancing ladies and gentlemen and Dr. Woodson's tale about a daring, adventurous young boy could be typical nostalgic reminiscences depicting a glamorous or heroic past.

However, by presenting the tales in the telling, Welty reveals the exaggeration as it takes place and simultaneously undercuts it, in a number of ways. In the first place, although the narrators' attitudes toward the events they describe are nostalgic, the conversational, everyday language with which they speak prevents the tales from having a poetic or romantic effect. The glamor of the seamstress's tale is undercut further by the unpoetic gesture which she uses in dramatizing her narration (she "drew out her arm as though to measure a yard") and by the reader's doubt that the seamstress would have been the one to lead out the dance with Clint McKelva if in fact such dances did once occur at his house. Miss Verna is "out of her mind" and her words, though tolerated, are not taken seriously by the community. Dr. Woodson's attempt to tell a comically heroic tale about his dear old friend falls flat because of the trivial interrupting remarks of people around him—

"Is this it, Aunt Sis?" Wendell Chisom asked. "Is it the funeral yet?"
"It'll be the funeral when I say so," said Sis.

—and because of some of the precise details that he includes, which, like Miss Verna's gesture, are natural to oral narration but inconsistent with a poetic effect: " 'But there's houses in sight by then. It's where the Self-Serve Car Wash is now.' " Furthermore, though Woodson's tale starts as a typical reminiscence glamorizing a now-dead hero, by the time it ends it is not at all in that tradition, for Woodson indiscreetly includes a circumstance that makes himself, not Clint, a hero. When Clint fell from his swinging vine and cut himself, the doctor (so he remembers) had to carry Clint into town on his back: " 'I reckon I'm to blame for saving Clint's life for him that time!' "

As presented through the actual words and actions of its narrator, then, the nostalgic reminiscence may appear more amusing than sublime, and it may say far more about the personality of the speaker and the process of oral narration than it does about the past or a generation's view of the past. Verna Longmeier, a seamstress who has spent her life working in the back rooms of other people's houses and being taken for granted, has exalted herself through her narration, imagining herself as a glamorous belle. And Dr. Woodson, attempting in his grief to honor the memory of his dear friend as best he can, says spontaneously what comes to his mind. If their tales seem unpolished, it is because Welty depicts lifelike narrators speaking in convincing human speech.

Though Faulkner and Porter and most other Southern writers do not as a general principle portray the oral tradition in its oral form, certain situations do elicit from them an inclination for the tale's oral form. Traditionally, writers have found everyday language, because of its lack of elegance, acceptable for the expression of low passions and descriptions of low subjects but unfit for higher themes and subjects—suitable for comedy but not for tragedy or romance. Just as Shakespeare renders comic scenes involving servants in prose, just as the Southwest frontier humorists use an exaggerated idiom of the plain folk, so do many post–Civil War and twentieth-century Southern writers regularly turn to oral narration when the tales or their narrators are appropriate, in this traditional sense, for comedy. In the short story "The Cracked Looking-Glass," Porter lets Rosaleen, a superstitious Connecticut housewife, narrate fantastic tales about a pet cat that disappeared and then spoke to her in dreams. In *Sartoris*, Faulkner lets Aunt Jenny partially narrate in her own brash way a tale about two little Sartoris boys in long curls doing battle on the school ground to defend their male pride, childhood wars seeming more mock heroic than truly heroic. He also frequently supplies narrators for tale-telling about horse-trading and goat-buying and barn-burning, about tricksters and dupes. In such tales as those told by V. K. Ratliff in *The Hamlet* (1940), there is little nobility or chivalry but much cunning and self-striving and duplicity, activities conventionally thought to be described fittingly in ordinary speech. While Faulkner prefers an elevated style for storytelling about noble, chivalrous ancestors, he may render tales about comic heroes and folk customs in folksy language.

But, like Thomas Nelson Page, he also chooses oral narration for tales about heroism if the narrator's speech is particularly quaint and illiterate, and thus entertaining in itself. Old Man Fall's tale about Colonel John Sartoris's escape from the Yankees is an example: " 'Cunnel was settin' thar in a cheer, his sock feet propped on the po'ch railin,' smokin' this hyer very pipe. Old Louvinia was settin' on the steps, shellin' a bowl of peas fer supper. And a feller was glad to git even peas sometimes, in them days . . . ' " (*Sartoris*, 20). But Fall does not tell a sentimental tale in this quaint language; rather, his tale is appropriate, in the conventional sense, for ordinary speech or dialect. For in his storytelling Fall does not spotlight the heroism of Colonel Sartoris's action (though he is aware of it), but the comedy and cleverness of Colonel's tricking a whole force of Yankee soldiers. The tale recalls the frontier humor tradition, where underdogs outsmart more powerful opponents. However, when the content of Fall's reminiscence changes from this comedy to the heroic tragedy of Sartoris's death, Faulkner suddenly drops Fall as narrator and resumes use of a dreamy rhetoric: "It showed on John Sartoris's brow, the dark shadow of fatality and doom, that night when he sat beneath the candles in the dining room and turned a wine glass in his fingers . . . " (p. 23).

Welty differs from Porter and Faulkner in that she generally puts the tale in the language of the speaker no matter what the nature of the tale or the background of the speaker. Neither India Fairchild, daughter of plantation owner Battle Fairchild, nor Dr. Woodson would be considered one of "the folk." Their language is conversational but not picturesque. In fact, the language of none of her storytellers is as illiterate or quaint as that of Old Man Fall or Page's ex-slave narrators. Nevertheless, the oral-dramatic mode promotes comedy, and Welty uses it for that reason as well as for its realism. About its use for *Losing Battles*, she explains, "The thought, the feeling that is *internal* is *shown* as external. I wanted the whole thing externalized. That was why it was a comedy. Because anything that is done in action and talk is a comedy." [20] Welty achieves some common ingredients of comedy—action, motion, immediacy, dramatic irony—by recording the tales in their natural or original form. There is not only the action which the tale itself recounts but also the immediate action and motion involved in the present retelling of the event, such as in the interplay between India and her audience. Welty depicts the total situation—speaker, audience, place, passers-by—and often increases the possibilities for comedy by having the tales told at times when large numbers of people are gathered together.

Just as frequently, the oral mode causes revelations at once comic and realistic about the process of oral narration itself. One of many possible examples from *Losing Battles* is the passage below from the Beecham family's long and intricate tale about why Jack Renfro had to go to "the pen." According to the story, Jack's plight was precipitated when Curly Stovall, owner of the local general store, confiscated as payment for long-overdue Renfro bills a family heirloom, an old wedding ring, carried by Jack's younger sister. Here is part of the interaction between the narrator, Uncle Percy, and his audience:

"And [Curly] put out his great paw and taken it [the ring]. Of course she right away asks him to please kindly give that back."
"And he wouldn't give it back?" A chorus of cries came, as hilarious as if none of them here had ever heard. "And what excuse did he offer for such behavior?" said Aunt Birdie in sassy tones. (p. 24)

Uncle Percy's listeners have obviously heard the tale before and love it so much that they cannot remain still. They want to help the tale along and join in the fun of the telling. Their questions are not questions to elicit information but simply their contributions to the narration itself. And Welty understands precisely the way they would ask their questions. Playing their role very well, they act as if they are totally surprised by, even aghast at, the events of the tale—" 'And he wouldn't give it back?' a chorus of cries came as hilarious *as if* none of them had ever heard"—although any one of them could tell the tale, and may have previously told it. And Aunt Birdie's question is the type that *requires* the "sassy tones" she gives it. While the quoted passage is inessential in regard to both the actual content of the tale and the portrayal of individual personalities, it represents perfectly one element in tale-telling as practiced by a family of talkers. Here, and elsewhere, Welty's subject includes the nature of an oral tradition.

Welty's fiction is frequently spoken of in terms of sight; she paints scenes and characters with an artist's or photographer's touch, so vividly that we can visualize them. Surely it is equally appropriate to speak of her fiction in terms of sound. But while the dominant mood of her fiction as a whole is comic and the dominant sound that of the human voice, the silences and the potentially tragic are not to be denied. Just as her comic scenes usually vibrate with talk and action (or talk-as-action), her noncomic ones exude silence. The scenes of the first 130 pages of *The Optimist's Daughter*, in which everything is "externalized" in talk, are largely comic. But the comical shifts to the solemn as the action shifts to the thoughts and feelings of Laurel. When the talking stops, temporarily, so does the humor.

Significantly, the talking and the silences play off one another, emphasizing one another through contrast. In stories about lonely or alienated persons, the typical major character seems to live in a silent world alone, and this silence and his or her loneliness are magnified through indirect contrast with the vocalness of characters in other stories and sometimes by direct contrast with the talking of people who share a sense of community in the immediate story. "No Place for You My Love" (*BI*) illustrates the latter. Here, the alienation of two strangers, Northerners sharing a car ride yet hardly speaking, is set against the easy and natural conversation of rural Louisianans whom they meet along the way: the teasing, joking, jostling crowd crossing a river on a ferry; the people at a backwoods cafe playing cards, playing music, playing the slot machine, laughing and talking. In the novels, the contrast between sound and silence is most pronounced in *The Optimist's Daughter* but occurs elsewhere as well. Much of the time in *Delta Wedding* we see people scurrying about, going, doing, talking, visiting; but this is only the external side of life on the plantation, the community side uniting the Fairchilds as one. The other side is the private life of the individual, the thoughts and feelings which separate Dabney from Shelley, Laura from India, and which show Ellen sensitive to all. Much of this side we get obliquely, externalized through the talk and action, but sometimes the thoughts are given directly. Even in *Losing Battles* the riot of human voices is finally stilled, at bedtime, and we hear one voice alone (young Vaughn's), not the community voice; we are shown one person's thoughts. We need the individual voices in order to see so well the community voice, and vice versa.

The silences, the inner lives of the characters, have been written about many times before. It is time we gave ear to the preponderance of sounds.

3
PLACE AND THE CONVERSATIONAL ARTS

> The arts of the section . . . were the eighteenth-century social arts of
> dress, conversation, manners, the table, the hunt, politics, oratory, the
> pulpit. These were arts of living and not arts of escape: they were also
> community arts, in which every class of society could participate. . . .
> The South took life easy, which is itself a tolerably comprehensive art.[1]

In the image of the South advanced by the Agrarians of *I'll Take My
Stand* (1930), the oral tradition is a social art organic to a leisurely,
humanistic way of life in which community and family are highly valued. This favorable interpretation of the Southern culture has had many
supporters. In interviews, Eudora Welty herself has spoken admiringly
of a Southern sense of community and has linked the region's narrative tradition to it. "Southerners," she said in 1965, "tend to live in
one place, where they can see whole lives unfold around them. It gives
them a natural sense of the narrative . . . a form of the story comes
readily to hand."[2] And in her little-known short story "Kin" *(BI)*,
this positive image of a relatively stable South appears in a convincing
and delightful portrait.

In "Kin," Dicey Hastings has returned from "up North" to her
childhood hometown in Mississippi for a visit with her double first cousin
Kate and her Aunt Ethel, Kate's mother. Life in this small town is
slow-paced, everybody growing "some of the best of everybody else's
flowers" and living "as if they had never heard of anywhere else, even
Jackson" *(BI,* 114). Kate has easily taken off from a job at the bank
for the duration of her cousin's stay. The story opens on a bright sum-

mer morning as Dicey, Kate, and Aunt Ethel visit together in Aunt Ethel's bedroom. Aunt Ethel, an invalid, is propped up on pillows reading aloud, in spurts, a letter from a distant relative known as Sister Anne. The two younger women giggle and talk and move about, one infected with a case of "company excitement" and the other with a case of "trip excitement." For the first twelve pages of the story, mere visiting takes place. The women are shown enjoying one another's company, catching up on family news, and laughingly recalling events of the past. Their conversation, initiated by the letter from Sister Anne, who is presently staying with Uncle Felix out in the country at the old family homeplace, is undeniably Southern in its animation, exaggerations, dramatic tonal emphases, and idioms.

"She'll be coming to you next if you don't hush about her," said Kate [to her mother]. . . .
"But who is she, pure and simple?" I said.
"You'd just better not let her *in*," said Aunt Ethel to Kate. "That's what. Sister Anne Fry, dear heart. Declares she's wild to lay eyes on you. I *should* have shown you the letter." (p. 115)

The women relate several old family stories, including one about Sister Anne falling in the well and another about Uncle Felix as a "born speller" whom Aunt Ethel managed once to spell down with the word "knick-knack." Then Aunt Ethel decides the girls must go right out to see Sister Anne and Uncle Felix (" 'Oh, curses!' " cries Kate) and take them some green tomato pickle and the freshly baked Lady Baltimore cake. " 'Poor Sister Anne can't cook and loves to eat. She can *eat* awhile,' " Ethel says (p. 121).

The extended conversation of the three women contributes to the portrayal of a much-enjoyed leisurely existence in which visiting and family are valued and conversation is a pleasurable social art. Indeed, "Kin" would seem to support those who have concluded that Welty's vision of the South is charming but regrettably uncritical.[3] But this scene represents only part of Welty's picture of an unrushed society and its oral culture. In her fiction as a whole, this favorable image is balanced by implications to the contrary.

For many of Welty's characters, life in the country or a small town is not a graceful, leisurely existence; rather, life there is dull, changeless, and often lonely, and the so-called art of conversation is one of the few means of entertainment. "Kin" itself offers a double view of the society. In the second half of the story, when the scene shifts to Mingo, the old family homeplace way off in the country, boredom and loneliness appear as incentives for the Southerner's inclination to talk, linger, and visit. The country folk who have gathered at Mingo from miles around to have their pictures taken by an itinerant photographer welcome this break in their usual isolated existence. (" 'My little girl says she'd rather have come on this trip than gone to the zoo,' " p. 130.) Everyone arrives early and stays all day, sitting and talking. (" 'I believe Old Hodge's mules done had an attack of the wanderlust. Passed through my place Tuesday headed East, and now you seen 'em in Goshen,' " pp. 128–29.) And Sister Anne, one of Welty's best talkers and most vivid characters ever, has allowed the photographer to set up his one-day shop in the front parlor because she is lonely and needs the company: " 'I hadn't seen a living person in fourteen days. . . . I made him open and show me his book. It was chock-full. All kinds of names of all kinds of people from all over everywhere. . . . I flatter myself I *don't get* lonesome, but I felt sorry for *him*' " (p. 133).

Welty had first hinted that the rural environment promotes a lonely existence in a few of her early stories. In "The Wide Net," the loneliness of rural life for women is taken for granted:

"How come Hazel to go and do that way?" asked Virgil as they started out. William Wallace said, "I reckon she got lonesome."
"That don't argue—drown herself for getting lonesome. My mother gets lonesome." (*WN*, 36)

Young women confined to country homes all day—Ruby Fisher ("A Piece of News"), Livvie ("Livvie"), Jenny Lockhart ("At the Landing")—are susceptible to the attractions of anything that interrupts the monotony of the day, such as the unexpected appearance of a wild young man, a traveling salesman, a saleswoman and her cosmetics, or a newspaper story that inspires romantic and violent fantasies. Life in the unprogressive small town can be equally dull and lonely since not much happens, or the same things happen over and over. But here, as in a large family, one at least can find someone to talk to, and talking becomes a necessary means of amusement. In several short stories, the post office is the place people go to spread or receive news, to see people and to be seen, to escape the humdrum of home, to hope for the thrill of a letter. In "At the Landing," when Jenny goes there to announce her grandfather's death, the postmaster is narrating a long tale about the last big flood to an audience of seven idling men.

In fact, just as the silence of characters in some of Welty's early stories is a consequence of a lonely rural existence, so is the loquaciousness of others fostered by a boring, seemingly changeless existence. In the early stories, the oral tradition rarely appears except in this role. The neighbors who watch from windows and gossip about Mrs. Larkin in "A Curtain of Green" have few other ways to entertain themselves, and little else to do. The three ladies of "Lily Daw and the Three Ladies" occupy themselves by being first-rate busybodies who try to manipulate other people's lives, but their everyday staple in the battle against the uneventfulness of life is their talking. The supreme examples of early characters who stay busy talking, however, are Sister of "Why I Live at the P. O." and Leota of "Petrified Man." Leota, a beautician, seeks out whatever diversions are available—she and her friend Mrs. Pike visit the traveling freak show and fortune tellers whenever these come to town—but she survives the shallowness of her culture and the tedium of her work mainly by talking a blue streak every day. Similarly, Sister of "P. O.," a postmistress, filled her days when she lived at home with nonstop fussing, gossiping, and tale-telling, but now that she has taken up residence in the post office, her nights are no doubt lonely and her days dull in between the arrival of customers who, all ears to hear her tale about her recent breakup with her family, come in under the pretense of needing stamps. Speaking to such a patron, Sister unintentionally reveals that she regrets missing the enticing tales she imagines being told at home: "And that's the last I've laid eyes on any of my family or my family laid eyes on me for five solid days and nights. Stella-Rondo may be telling the most horrible tales in the world about Mr. Whitaker, but I haven't heard them." Even as she insists that she loves living alone in the post office, she exposes her loneliness: "Of course, there's not much mail. My family are naturally the main people in China Grove, and if they prefer to vanish from the face of the earth, for all the mail they get or all the mail they write, why, I'm not going to open my mouth. . . . I want the world to know I'm happy" (*CG*, 109–10).

While life in Midwestern small towns and on Great Plains farms has frequently been depicted as static and boring, the same suggestion about life in the small town and rural areas of the South is less common, though not exceptional. Rarely, however, has the Southern writer linked the oral tradition to this monotony of life. Flannery O'Connor and Faulkner seem to do so in a few works; Grace King does so briefly in the introduction to *Balcony Stories* (1892); and Edith Summers Kelley does so in *Weeds* (1923) through the talking and visiting of poor, hard-working, tobacco-farming families of Kentucky: "Bill dearly loved to rest and visit. They were his favorite pastimes and indeed about the only ones that the circumstances of his life offered to him."[4] By dem-onstrating that the sense of community may be an outgrowth of the limitations of the environment, these works add a realistic dimension to the conventional portrait of the Southern oral tradition. This dimen-sion in Welty's fiction appears both more frequently and with more far-reaching implications, however. For Welty applies it to the story-telling and conversations not just of the "folk," as do Faulkner, O'Connor, and Kelley; or of New Orleans women made idle by the climate, as does King; but to that of all social levels, including the plantation owners and community leaders, whose conversational cus-toms have traditionally been represented as an outgrowth not of bore-dom but of a love of the past and an enviable slow-paced life permit-ting the cultivation of "the social exchanges which reveal and develop sensibility in human affairs."[5]

The Ponder Heart makes comically explicit Welty's earlier impli-cations about the oral tradition in the rural environment, and this time the compulsive talkers are products of the plantation South. Although "[i]t took Grandpa years to catch on it was lonesome" living way out in the country away from everybody (p. 44), his son Daniel has al-ways found the country dull. Uncle Daniel prefers his niece's boarding house in town to the family plantation because in town he has "a little better audience" for his tales (p. 48) and "a world more to see and talk about here" (p. 66). His niece Edna Earle asserts, "There's something I think's better to have than love, and if you want me to, I'll tell you what it is—that's company" (p. 56). Edna Earle hypoth-esizes that Uncle Daniel's young wife Bonnie Dee ran away to Mem-phis because she found living on the plantation boring: "She'd come up from the country—and before she knew it, she was right back in the country. . . . She was away out yonder on Ponder Hill and noth-ing to do and nothing to play with in sight but the Negroes' dogs and Peppers' cats and one little frizzly hen" (pp. 48–49). In Memphis, Bonnie Dee's sisters entertain themselves with shopping, movies, and sight-seeing. In the small town, as Edna Earle and her uncle demonstrate, one's entertainment is in keeping company and talking.

The suggestion that a static existence may be one impetus for the oral tradition parallels another less-than-reverent revelation emerging from Welty's portrayal of the Southern community and its oral culture. Her fiction shows that constant exposure to the "full circle of life" which the small community offers does not always encourage the amiable conversations, loving reminiscences, and amusing anecdotes implicit in the conventional reference to the oral tradition as a "community *art*" or "conversational *arts*." Neither Sister's spiteful narrative about her breakup with her family in "Why I Live at the P. O." nor Leota's petty and needling comments to her customer in "Petrified Man" reflect favorably on the oral tradition or the Southerner's interest in neighbors. Moreover, Welty acknowledges that day-to-day events and memories do not furnish the small-town citizen with very bountiful or always satisfactory materials for conversation. How is this scarcity of subjects overcome? For many people, the problem never seems to arise, for they simply repeat the same stories over and over again. Just as the Fairchilds of *Delta Wedding* repeat the Yellow Dog train tale frequently, so does Uncle Daniel Ponder retell the story of his runaway wife every night at the supper table in the boarding house. But another answer is also possible. It is implicit throughout *The Golden Apples*: a little imagination will go a long way in converting local happenings into engaging tales.

From the beginning to the end of *The Golden Apples*, Morgana, Mississippi, reeks with stagnancy. Nothing reveals the limitations of small-town life better than to see people, usually young people, riding back and forth up and down the town's one major street, hoping to be seen and to see somebody exciting.[6] The motives for Ran MacLain's recurring trips on Morgana's main street in "The Whole World Knows" are complicated by the frustration he feels because of his separation from his wife, but the trips themselves are common local pastimes: "I got in my car and drove up the street, turned around at the foot of Jinny's driveway (yonder went Woody) and drove down again. I turned around in our old driveway, where Miss Francine had the sprinkler running, and made the same trip. *The thing everybody does every day*, except not by themselves" (*GA*, 139, emphasis added). Ran picks up Maideen Sumrall, and they drive "idling along, up and down a few times more,'' Maideen exchanging waves repeatedly with the same persons standing in doorways or riding in other cars.

As they ride, Maideen recounts to Ran all that she has seen and heard while clerking in the Feed and Seed store that day. She may do what many other Morganans do in order to make interesting tales of observed experiences. With just a small twist, a half-unconscious twist, they add a little zing to the mundane and they make more spicy the unusual. Eagerly embracing Ran and Jinny's marital trouble as a relief from Morgana's wearing stability, the townspeople feed on this tasty crumb and mold it into a sensational tale to swap with the neighbors:

He walked out on her and took his clothes down to the other end of the street. Now everybody's waiting to see how soon he'll go back. They say Jinny MacLain invites Woody out there to eat, a year younger than she is, remember when they were born. Invites, under her mama's nose. Sure, it's Woodrow Spights she invites. . . . They don't say when it started, can anybody tell? At the Circle, at Miss Francine's, at Sunday school. . . . [Ran] won't divorce Jinny but he'll do something bad. Maybe kill them all. They say Jinny's not scared of that. Maybe she drinks and hides the bottle, you know her father's side. And just as prissy as ever on the street. (*GA*, 144)

This narration begins with repetition of common gossip—"they say" this, "they say" that. But as twists and exaggerations creep in, the tale becomes a melodramatic fantasy about a triangular love affair which forecasts a murdering husband and a drunken wife.

Though a few Morganans boldly seek and create their own excitement, the standard escape from the town's uneventfulness is through exchanging such imaginative and titillating tales. *The Golden Apples* opens with Katie Rainey's recital of the legends about Ran's unconventional father, King MacLain, a habitual wanderer from home. As she sits all day at her roadside market, Katie passes the time—as do Leota and Sister of the early stories—by talking to anyone who will stop and listen. Katie's interest in King is spurred because he is unpredictable and outrageous while her own husband "ain't got a surprise in him, and proud of it" (p. 6). That her chatty, colorful tales about King make the time pass more pleasantly for her is suggested not only by their gossipy nature but also by the barrenness and solitude of her life years later when she no longer operates the roadside stand and hence no longer has anyone to delay with a yarn. In the last story of *The Golden Apples*, Katie is seen, before her death, as an old woman alone and lonely, standing in her front yard where she used to have the produce stand, now only watching the world go by as she waits silently for her daughter to get home from work. Passing by, old countryfolk stare at her, teenagers "giggle at her," and "small children and Negroes . . . [take] her for granted like the lady on the old Dutch cleanser can" (p. 204).

An aristocrat by local standards, the dazzling son of an old and once powerful family, King MacLain has become the town's hero, the chief subject of community tales. Though he is not dead, his perpetual absence from Morgana lends him a romantic aura not unlike that of the typical dead hero of reminiscence in other Southern fiction; and in their tale-telling and daydreams the people embellish his real exploits and imagine exploits he might have. "Everybody to their own visioning," says Katie in "Shower of Gold" (p. 10). King has escaped the confines of Morgana's sameness, as so many other Morganans wish they could but do not dare, and thus has become a legend in his own time.

As one who remained aloof from Morgana's customs and whose daily life was something of a mystery and curiosity, Miss Eckhart too was a likely subject for local tale-telling. Yet the twists the townsfolk give their tales about this unpopular and uncommunicative piano teacher after she moves away are different.

Then stories began to be told of what Miss Eckhart had really done to her old mother. People said the old mother had been in pain for years, and nobody was told. What kind of pain they did not say. But they said that during the war, when Miss Eckhart lost pupils and they did not have much to eat, she would give her mother paregoric to make sure she slept all night and not wake the street with noise or complaint, for fear still more pupils would be taken away. Some people said Miss Eckhart killed her mother with opium. ("June Recital," *GA*, 57)

Through the tale-telling, the piano teacher is changed from a nervous, lonely figure into a secretive, heartless witch. Whereas Morgana makes a hero of the handsome King of the old, established MacLain family, it makes a villain of "the foreigner" Miss Eckhart.

With many of the gossipy tales of *The Golden Apples*, Welty departs from her standard method for depicting the tale-telling (discussed in Chapter 2). The narrations about Ran and Jinny and Miss Eckhart are not presented as the words of an identified speaker. And no quotation marks are used, suggesting that the tales this time are not necessarily in their original, oral form. Nonetheless, in the tale about Ran and Jinny, the language, sentence structure, the use of present tense, and the repetitions indicate an oral account. This narration is one representative tale among many told about the couple, while the passage about Miss Eckhart is a summation of many tales told about her. But both approaches capture the essence of gossipy tales. The repetition of the phrase "they say" in the one and of "people said" in the other testifies to the passing of rumors from one person to another, with exaggerations no doubt occurring with each exchange. The fact that no speaker is identified contributes to the characterization of the passages as rumor and gossip, the origins of which are seldom traceable to any one person. Rather than the personality of an individual, the narrations reflect the personality of the community, Morgana, itself a character in the book.

Welty thus discloses that a significant part of the much-lauded Southern oral tradition is the gossipy enlarging of people and events to add spice to a sometimes monotonous existence. In the countryside and small town, other means of entertainment are scarce. Welty herself said as much in an interview while discussing her short story "Why I Live at the P. O.": "I was trying to write about the way people who live away off from nowhere have to amuse themselves by dramatizing every situation that comes along by exaggerating it—'telling it.' . . . It's just the way they keep life interesting—they make an experience out of the ordinary."[7]

This "making an experience out of the ordinary" is endemic to life in rural areas and occurs in actions as well as in words. It lies behind the comically extreme actions of certain of Welty's early characters. Sister of "Why I Live at the P. O." is not "a terrifying case of dementia praecox" or an example of R. D. Laing's " 'unembodied self' "[8] but a comically exaggerated version of a rural Southerner who unconsciously dramatizes every situation that comes along. On a hot July 4, in the very small town of China Grove, Sister's ridiculously extended spat with her family is a family diversion (as her tale about it is a community diversion), and her overly dramatic gesture which climaxes the spat is another: she stomps out of the house with all her belongings and moves into the post office. When there is no company on hand, no murder trial (*The Ponder Heart*) or freak show ("Petrified Man") to take in, one may have to make one's own entertainment. That's exactly what the three women of "Lily Daw" are unconsciously doing by taking it upon themselves to send the simple-minded Lily to an insane asylum—and then again by opting to get her married instead. In "The Wide Net," William Wallace Jamieson amuses himself with a night out with the boys and "a carnival at Carthage," and when he arrives home the next morning and finds his wife missing, he gets a chance for another diversion. Although he does not seriously believe that Hazel has drowned herself (though he will argue that she has), he calls on all the males in the hollow to join him in a river-dragging, and with gusto they turn this "sad" occasion into a game and a celebration of life. It gives them something to do, a reason to be together, another chance to play. Virgil tells William Wallace, " 'You're feeling as good as you felt last night' " (WN, 59). William Wallace has turned an ordinary thing, trouble between himself and his wife, into a happening—just as his wife Hazel, left alone and bored at home, had done in the first place by pretending to drown herself.

But words are the most common and handiest means of keeping life interesting. And from Sister of "P.O." to the Beechams and Renfros of *Losing Battles*, Welty's characters "make experiences out of the ordinary" with talk and tales, thus entertaining themselves and the reader.

Several unorthodox implications about the oral culture emerge even as Welty shows the oral tradition fulfilling orthodox purposes for her characters. Many of the characters, surrounded by talk since birth, consider conversation to be a natural and desirable part of life and tale-telling to be second only to a good meal as the best treat to offer guests. They cultivate the oral tradition as social amenity. Moreover, some of their tales fulfill two or more of the usual purposes of family reminiscences as depicted in the Southern literary tradition: besides entertaining, they serve to honor ancestors, to please the descendants, and to pass on local history and family values. However, though these characters hold a conventional view of the "conversational arts," Welty does not. As we'll see here, she draws a complex portrait of the family's attitudes toward the past, distinguishing between the attitudes not only of generations but of individuals. And as we'll see later, she achieves incisive revelations which challenge the effectiveness of the oral tradition as a cultural amenity.

The Fairchilds of Shellmound plantation know and love stories of the family's past. George Fairchild, for example, "evidently felt that old stories, family stories, Mississippi stories, were the same as very holy or very passionate" (*DW*, 191). The Fairchilds tell tales about uncles killed in war, a grandfather killed in a duel, a grandmother who, after a cyclone, insisted on having her lace curtains retrieved from the tree tops. Thus this family, like other plantation families in Southern literature, maintains a unity with the past through its saga tradition.

The tale told by Aunt Jim Allen and Aunt Primrose about their Aunt Mashula is a typical Fairchild tale about ancestors. The two living aunts have just given their niece Dabney a cherished family heirloom, a little night light, and Jim Allen begins narrating the lamp's history.

"And Aunt Mashula loved it—that waited for Uncle George, waited for him to come home from the Civil War till the lightning one early morning stamped her picture on the windowpane. *You've* seen it, India, it's *her* ghost you hear when you spend the night, breaking the window and crying up the bayou. . . . "

. . . .

"When did that Uncle George come back?" asked India.

"He never came back," said Aunt Primrose. "Nobody ever heard a single word. . . . and yet she hoped. . . . Only this little night light comforted her, she said." (*DW*, 45)

This tale, only part of which is repeated here, may seem to have little significance to *Delta Wedding*. It appears only this once, and it does not affect subsequent action. It is just one of many Fairchild stories about a host of relatives. Nonetheless, the narration has a definite role; it is one step in the author's gradual but steady development of the Fairchilds' extensive oral tradition, their relationships to the past, the differences between the older and younger generations, and the personalities of individual characters.

Heirlooms give the Fairchilds an important link to the past. The portraits of ancestors hanging on the walls, the old muskets propped in the corner, the Irish lace curtains at the windows all have their tales. Each item is identified by its story—the night light is not just any night light but the night light which Aunt Mashula waited by. For Aunt Jim Allen and Aunt Primrose, who live alone with their meticulously cared-for keepsakes, the past is very real indeed. Just as Jim Allen " 'wants all the ghosts kept straight,' " Primrose becomes nervous when people "don't keep their kinfolks and their tragedies straight" (p. 45).

But the youngsters who listen to the aunts' story about the night light have a different attitude toward the past. India's questions illustrate not so much a sincere interest in the family's past as a nine-year-old's natural fascination with hearing a story told (especially one that includes ghosts). Though she cries when Dabney later breaks the lamp, the tears are for the loss not of a family heirloom but of a prized and mysterious possession, loved since infancy. Uniquely designed with "an amazing little teapot" on its top, the lamp seems to her "the most enchanting thing in the world"; it is "the bribe" they "had all come to see when they were little" (pp. 49, 44). Whereas India, who is more delighted with her sister's bridal gift than is Dabney herself, asks questions to encourage the aunts' narration because she loves to hear a story (any story) told, Dabney remains silent and apparently uninterested. A seventeen-year-old, she considers the story not just a story but a story about the past, and as a bride-to-be, her interest is in the present and future. Though when she was India's age she too showed interest in the stories (see *DW*, 121), she now considers the past and family tradition silly and unimportant: "Sometimes, Dabney was not sure she was a Fairchild—sometimes she did not care, that was it" (p. 32). She is proud to be defying the family code in marrying the plantation overseer; she scorns the family value of honor preached to the children of each generation through tales about the past ("Honor, honor, honor, the aunts drummed into their ears," p. 20); and shortly after its history is narrated, she carelessly breaks the cherished night light, emblem of the family's unity with the past, while running to greet Troy, the overseer who is her fiancé, emblem of her break with family tradition.

The meaning of the past to the Fairchilds is epitomized in their differing attitudes toward the night light and the tale about it. The past does not mean the same thing to all the family, and their individual reactions to it depend on a number of things, not their generational identities alone. As Dabney and India illustrate, their specific ages, their personalities, their immediate situations and concerns are all factors.

But generational differences are not to be discounted. Though Fairchild youngsters such as India love stories about ancestors because, being children, they love any storytelling, their interest in these tales is fleeting. Not surprisingly, they give their attention more often to the present than to the past: "They were never too busy for anything, they were generously and almost seriously of the moment: the past (even Laura's arrival today was past now) was a private, dull matter that would be forgotten except by aunts" (p. 15). The children have much more enthusiasm for tales about recent events, about themselves and their living relatives, than for tales about dead ancestors—as is illustrated by their frequent retelling of and enjoyment of the Yellow Dog story, a tale about an adventure which they all shared two weeks earlier. Tales about recent events represent reality for them, but tales about ancestors affect them much as would stories read in books. It is hard to imagine a Fairchild youngster's becoming obsessed with or even genuinely concerned about events of the past, as have members of younger generations depicted in other Southern fiction.[9] The Fairchild youngsters feel no more challenged to compete with the heroics of ancestors than they would feel to compete with those of characters from a romantic novel such as *Quo Vadis*, which Roy reads amidst the helter-skelter of the wedding activities.

The exploits of a living "hero," handsome, sensuous George Fairchild, affect them much more. Each one, from tiny Bluet to the visiting cousin Laura to Dabney the bride, desires George's attention and love. Nine-year-old Laura hides George's pipe so that she can please him by later discovering it; influenced by George's heroics in the Yellow Dog story, eighteen-year-old Shelley daringly drives over the railroad track just as the Yellow Dog train approaches; and Dabney proudly compares her own defiance in marrying the plantation overseer to George's defiance in marrying the clerk of a general store. Denis Fairchild, George's dead older brother, immortalized in family tales, outshines George in the older folks' eyes—"Dabney, who loved her father and adored George, knew beyond question when Aunt Tempe came and stated it like a fact of the weather, that it was Denis and always would be Denis that they gave the family honor to" (p. 116)—but not in the eyes of the young. The young can more easily relate to the living and the visual, and for them Denis is dead and, for many of them, was never seen.

Of course, it is entirely possible that, as they grow older, the past will come to mean more to these younger Fairchilds, but it will be a past that they have experienced or observed themselves. The story of George and the Yellow Dog train which they so love now will be repeated and modified through the years, and some day *their* children will find *it* just a momentarily diverting story told by elders. Similarly, and naturally, the tales which mean most to the aunts are not ones about ancestors whom they never knew but ones about relatives and events which were part of their own lives. Jim Allen and Primrose actually remember *their* Aunt Mashula sitting by the window with the night

light (" 'We little children would be envious to see her burn it every
dark night,' " p. 45).

In her realistic portrayal of the reminiscing tradition, then, Welty
avoids implications common to much Southern fiction. Just as she does
not show a younger generation anguishing over events of the past, neither does she suggest that the Fairchild youngsters' lack of wholehearted respect for the past reflects the dying of old values. The
youngsters are not portrayed as products of a materialistic present which
has no time for things of the past. In fact, change is only beginning to
touch the isolated and protected Fairchild environment. Instead, the
general difference between the youngsters' attitude toward the past and
the attitude of those older is simply a normal difference between the
dispositions of an older and a younger generation. But Welty does not
develop group differences only; she also depicts variations in attitudes
of Fairchilds of the same generation. Her insight into the subtleties of
the meaning of the past is rare and convincing. Although the suicidal
obsessions with the past of some of Faulkner's characters are more
thrilling and engrossing than the reactions to the past of Welty's characters, surely the Fairchilds' attitudes are more common. In her realism of the ordinary, Welty portrays typical rather than extreme cases.

Though the members of the Fairchild family differ in their views
toward the past as represented through their tales, they all accept narrations of family adventures as a treat to offer to their guests. Again,
through the oral-dramatic form, Welty challenges this traditional view
of Southern conversation as a gracious cultural amenity. With comic
irony, she suggests that the tales may not be all the Southerner thinks
they are.

When Mr. Rondo, a Methodist preacher, arrives at the Fairchild home
unexpectedly and, unfortunately, too late for dinner, Mr. Fairchild immediately turns to the family's stories: " 'Well, entertain Mr. Rondo.
Tell him about George on the trestle—I bet he'd like that.' " India's
performance of the Yellow Dog story is the result. The family hardly
knows Mr. Rondo—he has dropped by, Ellen Fairchild realizes, because it seems to him the appropriate thing to do since he will soon
conduct the marriage ceremony for one of the Fairchild daughters. Obviously ill at ease among the chatty Fairchilds, he does not know what
to make of India's tale; but because the family watches him closely
throughout her narration, expecting him to be greatly entertained, he

attempts to make appropriate responses. His most effective response, the one that pleases the family most, comes as India describes the train bearing down on the family on the trestle:

> "We said, 'Wait, wait! Go back! Stop! Don't run over us!' But *it* didn't care!'"
> "Mercy!" said Mr. Rondo. Bluet, who had never taken her eyes off him, laughed delightedly and circled around him.

However, Mr. Rondo is not, in general, able to give India's tale its expected due. When India surprises him with a question which he considers only rhetorical, he has to put forth real effort to respond:

> "Everybody knows there isn't any water in Dry Creek in the summertime. Did you know that, Mr. Rondo?"
> "I believe that is the case," said Mr. Rondo, when India waited.

His confusion when the family expects of him a dramatic reaction is illustrated in the following excerpt:

> "It was coming fast!" cried Dabney. "Mr. Rondo, the whistle was blowing like everything, by that time!"
> Mr. Rondo nodded, in a pleasant, searching manner.

And at the end of the tale, the only thing Mr. Rondo can think to do is to ask a polite question: " 'Who is Maureen?' asked Mr. Rondo pleasantly. 'Is she this little girl?' " (pp. 59–61).

Evidently, the Fairchilds have enjoyed the tale much more than has their guest. Immediately after the narration ends, he leaves—hurriedly, one suspects. Through the long, dramatic narration, Welty illustrates many things about the Fairchild family and the nature of oral narration, but at least one thing in particular about the oral tradition as cultural amenity: the family, or the in-group, is likely to enjoy its tales more than do those whom the tales are intended to entertain. One cannot help wondering if Katie Rainey's customer ("Shower of Gold") and Edna Earle's boarding house guest (*The Ponder Heart*) are as uncomfortable as is Mr. Rondo. Strangers cornered by garrulous storytellers, are they not also too polite to leave abruptly before the end of the narrations? Welty's suggestion, comically rendered, is that the oral tradition may not be all it is reputed to be; it may be effective as an in-group pleasure but not necessarily as a social amenity.

Situations in two other works, *The Golden Apples* and *The Optimist's Daughter*, offer additional Weltian comment on the nostalgic reminiscence as cultural civility. Special occasions which bring the family or community together are times when tales are sure to be repeated—reunions, funerals, weddings. In "The Wanderers" and *The Optimist's Daughter*, tales are told about Katie Rainey and Judge McKelva in the days following their deaths. Two of the tales are similar, and like tales about Aunt Amy of "Old Mortality" and Carolina Bayard Sartoris of *Sartoris*, they depict Katie and the Judge as daring, vivacious free spirits. King MacLain remembers Katie as a reckless, independent young girl who set fire to her stockings on a dare, and Major Bullock recalls that Judge McKelva was " 'a fearless man! Fearless man' " who once single-handedly and with moxie turned away an angry mob from the courthouse door. Apparently neither tale is entirely true, yet neither is the usual literary depiction of a Southern romanticization of the past.

King simply makes a mistake—it wasn't Katie but Nellie Loomis who set her stockings on fire, according to King's wife Snowdie. Thus King's tale says very little about the past or about a character's attitude toward the past, but the narration is ironically revealing about King himself: the vital, virile hero of the book's earlier legends has become an old man with an old man's normal slips in memory. It is ironic, too, that King, who has a reputation in the community as an exciting nonconformist, should recite such a conventional reminiscence, and on such a conventional occasion. That he does so hints at just how firmly ritualized such nostalgic tale-telling has become in the small community, an implication Welty would make more emphatically in *The Optimist's Daughter*.

Elderly Major Bullock's narration about his friend Judge McKelva presents a rare case in Southern fiction. His romantic tale is not a spontaneous, largely unconscious embroidering of a past event, as nostalgic reminiscences usually are. Rather, Bullock apparently deliberately falsifies the past. Stationed at the foot of the Judge's coffin, he "suddenly burst[s] into speech": " 'Remember the day, everybody, when Clint McKelva stood up and faced the White Caps? . . . The time Clint sentenced that fellow for willful murder and the White Caps let it be known they were coming to town out of all their holes and nooks and crannies to take that man from the jail!' " But Bullock does not speak in his normal voice; he speaks far too loudly: "The floor creaked agonizingly as he rocked back and forth on his feet and all but shouted, filling the room, perhaps the house, with his voice'' (*OD*, 79). Major Bullock is nervously and self-consciously trying to fulfill the role which he thinks incumbent upon him as best friend of the deceased; he must eulogize McKelva with a highly favorable tale. Though the basis of his story is probably a real incident, he exaggerates McKelva's part in it, making him a romantic hero. A sweet, gentlemanly (if somewhat silly) man, Bullock is out of character with his boisterous, folksy narration, and the fantasy of the tale and his uncomfortableness as narrator are clearly evident in his awkwardness. This fantasy is underscored further by the inconsistency between the bravado of the man described in the tale and the quiet modesty of the real Judge McKelva introduced to the reader shortly before his death.

Despite Bullock's obvious fabrications, Judge McKelva's daughter Laurel, who has returned to Mount Salus from her designing career in Chicago during her father's illness, is the only listener who objects, and her objections cause Bullock's self-consciousness to intensify and his exaggerations then to increase. The Mount Salus mourners are hardly aware of the romanticization, it being a common element in a community ritual. When Laurel tries to deter the narrator, her friends seek to pacify her:

"He says, 'Back to your holes, rats!' And they were armed!'' cried Major Bullock, lifting an imaginary gun in his hands. .

"He's trying to make father into something he wanted to be himself,'' said Laurel.

"Bless his heart,'' mourned Tish [Bullock's daughter] beside her. "Don't spoil it for Daddy.'' (p. 80)

Through this tale and others narrated about McKelva before his funeral, Welty shows such tale-telling to have a special role in the ceremonial "pageant of grief" which, according to John Crowe Ransom, traditional communities stage in order to turn attention away from "the deadness of the body" and "the riddle of mortality." [10] The tales are a form of politeness and a means of expressing grief. The truth or falsity of the tales is irrelevant to the practitioners since the tales are not intended primarily as accounts of the dead friend's past but as a means of honoring him or her and as compassionate sympathy cards to the most bereaved. The tales, like funeral flowers, are offered as beautiful conclusions to the deceased's life.

"What's happening isn't real," Laurel said low.
"The ending of a man's life on earth is very real indeed," Miss Adele said.
"But what people are saying."
"They're trying to say for a man that his life is over. Do you know a good way?" (p. 82)

A few days after the funeral, Laurel's friends continue to grieve and to express sympathy for Laurel through tales about her dead parents. Whereas Major Bullock's tale exaggerated McKelva's bravery, these later ones comically exaggerate the parents' humanity. The friends hope to make Laurel smile. One tale is about an absurd party dress of " 'Beaded crepe! Shot beads! Neck to hem, shot beads,' " which Judge McKelva bought as a gift for his first wife (Laurel's mother), and which Becky wore, despite its gaudiness, because of her love for her husband. Tish says, " 'Oh, they'd do anything for each other! Sure she wore it. And the weight she had to carry! Miss Becky told Mama in confidence that when she wasn't wearing that dress, which was nearly a hundred percent of the time, she had to keep it in a bucket!' " The friends' tale, which seems a natural, not a deliberate, exaggeration of qualities of Laurel's parents, is, like Major Bullock's tale, part of the mourning ritual. When Laurel attacks her friends for laughing at her parents—" 'Are they just figures from now on to make a good story?' "—Tish reminds her of the purpose of the tales:

"Polly! . . . We weren't laughing at them. They weren't funny—no more than . . . all our fathers and mothers are! . . . Aren't we grieving? We're grieving *with* you."
"I know. Of course I know it," said Laurel. (pp. 126–27)

While the falsity of King MacLain's tale about Katie Rainey is simply the honest mistake of an old man, a tale other Morgana mourners tell about Katie Rainey in "The Wanderers" is more akin to the romantically or comically embroidered ones about Judge McKelva in *The Optimist's Daughter*. The mourners recall that Katie used to sell produce by the side of the road but in her later years could not because " 'Now the road went the wrong way.' " As the omniscient narrator and Katie's daughter Virgie realize, this tale is "like a sad song" but is not true: the road continues as before, only "now the wrong people went by on it." The local folk who used to linger along the way have been replaced by people in big trucks, heavily loaded, rushing from the nearby woods to the saw mill. The mourners ignore the real details about the end of the forest and the coming of industry because those things seem inappropriate to beauty and sadness. They wish their tale to be "like a sad song"—a benediction to Katie's life. Katie's daughter Virgie weeps "because they could not tell it right, and they didn't press for her reasons" (*GA*, 213–14). Funeral decorum requires tears from the bereaved relatives and beautifully sad or comically heroic tales about the deceased from the community mourners. Virgie and Laurel object to the romantic tales told about their parents because they have become outsiders, in their emotions, to the customs of their hometowns, and thus do not recognize or are unwilling to accept the purpose of the romanticizations.

The death of King MacLain's son Eugene a few years earlier had presented a special challenge to Morgana, for in his last years Eugene was a bitter, scornful man who isolated himself from his neighbors. Good manners prevented the citizens from saying anything negative about him at his funeral, yet tradition demanded that they say something. Morganans proved themselves equal to the task; they praised Eugene for doing nothing: " 'He never did bother a soul,' they said at his graveside that day, forgetting his childhood" (*GA*, 241). That, too, is like a sad song.

The significance of these funeral tales is at least two-fold. The tales illustrate that invention, under the cloak of civility, is inherent in and even a formalized part of the traditions of the polite, old community; and the pain which the tales about their parents give Virgie and Laurel is another indication that the Southern oral tradition has been over-glorified as a social amenity.

Repeatedly through their storytelling, Welty's characters are seen presenting biased accounts of events. Whether their tales result from boredom, from a long habit of talking, from nostalgia for the past, from a desire to entertain, from an attempt to honor and please others, or from a combination of these, the family and community do not recount events as they actually occurred but instead reshape the reality behind the tales to accord with their needs and values. The society's roots are not in the past but in a personal interpretation of the present and the past.

Of course other Southern writers have also suggested that Southern storytelling is romantic, but they refer in such cases almost exclusively to nostalgic tales about the past and the dead, tales which serve to exalt favorites or to magnify unusual community figures or events. Welty offers a more complex picture of the nature of her characters' romanticizing and more numerous reasons for the romanticizing. Her characters' oral remolding of events ranges from simple and sometimes malicious gossip to nostalgic tales about the dead, and from the creation of heroes to formalized rituals. This complex portrait of a many-dimensioned oral tradition both complements the usual literary portrait of the oral culture and makes apparent the limitations of the usual portrait. In its variety, the narrative reshaping of events pervades life in Welty's South.

4

"WELL, BELIEVE WHAT YOU WANT TO"

Interviewer: Would you say that Southerners—Deep Southerners—are more open than Northerners?

Welty: I think we have a sort of language we all understand and speak—a shorthand of some kind, based on familiarity—but I'm not sure we're more open. We may not tell as much as we think we do, and we may not hide as much as we think we do. We're just more used to talking. . . . [1]

The view that Welty has not dealt significantly with "the larger cultural, racial, and political themes" thought reflective of the Southern Renaissance—that she does "not place the South at the center of her imaginative vision"—has been expressed or implied frequently but never stated more blatantly than by Richard H. King in a book on the Southern Renaissance published in 1980.[2] Such a view would seem to suggest either a very shallow reading of Welty's fiction or a very narrow preconception of what themes define the Southern Renaissance. Welty's portrayal of the oral culture of her characters creates incisive pictures of Southern life, pictures encompassing concerns common to Southern fiction. Moreover, through much of her fiction she has progressively developed a telling theme about a Southern outlook on life, an outlook she shows to be reflected in and served by the oral culture. She introduces the theme in *Delta Wedding*, but a hint of it appears near the end of one of her earliest short stories, "Keela, the Outcast Indian Maiden."

Most of this story consists of Steve's obsessive narration of the injustices heaped upon Keela, a victim of exploitation by a circus. Costumed as a wild Indian maid, Keela was put into a cage and forced to eat live chickens as a stunt. Steve, formerly a barker with the circus, tells his tale to Max in front of a shack in a field where the two white men have gone in search of Keela, who was freed from imprisonment two years before. Steve's confessional tale, deriving from a personal sense of guilt concerning Keela's ordeal, does not illustrate a cultural pattern of oral narrative. But a tale begun by Keela at the end of the short story does. Actually a diminutive club-footed Negro man named Little Lee Roy, Keela sits on the steps of his shack listening gleefully to Steve's tale and then later speaks to his children: " 'Today while all you all was gone, and not a soul in de house,' said Little Lee Roy at the supper table that night, 'two white mens come heah to de house. Wouldn't come in. But talks to me about de ole times when I use to be wid de circus—' " (*CG*, 87–88). With these words, Little Lee Roy becomes the first of Welty's characters to reminisce nostalgically.

Rather than remembering his time with the circus as the gruesome experience that it apparently was, Little Lee Roy recalls it fondly. Though "Keela" is not about nostalgic reminiscences—Little Lee Roy's tale-telling merely provides the story a shocking and ironic ending— this incident nonetheless anticipates one of Welty's major themes as it relates to oral narrative. Obviously, Little Lee Roy romanticizes the past through his tale-telling. Given the bizarre reality behind his tale, however, "romanticize" hardly seems a strong enough word. Little Lee Roy does not simply glamorize or exaggerate the past, the meaning we usually intend when we speak of a romanticized past. He, in fact, remolds the past, blocking out its horror. In subsequent works, this brief hint concerning the reminiscing process is more fully and more explicitly developed. Notably, in *Delta Wedding*, while listening to her family's hilarious narration of an event that was in reality a near-tragedy on a railroad track, Ellen Fairchild thinks: "No, the family would forever see the stopping of the Yellow Dog [train] entirely after the fact—as a preposterous diversion of their walk, resulting in lovers' complications, for with the fatal chance removed the serious went with it forever, and only the romantic and absurd abided. They would have nothing of the heroic, or the tragic now . . . " (p. 188). This explanation of the way the Fairchilds look at the unpleasantness in their lives—or, rather, do not look at it—might apply to Little Lee Roy's view as well. With the horror of his circus days ended and his confinement on his crutches to his small yard and small home in a Mississippi field, his adventure in the larger world does not seem so bad. It becomes nostalgically "de ole times when I use to be wid de circus." And the time two white men unexpectedly broke the monotony of his day is also enlarged upon; Little Lee Roy is already romanticizing their visit.

That the Fairchilds of *Delta Wedding* remold the uncomfortable past through their tales is indicative of their general outlook on life. They live by an unstated principle of overlooking whatever seems unpleasant and ugly in life. Just as senile Aunt Mac washes and irons the money to be used in paying the plantation payroll each week, so do the Fairchilds try to make the world of Shellmound plantation clean and pure, a world suitable for princesses and princes, or Southern ladies and gentlemen.

The family code is seen in the pretense by its most dedicated supporters that sex and passion do not exist. While affection is encouraged, the smallest allusion to anything sexual is taboo. Hence Dabney surprises herself and India and embarrasses their middle-aged spinster aunts when she brazenly declares that she hopes she will have a baby soon after getting married: "Aunt Primrose took a little sacheted handkerchief from her bosom and touched it to her lips, and a tear began to run down Aunt Jim Allen's dry, rice-powdered cheek. They looked at nothing, as ladies do in church" (pp. 48–49). Rather than rebuking their niece for her impropriety, the aunts try to ignore her remark, as they ignore all disagreeable things. Though the nieces and aunts part warmly, they are all silently aware that Dabney has broken the family code: "It was late, and the aunts might have been going to insist that they stay to supper, if Dabney hadn't said something a little ugly, a little unbecoming for Battle's daughter" (p. 49). Similarly, when Troy, Dabney's bridegroom, displays a wedding gift of quilts from his mother, points out the one he intends to sleep under with his bride, and speaks of having a baby, the aunts' discomfiture is evident: "Aunt Primrose darted her little hand out, as if the quilt were hot and getting hotter . . . " (p. 113).

But simply overlooking the disturbing and improper is not always possible. Thus the Fairchilds unconsciously rely on well-established

habits, including several which are part of their oral tradition—euphemisms, evasions, and creative tale-telling—in their endeavors to make
of life what they would like it to be.

The family's sensitivity to any subject which borders on the sexual
frequently requires the use of euphemisms. "Predicament" is a Fairchild euphemism for marital troubles and sexual matters, used by the
aunts in reference to George Fairchild's separation from his wife and
by eighteen-year-old Shelley in referring to her mother's present preg-
nancy: " 'How could you keep getting Mama in this predicament?' "
she asks her father; and when Battle asks what she means by a predicament, she, confused, replies, " 'I thought that was what people call
it' " (p. 229). Shelley could have learned her lesson in indirect language from not only her aunts but also her mother Ellen. In warning
a beautiful wandering stranger about the sexual passion of men, Ellen
says, " 'Way out here in the woods! . . . You'll bring mistakes on
yourself that way.' " Trying to clarify her warning, she can only add,
" 'I suppose I was speaking about good and bad, maybe. I was speaking about men—men, our lives' " (p. 71). Ellen's astonishment is understandable, then, when her handsome brother-in-law George later
bluntly remarks to her that he discovered the beautiful stranger in the
woods and " 'slept with her.' " She thinks, "Sometimes he, the kind-
est of them all, would say a deliberate wounding thing . . . " (p. 79).

It is frequently in relation to George Fairchild that the family finds
evasions and protective tale-telling convenient, for George with his
"wild, free kind of self-assertion" (p. 79)—in both word and action—
is a perpetual threat to the Fairchild principle of harmony and pleas-
antness. An incident during a family picnic illustrates this point. George
jumps into the river in pursuit of his wife Robbie, who is teasing him,
and after the "rescue" he strips off her outer clothing in front of the
whole family. Most of the observers are decidedly embarrassed and
offended. Their initial defense is to try to ignore the sexual play, instead resorting to an evasion in their criticism of Robbie: "They had
chided Robbie, she had endangered George—he could not swim well
for a wound of the war" (p. 25). Weeks afterward, another defense is
adopted; as is their custom, they remold the unpleasant experience into
a humorous tale to be laughed over, entitling it the "Rape of the Sabines." The taboo topic of sexual passion is admissible publicly in the
Fairchild world only in comic, not serious, terms.

One of the Fairchilds' major forms of self-protection, in fact, is their refusal to take *any* disturbing idea or action seriously. If viewed as little more than a joke, it will not appear threatening. This defense is illustrated in a second example involving the family's reactions to disturbances created by George. This time, the offensiveness is not sexual in nature. Rather, it seems to portend a violation of that most cherished of Fairchild values, devotion to family and family tradition, and it consists of George's assertion that he may move his sisters out of a house he has given them and set up a vegetable farm in cotton territory. Momentarily jolted, the Fairchilds finally refuse to consider George in earnest. " 'But I don't understand George at all,' Tempe began, as if George himself were not there, and he kissed her too. 'You just want to provoke your sisters, you're just teasing.' " George's remark is taken to be a ridiculous joke: " 'Watermelons and greens!' Tempe still fumed softly. 'Sisters out in the cold. George, sometimes I don't think you show the most perfect judgment.' Then they both laughed gently at each other" (p. 246).

Actually, Tempe may be right; George's remark may have been another of his playful attempts to shock them, his "plan" for a truck farm merely an impulsive thought. And Tempe's repeated objections could be part of the game. After getting over her initial shock, though she does not take George's plan seriously, she enjoys pretending to worry about it. Trouble, if it in fact foreshadows no real harm or pain, is attractive to them: "the Fairchilds half-worshipped alarm" (p. 161). They enjoy and even court the excitement of alarm—as Dabney demonstrates with her impetuous remark about hoping to have a baby, as India demonstrates when she is thrilled by Dabney's daring in making the remark ("India saw Dabney's jaw drop the moment it was out, just as her own did, though she herself felt a wonderful delight and terror that made her nearly smile," p. 48), as George demonstrates with his "deliberate wounding" statements. Yet, at the same time, they resist acknowledgment of real trouble and pain.

The nature of the family's Yellow Dog story, about a recent incident on a railroad trestle, illustrates their "worship" or enjoyment of alarm—" 'We said, "Wait, wait! Go back! Stop! Don't run over us!" But *it* didn't care!' "—as well as the way they, through their tale-telling, convert a near-tragedy, a real danger, into a humorous story. And they evade recognition of Robbie's distress, her concern and jealousy over her husband's deliberately risking his life on the railroad track when his niece's foot is stuck. In the family's tale, Robbie is portrayed

as acting silly, her anxiety becoming merely part of a comic and romantic lovers' quarrel, something the family can laugh together about.

> "Now wait. Tell what Robbie said when it was all over, India," said Bat-
> tle, turning the corners of his mouth down. "Listen, Mr. Rondo."
> "Robbie said, 'George Fairchild, you didn't do this for *me*.' "
> Battle roared with cross laughter from his stool.
> Dabney cried, "You should have heard her!" (p. 61)

When real pain and suffering later cross their threshold in the form
of Robbie's despair over her separation from her husband, the Fairchilds are displeased. They feel that Robbie's open expression of her
distress is vulgar, and they try to escape any confrontation with her
trouble. A servant voices an "alarm"—a bird has gotten into the
house—and the family, from the children to the men, buoyantly give
chase, thankful for the diversion: "Ellen looked after them. It was not
anything but pure distaste that made them run; there was real trouble
in Robbie's face, *and the Fairchilds simply shied away from trouble
as children would do*" (p. 159, emphasis added).

Fairchild youngsters learn from their elders the practice of closing
their eyes to the dark side of life, discovering or creating instead the
comic and playful. From the beginning of India's vibrant and humorous tale about the Yellow Dog episode, her father Battle directs and
encourages her to look for the entertaining and light. " 'Well, entertain Mr. Rondo. Tell him about George on the trestle—I bet he'd like
that,' said Battle" (p. 58). It is Battle who reminds India to add the
comic ending about Robbie's anger, and he roars with laughter when
she does. In discovering only the happy and comic in the adventure,
India might be influenced not only by her father's guidance but also
by the similar storytelling of her elders. Though her mother Ellen is a
sensitive observer capable of detaching herself from the group and recognizing their foibles, even she is a storyteller who paints the painful
past with comic strokes, as in the following example.

In answer to family request (" 'Tell about when your mama came!'
Was that Orrin or Battle?"), Ellen repeats a much-loved Fairchild
reminiscence about the time her mother came to Shellmound from Virginia to assist with the birth of her first child, Shelley. Like the Yellow
Dog episode, this event, too, was almost a tragic one, but Ellen's tale
makes it seem delightfully preposterous.

"Dr. Murdoch . . . was a young man starting out and he brought a brand-new gas machine with him. . . . As soon as he got here he just sneered at me, the way he would now, and said fiddle, I had all the time in the world and he was going to go and we could call him when I was good and ready. But Mama thought that was so ugly of him, and it was, Dr. Murdoch!—and she said, 'Don't you fret, Ellen, I'll cook him such a fine breakfast he wouldn't dare go.' " (p. 215)

According to the narration, the doctor became incapacitated by eating the huge breakfast and ended up, sick, on the same bed with Ellen. Then first Ellen's mother and next the doctor passed out from taking test breaths from the gas machine, and Ellen had to deliver the baby herself with the assistance of the Negro cook.

Whether or not Ellen exaggerates the mishaps to improve the comedy is unclear, but she does focus the story on the mishaps and on a comic rivalry between Dr. Murdoch and her Virginia-born mother, who took a condescending attitude toward the doctor from the Mississippi Delta. Moreover, Ellen carefully avoids any reference to pain she felt during her labor or to fear she might have experienced when the doctor could not help her with the birth of this, her first child: "They laughed till the tears stood in their eyes at the foolishness, the long-vanquished pain, the absurd prostrations, the birth that wouldn't wait, and the flouting of all in the end. *All so handsomely ridiculed by the delightful now!* They especially loved the way it made a fool of Dr. Murdoch, who was right there . . . " (p. 216, emphasis added). Repeated many times since Shelley's birth eighteen years before, this nostalgic reminiscence, like the typical well-made short story, has acquired a pat and effective dénouement:

"Mama, don't tell how much I weighed," Shelley begged. . . .
"You weighed ten pounds," said Ellen helplessly, for that was the end of the story. (p. 216)

This is the "fairy Shellmound world" (p. 149) where every attempt is made to exclude the unattractive parts of reality. As Ellen's and India's stories illustrate, near-tragic events may be metamorphosed into comic tales, just as the embarrassing sexual openness during the family picnic is transformed into a comic "Rape of the Sabines." Actual tragedies, however, cannot be taken quite so lightly. The Fairchilds tend to treat them in a different but still self-protective way, making of them beautiful, sad songs wherein suffering appears heroic rather than painful and unpleasant.[3] The story about Aunt Mashula's long, patient waiting for the return of her Confederate husband is a sad love story about a devoted wife; tales about the many Fairchild men killed in the Civil War are bloodless stories about brave, loyal brothers and husbands; and the story of the Fairchild ancestor who was killed in a duel is a painless tale about a man of principle.

Much in the Shellmound universe allows and encourages the family to avoid reality. Isolated from the larger world on their idyllic plantation and exposed to little reading material other than romantic novels, the children grow up sheltered from the pain and suffering of those outside the family. And with servants aplenty to do the undesirable tasks, the children can be little princes and princesses; even pre-schooler Ranny knows how to give orders to grown black women (p. 208). Fairchild youngsters and women have little familiarity with their servants' lives outside the Fairchild house. Stories about knifings and fights among the Negroes do not disturb the family, for the point of the tales is not the suffering of the blacks but, typically, the authority and realm of Battle Fairchild: "When Negroes clear to Greenwood cut each other up, it was well known that it took Uncle Battle to protect them from the sheriff or prevail on a bad one to come out and surrender" (p. 12). In addition, the plantation overseer usually stands between the family and trouble among the field hands, as is demonstrated by the juxtaposition of two scenes which occur simultaneously. In one, the Fairchilds all gaily lounge, eat, and dance around the house in frilly summer clothes before the wedding rehearsal begins, while in the other, Troy, the overseer-bridegroom, is in the plantation office shooting an icepick out of an angry Negro's hand and then using the same icepick to dig buckshot out of the buttocks of another Negro. Shelley, who witnesses the violence when she goes to fetch Troy, is frightened, but afterwards she easily separates the office scene from her own world; it belongs instead to Troy's inferior world: "Running back along the bayou, faster than she had come, Shelley could only think in her anger of the convincing performance Troy had given as an overseer born and bred" (p. 196).

At the top of their world in power and status, the Fairchilds consider themselves masters of their own fates and the fates of others. They pass houses around among themselves with simple words; they bring dead Denis Fairchild's retarded daughter into their household but exclude his insane wife; they decide, without consulting the child's father, that motherless Laura McRaven should remain at Shellmound, confident that her father would be willing to give her up (" 'Your father would listen to reason, he hopes you'd be happy too,' " p. 237).

In depicting the family of Shellmound plantation as leading sheltered lives, Welty is very close to Ellen Glasgow, who actually entitled a novel about the protective environment in which young Jenny Blair Archbald grows up *The Sheltered Life* (1932). But Welty draws a direct relationship between the fairy-like lives of the Fairchilds and the Southern oral tradition. The magical glow of the characters' days depends not only on the bumper between them and reality provided by the servants, the overseer, and their own status and power but also on the tales and conversations which remove from reality the dull and dark. Dabney Fairchild herself momentarily realizes this crucial point: "Nobody had ever told her anything—not anything very true or very bad in life" (p. 122).

While other writers have shown their Southerners romanticizing the past through their tales, Welty suggests the precise nature and effect of many of these tales. Her implications apply readily to much storytelling depicted by other writers. Tales about tragedies become beautiful sad songs. Friends and ancestors in such tales usually die beautiful, gallant, and heroically tragic deaths, not painful, useless, disgusting, or bloody ones—Aunt Amy in her family's reminiscences in "Old Mortality," Marse Chan and Marse Phil in tales narrated by servants in Page's short stories "Marse Chan" and "Meh Lady: A Story of the War," Confederate leaders in tales told by the McGehees in *So Red the Rose*, the Bolling men in tales told by their relatives in Walker Percy's *The Moviegoer*.[4] If not made pure and almost holy, that which was disturbing at the time it occurred may be transformed into the comic. In *The Moviegoer*, in telling a tale about her first husband's depressive cycles, Binx's mother Mrs. Smith underplays the gravity of her husband's condition and her own anxiety by emphasizing what now appears comic: she had tricked him back into good health by distracting him at meal time. As long as she would read to him, he would eat. But the next time depression set in, her method did not work, another circumstance which she recalls with humor: " 'He said my treatment was like horse serum: you can only use it once' " (pp. 153–55).

As is true of the reminiscences portrayed in the works of these other Southern writers, the Fairchilds' tales embody family values. The val-

ues are obvious in the sad stories about family tragedies. "Honor, honor,
honor" is the theme of the tale about the ancestor who was killed in a
duel, eternal devotion to one's husband the theme of the tale about
Aunt Mashula and the night light, loyalty and sacrifice that of tales
about Fairchild men killed in war. But the values suggested by the
family's humorous tales are not so immediately obvious. Spoofing their
figures in the tradition of folk humor, the tales may seem only amusing anecdotes. The Yellow Dog story pokes good-natured fun at all
those who walked down the trestle, permitting "nothing of the heroic,
or the tragic," and the tale of Shelley's birth mocks both Dr. Murdoch
and Ellen's mother. But, then, the travesty that the Fairchilds make of
such near-tragic adventures itself reflects a primary Fairchild value: the
valuing of a world of happiness and innocence. The comic ridicule
prevents the Fairchilds from dwelling on the opposites of these and
thus helps to sustain the family's sense of well-being: "How the Fairchilds did talk on about their amazing shortcomings, with an irony that
Ellen could not follow at all, and never rested in perfecting caricatures, little soulless images of themselves and each other *that could
not be surprised or hurt or changed!*" (p. 80, emphasis added). Ellen's (or Welty's) insight here is relevant to the storytelling of many
Southerners or Southern characters, such as that of Mrs. Smith in *The
Moviegoer*. Through the previously mentioned comic tale which she
tells of her husband's illness, Mrs. Smith has perfected a caricature of
her dead husband, a little soulless image that cannot be hurt or changed.
As his mother begins her tale, Binx sees his father disappear again "into
the old emblem" (p. 153).

Other values are often embodied, indirectly, in the comic tales as
well. Somehow, George's apparent willingness to sacrifice himself for
his dead brother Denis's child on the railroad trestle shines through the
mass of comic details contributed by India in her narration. When Roy
describes the Yellow Dog adventure to her, Aunt Tempe, more forth-
right than the rest, bluntly states what many of the others have assumed but been modestly silent about: " 'Naturally . . . he did it for
Denis' " (p. 115). Perhaps the tale of Shelley's birth stirs similar
emotions in them; they may take silent pride in the snobbishness of
Ellen's Virginia-born mother and in Ellen's own endurance and self-
sufficiency in managing the delivery of her baby herself (with the cook's
help, of course). In these tales, the Fairchilds' sense of decorum deters
them from putting emphasis on the heroic since these tales are about

living people, ones present, in fact, when the tales are narrated. Through such lively, burlesquing stories, the Fairchilds shun the reality of danger and potential death (the scene would have been gruesome indeed had George and Maureen actually been hit by the train) and at the same time pay tribute to family bravery through modest indirection.

In the sheltered Shellmound world, the Fairchilds' outlook is excessively and naively optimistic. "[T]heir legend was *happiness*. 'The Fairchilds are the happiest people!' They themselves repeated it to each other" (p. 222). It is a legend which they have created and attempt to perpetuate, with the help of their oral tradition. Their extravagant verbal threats, common to the Southern oral tradition, epitomize their attitude toward life. The aunts say of Ellen, " 'We're going to have to whip her or kill her before she'll lie down in the afternoons, even' " (p. 20); Battle threatens little Bluet, " 'Go back to sleep or I'm coming to break your neck!' " (p. 230); and Shelley warns Laura, " 'If you tell what I did, Laura, . . . I'll cut you to pieces and hang you up for the buzzards' " (p. 234). The Fairchilds would make life as playful and harmless as are these preposterous threats.

However, the appearance of well-being does not prevent individual Fairchilds from experiencing doubts and dissatisfaction in private moments. And the blinders they wear can only hide, not eliminate, the genuine harm and pain which do occur within their paradise—such as the injuries to Negroes during bloody fights and the death of the beautiful wandering stranger, who is killed by the Yellow Dog train not long after George "slept with her."

Perhaps only in cartoons and farces is life continually as harmless and fun as the Fairchilds would like to think life at Shellmound is. Welty's short novel *The Ponder Heart* (1954) depicts just such a fun-and-games world. In this work, as narrated by Edna Earle Ponder, (1) a father has his son committed to the state mental hospital to teach him a lesson, (2) a mistake is made and the father is confined while the son is released, (3) the son in middle age takes a very young wife, who insists that they not live together, (4) the son, Uncle Daniel, accidentally tickles the wife to death during a storm, and (5) at his ensuing trial for murder, the generous-hearted defendant unwittingly gives all his money away to the jury and crowd and is acquitted. In spite of all this, the only admitted suffering in the story is Uncle Daniel's; he frequently suffers from lack of company with whom to share his tales.

The Ponder Heart is, in fact, a Southern farce—or a tall tale. The combination of the colloquial language, the exaggerated comic actions, the triumph of the naif (Uncle Daniel) over more powerful and more intelligent forces in several incidents, and the comic courtroom scene places the novella in the tall tale tradition.

But Edna Earle does not mean to be telling a tall tale; she is recalling Uncle Daniel's history as faithfully as *she* is able. Rather, *The Ponder Heart* is Welty's own tall tale. That it is also Edna Earle's reminiscence reflects a significant development in Welty's implications about the family saga tradition. Here, for the first (but not the last) time, Welty humorously reveals that the Southern reminiscence and the tall tale share some essential ingredients. With the romanticizing inherent in it and with the exaggerations and dramatic performance which a Southern narrator naturally brings to it, the reminiscence will appear—if taken to its comic extreme—very much like a tall tale.

In her tall tale, Welty employs for hilarious effect an aspect of the oral culture which she had earlier depicted in *Delta Wedding*. Following his wife's sudden death, Uncle Daniel is brought to trial for her murder because the prosecution takes literally one of his exaggerated verbal threats—threats identical in nature to those harmless ones of the Fairchilds. On the witness stand, Edna Earle (according to her narrative) is asked to explain what her uncle meant when he threatened to kill his estranged wife " 'dead' " if she did not take him back.

"Meant he got it straight from Grandma," I says. "That's what it means. She said 'I'm going to kill you' every other breath to him—she raised him. Gentlest woman on the face of the earth. 'I'll break your neck,' 'I'll skin you alive,' 'I'll beat your brains out'—Mercy! How that does bring Grandma back. Uncle Daniel was brought up like anybody else." (p. 111)

"Like anybody else"? Well, certainly Uncle Daniel was brought up like the Fairchild children; or, to be exact, his upbringing is a tall tale version of the overly protective rearing many Southerners experience. And in Uncle Daniel, Welty shows, comically, what might become of a person who literally lives all his life in a sheltered fairyland. At age fifty, Uncle Daniel is still an innocent child, described by his niece as "good as gold" (p. 16), who loves indiscriminately and thinks the world is pure goodness. First his father and after the father's death Edna Earle and the family lawyers conspire to protect Daniel from the world. They see his legend as happiness; even in the insane asylum, he "had the time of his life.'' Yet to the reader Uncle Daniel appears sweet and generous but simple-minded. The advantages of the Ponder money and status and the over-protection of those who love him have ill-prepared him to live in the larger world. He must remain under the protective wing of his niece in the haven of her boarding house in Clay, Mississippi.

Although not published for another fifteen years, Welty's next novel, *Losing Battles*, combines the tall tale approach of *The Ponder Heart* with *Delta Wedding*'s more serious treatment of a Southern family's efforts to make life rosy by, if necessary, pretending the disagreeable does not exist. The author presents in exaggerated form the family's attitude that life is a harmless game—to be played within the protecting confines of the family circle. This attitude is demonstrated through the events taking place in the present, on the day of the family reunion, and is reflected in the family's interpretation of the past through their tales.

Jack Renfro, the apple of the family's eye, arrives home from prison only to discover that en route he has unknowingly given assistance to a family enemy, Judge Moody, who had sentenced him to prison. So now, to vindicate family pride and provide entertainment for the reunion, he must push the judge's car into a ditch. His little sisters follow him on his assignment and periodically run home with bulletins of his progress. Dialogue and actions indicate that the characters view the adventure as a game. Etoyle, sitting up in a tree as a lookout, sees the judge's car approaching and calls down to her brother, " 'Is it fair for me to warn him?' '' (p. 118). Once the car ends up dangling over Banner Top Cliff after the judge swerves to avoid hitting Jack's wife and baby, Jack feels obligated to help get it down; and his mother, Beulah, goes to Banner Top in the rain to watch her son's performance, just as she would go to watch him play basketball: " 'I'm going to Banner Top! Why, you couldn't hold me! . . . If my boy's ready to turn in the performance I think he is, it's a mother's place to be there and see it done right!' '' (p. 375). Wanting to join in the game, another local family had tied cowbells to the bottom of Moody's stranded car during the night. When Curly Stovall, Jack's bosom enemy and friend, sees that assisting in the car rescue may be dangerous, he yells, " 'I ain't playing!' ''; and Jack, like a team captain, replies, " 'If you want any glory, you can't quit now' '' (p. 383). At midpoint in the contest to retrieve the car, Miss Lexie, watching from the sidelines, announces a score—" 'From here, I would call things a tie' " (p. 384). The family's optimistic, extravagantly playful outlook not only exaggerates, then, the Fairchilds' "legend of happiness" but also the love of play often associated with Southerners.[5]

While getting even with Judge Moody and then rescuing his car later are games to Jack and his family—entertainments—they also serve another important purpose as well. Just as the new tin roof Mr. Renfro puts on the house to celebrate Jack's homecoming is intended to hide the family's financial trouble and put forward a bright front, so too does the game attitude assist in pushing aside the serious and potentially tragic. The game bolsters family pride, one of the few things the poverty-stricken family has left. The action-filled, often humorous tales narrated all day at the reunion also enable the relatives to avoid concentration on present hardships. When Lexie Renfro begins her tale about Julia Mortimer's suffering and death, the Beecham-Renfros try to hush her; like the Fairchilds, they want no reminders that life is not always merry and blissful. Furthermore, many of their tales reveal that they, like the Fairchilds, reshape events to hide actual unpleasantness in the past. Their humorous and heroic tale of the battle Jack had with Curly which resulted in Jack's ending up in prison veils the real hardships and hurt pride the Renfros suffered from the imprisonment, as does their comic tale about Jack's trial.

But some of the suffering creeps in, despite efforts not to admit it. With Jack absent, the Renfros had to double up on chores. Jack almost gets criticized: " 'Well, a son can do something that's a whole heap harder to bear than what Jack did,' " Aunt Birdie says, and Aunt Beck hastily adds, " 'Now I'm not *blaming* the boy!' " (p. 66). After the reunion has ended, the guests have gone, and everyone is in bed, Jack's mother cannot continue the facade of joy and hilarity expressed during the day in the tales about Jack's exploits. " 'My son in the pen,' Miss Beulah's voice said, travelling up the passage from the dark bedroom. 'My son had to go to the pen.' " Then she tells her husband, " 'I've got it to stand and I've got to stand it. And you've got to stand it. . . . After they've all gone home, Ralph, and the children's in bed, that's what's left. Standing it' " (pp. 359–60). The optimistic, game attitude is not always a sufficient bulwark against real grief and pain.

While with her realistic pen Welty reveals that the Beecham-Renfros do suffer from hardships, with her comic pen she depicts their reshaping of the past to suit themselves through their tale-telling as so

extreme as to appear outrageous. Without batting an eye, they convert
an incident of murder, racism, and self-mutilation into a tale of brotherly love and sacrifice (Nathan's tale); an incident of deserting parents
into a tragic love story (Beulah's tale); and an orphan of unknown parentage (Gloria) into the daughter of a man who was believed to be
incapable of begetting children.

Uncle Nathan is a one-handed wandering preacher who lives a life
of mere subsistence, sleeping on the ground and eating very little. Sus-
pecting that his tale would be dreadfully unpleasant, his family has never
asked him the reasons for his way of life. But naive Jack Renfro asks
at this reunion, and Nathan tells a startling tale: he killed a man, allowed a Negro to hang for his crime, and in penance cut off his own
hand and devoted himself to the ministry and a life of deprivation. His
listeners are shocked, and his sister acts to prevent him from saying
more. Granny, however, manages to whitewash this episode from the
past by giving it a heroic context. Nathan " '[d]id it for Sam Dale,' "
Nathan's brother who is now dead, she says (p. 345). The family's
unquestioning acceptance of this comment as a justification reveals the
perverse lengths they will go to in their desire to shun the horror in the
past. With her brief comment, Granny has remolded the tale of Nathan's heinous actions into a mysterious tale of brotherly devotion and
sacrifice.[6]

Another unflattering incident in the family's past is manipulated by
Beulah into a beautiful, sad story about the death of her parents
(pp. 215–19). The two were the handsomest couple around, Papa
" 'good-looking beyond the ordinary,' " and Mama so pretty that for
her husband it was love at first sight. According to Beulah's tale, the
loving couple drowned late one dark, stormy night when their " 'runaway horse' " fell through a hole in Banner bridge, and the rapid rush
of the flooding river " 'tore 'em out of each other's arms.' " But this
is not the whole story—it is just the version Beulah likes to remember.
Her brother Noah Webster, who as a child witnessed his parents' flight,
puts in, when Beulah blames him for not stopping the runaway horse,
that the horse was not running away but the parents were; they were
abandoning their children. This possibility the family refuses to face.
When an aunt asks where the drowned couple were going so late at
night, Uncle Curtis replies, " 'Beck, that part of the story's been lost
to time. . . . I think most people just give up wondering, in the light
of what happened to 'em on the way.' " The family evades such ques-

tions which threaten family harmony. So, through simply the will of the family, the story remains a romantic and tragic account of the death, one dark, stormy night, of a handsome and loving couple, not an account of deserting parents.

The most absurd example of the extremes the family will go to in order to conceal uncomfortable elements in their past is the tale which concludes with the group, in effect, voting to decide who were the parents of Gloria Short Renfro! During the course of the reunion narrations, the Beechams put several old tales together and reach the conclusion that Gloria, Jack's wife and an orphan of unknown parentage, is also his cousin, the daughter of the dead Sam Dale Beecham and Rachael Sojourner. This interpretation of history pleases all but Gloria, for it makes Gloria one of them whereas she has always held herself apart from and above them. The interpretation pleases them further because it means that Sam Dale, beloved favorite, got to be a father before his early death. By making Sam Dale a parent, the family can negate an unpleasant memory, a childhood accident in which Sam Dale was presumably made sterile when his sister Beulah threw a live coal into his lap. Now they quickly overlook this long-accepted bit of history in grasping the new story of Sam Dale as father. " 'Beulah's got more fortitude than some,' said Aunt Beck gently. 'Yet, if the right story comes along at the right time, she'll be like the rest of us and believe what she wants to believe' " (p. 267). When later remarks from Granny lead to another possible interpretation of Gloria's origins, suggesting that Sam Dale was not her father but was marrying Rachael Sojourner to " 'pull her out of a pickle,' " Beulah begs the old woman to decide on one story or the other, whichever is most pleasing. " 'Granny, which would you rather? Keep Sam Dale perfect [that is, not the father of an illegitimate child], or let him be a father after all?' " (p. 345). And Auntie Fay calls to her husband as he arrives late in the day, " 'You missed things. . . . Gloria's born a Beecham, she's Sam Dale's child—that's the best surprise that was brought us. She's here tonight as one of the family twice over.—Oh no she isn't!—Well, believe what you want to' " (p. 336).

"Believe what you want to" indeed! The notion about reminiscing tale-telling briefly hinted at through Little Lee Roy's narration in the early short story "Keela, the Outcast Indian Maiden" and realistically developed and expanded into a theme about a whole attitude toward life in *Delta Wedding* is exaggerated to the edge of the preposterous in *Losing Battles*. In the comic overstatement of *Losing Battles*, Welty shows Southerners to be not mere devotees of the past, not mere romanticizers of the past, not even mere censurers of the unpleasant past, but actual sculptors of a pleasing past.

In some of her early short stories, Welty gently probed the illusions which individuals, often isolated individuals, build around themselves and others. Soon, however, she took on a whole fantasizing tradition—Southern tale-telling and reminiscing—and she has been pricking her characters' illusions with ever-sharper pins.

5

HERO-MAKING AND
ALLUSIONS TO MYTH

What had drawn the characters [of *The Golden Apples*] together there
was one strong strand in them all: they lived in one way or another in
a dream or in romantic aspiration, or under an illusion of what their
lives were coming to. . . .
   The stories were connected most provocatively of all to me, perhaps,
through the entry into my story-telling mind of another sort of tie—a
shadowing of Greek mythological figures, gods and heroes that wander
in various guises, at various times, in and out, emblems of the characters' heady dreams. (Welty, *OWB*, 99)

Welty's frequent allusions to ancient mythology testify to the broad
familiarity with narrative traditions which her love of storytelling has
given her. In one way in which they operate, they testify as well to
her comic-realistic spirit. In connecting local figures or situations to
ones from myth, Welty is, Ruth M. Vande Kieft has said, hinting at
"what is permanent in the human race—in character types, rituals, and
heroic actions."[1] A close reading of Welty's fiction reveals that the
allusions often take on a special role in that regard: they serve as "emblems of the characters' heady dreams." It is this, the tendency to romanticize and the nature of the romanticizing, that the allusions imply
is permanent in the human race. Moreover, at the same time that they
signal the characters' romanticizing, the allusions undermine that romanticizing.
   As indicated in the preceding chapter, through their tale-telling Welty's characters remold the past in accordance with their needs and val-

ues, thereby creating personal or tribal interpretations determined by their cosmic views. The tales are held as truths by the people and passed on orally through many repetitions. The tale-telling resembles, then, the myth-making of primitive people. In effect, Welty depicts her Southerners' stories as hardly more accurate as accounts of people and events than myths usually are. Her allusions to mythology support this characterization, but they are double-edged. On the one side, the allusions associating a character with a figure from myth reflect the enlargement of that character to supramortal status by a community or family. On the other side, by alluding to selective aspects of the same myth, Welty manages subtly to deflate the character's glory. Thus, in these works the association of a local hero with a mythic one does not elevate him, as such allusions traditionally do, but instead mocks him. Through her use of myth, Welty both mirrors a group's mythologizing of a person and punctures that mythologizing.

Though not alone in portraying Southerners as myth-makers, Welty creates a portrait distinctive for its extensive implications and intricate web of allusions to myth. Impossible to discuss in isolation, the allusions are only the most subtle of the author's means of unveiling the fallible man beneath the magnificent legend and thus achieving comedy and insight into a myth-making, hero-worshipping society.

Welty frequently uses contrasting images from mythology in delineating differences between two characters. In some of her early short stories, the contrast between a free-spirited Dionysian figure and a restrictive Apollonian one represents a contrast between two approaches to life which an innocent young woman confronts. In *The Wide Net* collection, Cash McCloud of "Livvie" and Billy Floyd of "At the Landing" are portrayed as vital, uninhibited young men, symbolically associated with Dionysus, God of Wine, or other wood or field spirits. To Livvie in the one story and Jenny Lockhart in the other, Cash and Billy seem excitingly attractive. Cash contrasts with Livvie's elderly husband and Billy with Jenny's father, both represented as over-protective Apollonian figures.[2] In these stories, the Apollonian approach to life produces a dull and lonely existence, yet also an orderly and secure one. In offering contact with the world outside the home, the Dionysian way of life is more interesting but also potentially dangerous. Though Welty takes nothing away from either side, critics tend to conclude that she favors the adventurer, her implication being that to avoid knowledge of the larger world is merely to exist, not to live. Whereas in "Livvie" and "At the Landing" the Apollonian-Dionysian contrast is between two individuals and represents a choice which a third individual must make, in "Asphodel" (WN) the contrast becomes a comment on the nature of the rural Southern community. The authoritarian figure this time is not simply a restrictive individual within a family but actually represents the convention-bound Southern community; and the Dionysian figure, also more than an individual, represents a challenge to the usual orderliness of life in that community. Moreover, the symbolism plays an important role in Welty's depiction of the community's oral tradition.

The allusions to myth in "Asphodel" are numerous and fairly obvious. Don McInnis is the Dionysian figure, Miss Sabina the Apollonian one. In furnishing fruit for others' dreams and hopes, the unconventional Mr. Don is full of life and life-giving. At the same time, he is self-centered and irresponsible. Miss Sabina, the village's most influential citizen, is life-denying: she condemns any sign of freedom and vitality in those around her. The story's setting is itself suggestive of myth, the time high noon and the place the ruins of Mr. McInnis's mansion Asphodel, "a golden ruin: six Doric columns," set on a high hill. Untamed by human hand, vegetation grows lush and wild here, the woodsy setting thus being a perfect home for Pan or Dionysus and a picturesque locale for the exotic picnic enjoyed by the story's three narrators. Mr. Don's overgrown Asphodel contrasts with Miss Sabina's orderly, dark, square house of marble and stone, furnished with artificial nature (mahogany roses in the ceiling and chandeliers which "hung down like red glass fruit") and artificial gods (statues of Venus, Hermes, Demeter) and surrounded by a yard in which not one blade of grass will grow. This mythic short story has a Greek chorus; three virgins, all dressed in sheer, flowing dimity, narrate the tragic tale of Mr. Don and their mistress Miss Sabina, who has died that day. Though they speak one by one, their voices are "serene and alike" and the lips of the silent two move with those of the current speaker (WN, 98).

The significance of these extensive and explicit classical allusions is revealed through a second and equally detectable strand of allusions running through the story. For besides being aligned with figures from classical mythology, Miss Sabina and Mr. Don are exaggerated versions of conventional character types in romantic Southern literature.

In their tale, the women depict Miss Sabina in her youth as a Southern belle and beauty, Don McInnis as a dashing Don Juan. What befalls Miss Sabina and Mr. Don could conceivably become, depending on the treatment given it, the components of a Greek tragedy, a Shakespearean tragedy, or a sentimental love tragedy from Southern literature. Married through arrangement of Miss Sabina's father, who wishes to join the last lineage of two old aristocratic families, Mr. Don and Miss Sabina are ill-matched. The young Miss Sabina as Southern beauty later becomes a cold, domineering Apollonian figure, now playing a jealous Hera to Mr. Don's promiscuous Zeus. Their children die violent deaths, and Asphodel is destroyed by a suspicious fire, presumably with Don McInnis inside. Alfred Appel, Jr., draws the connection between the two strands of allusions, the classical or mythic and the Southern. Welty, he says, "has fun at the expense of the Old South's identification with a Golden Age; the ruins of 'Asphodel' point to that grand anachronism in the history of American style, 'the classical revival.' " He shows that Sabina and Don McInnis are "parodied versions of those staple, stock characters in historical fiction, the tempestuous Southern lovers," and he explains the purpose of "Asphodel" as an "oblique attack on the old ruling class and the ineffectuality of its descendants—a parody of the romantic view of Southern gentility as perpetrated by Margaret Mitchell's *Gone With the Wind* (1936) and a hundred other novels."[3] In his handsome, aristocratic sensuousness and his defiance of Southern propriety, Don McInnis is another Rhett Butler. Thus, the function of the extended classical allusions in this story apparently goes beyond the suggestions about two modes of living which were their function in "Livvie" and "At the Landing." As Appel suggests, through the allusions Welty mocks both the Old South's glorification of itself (its sense of itself as present-day nobility, inheritor of the Golden Age) and literature's similar glorification of Southern gentility.

But there is more to it than that. In his otherwise informative discussion of "Asphodel" as a parody, Appel does not account for the role of the three narrators. If, on the symbolic structural level, they are a Greek chorus, what is their role in the parody of the romantic view of the South? The answer is to be discovered in the fact that the women themselves have clearly romanticized the real events in Miss Sabina's and Mr. Don's lives. Their exaggeration is evident, for example, in Cora's description of Miss Sabina's domineering nature:

"She took her stick and went down the street proclaiming and wielding her power. . . . Her power reached over the whole population—white and black, men and women, children, idiots, and animals—even strangers. . . . At the May Festival when she passed by, all the maypoles became hopelessly tangled, one by one. . . . She . . . set the times for weddings and for funerals, even for births, and she named the children." (p. 105)

Appel finds the significance of the women's fantasizing in the psychological portrait of them which results, but this explanation is weak since throughout the story the women are presented largely as a unit, a chorus, rather than as individuals. A further and now obvious step is required.

Whereas on the level of the classical allusions the women are a Greek chorus, on the level of a parody of the romantic view of Southern gentility they compose a "Southern chorus"—they are members of a small community romanticizing the old nobility of that community, a recurring role in Southern literature. Indeed, the occasion for their tale is a common one for such reminiscences: the death of a community figure, in this case, Miss Sabina; and their picnic makes the occasion also a social event, as is characteristic of such occasions in fiction as well as often in life. The author's description of the women's narration could apply equally well to a tale from the classical myth tradition or the Southern reminiscing tradition: it is "an old story" which has grown through repeated tellings until now with Miss Sabina's death it is "closed and complete" (p. 109); it is an "old song they carried in their memory" (p. 98), "only part of memory now, and its beginning and ending might seem mingled and freed in the blue air of the hill" (p. 100).

In parodying the Old South's identification with a Golden Age (and the identification of the Old South with a Golden Age by subsequent generations and writers), Welty shows Miss Sabina actually to have given her children classical names (Minerva, Theo, Lucian) and the two aristocrats' mansions to be copies of classical architecture. But Miss Sabina and Mr. Don are not in fact superbeings. By suggesting a parallel between the women's reminiscence and the narration of a Greek chorus, Welty implies that such nostalgic storytelling grows out of and promotes the making of myths. Through repeated and increasingly exaggerated narrations, the Southern community makes superbeings of local figures who appear in some way different and hence exciting, even if menacing, in the small community in which conformity is the

norm. The villagers have always been in awe of the two old aristocratic families from which Sabina and Don McInnis come, and Sabina
and Don have inherited their families' images and legends. Irene says,
" 'A great profane man like all the McInnis men of Asphodel, Mr.
Don 'McInnis. . . . He was a McInnis, a man that would be like a
torch carried into a house' " (pp. 99–100). She and the other local
folk envy Don his flagrant defiance of the village's conformity and find
him sexually attractive for it. Yet only through their fantasizing and
tale-telling have they themselves dared escape the restraints and drab-
ness of their existence.

Thus, the implicit Dionysian-Apollonian contrast in this story has a
double meaning. While it symbolizes the essential differences between
two personalities, as in "At the Landing" and "Livvie," this time that
contrast has to be read in terms of the two characters' functions. First,
then, the Apollonian figure embodies the restrictive social code of the
ritualistic Southern community, and the Dionysian figure represents
sensuous defiance of that code. However, one of these characters is
seen entirely, and the other almost entirely, through the women's storytelling, and the story the women tell unquestionably romanticizes the
personalities and actions of the two. Second, then, the symbolic association of Sabina and Don with gods of myth reflects the female narrators' (and society's) attitude toward them. The women see the aristocratic and defiant Don McInnis as a sensuously thrilling but frightening
hero, radiant as a god, and the aristocratic, autocratic Miss Sabina as
a dark, threatening villain, powerful as a goddess.

This interpretation of the meaning of the allusions becomes clear near
the end of "Asphodel" when Welty has Don McInnis, so far seen only
through the women's tale, suddenly appear in the flesh. The contrast
between the women's fantasized view of him and his actual appearance produces much of the story's humor.

Although the village has long assumed Don McInnis to be dead, the
man who suddenly appears is real, not an apparition or a product of
the women's romanticizing, for his appearance is recorded by the author rather than by the women: "All at once there was a shudder in
the vines growing up among the columns. Out into the radiant light
with one foot forward had stepped a bearded man. He stood motionless as one of the columns. . . . He was as rude and golden as a lion.
He did nothing, and he said nothing while the birds sang on. But he
was naked" (p. 109). Stepping out from among the vines, bearded,

naked and golden, he might be a satyr figure, even Dionysus. However, seen close up, in naked flesh, under the revealing glare of mid-
day sun (Apollo's effect), he loses the mystery and romance of myth.

That this sudden and unexpected appearance awakens one of the
women, Cora, from her fantasizing so that she finally sees him as he
really is, an old man, not a superior being, is evidenced by her subsequent comments. She no longer speaks in a serene, solemn, poetic
tone, her language for once becoming common and idiomatic:

> "That was just as much Mr. Don as this is I," said Cora, "and I would
> swear to that in a court of law."
> "He was naked," said Irene.
> "He was buck-naked," said Cora. "He was as naked as an old goat. He
> must be old as the hills." (p. 110)

The comparison of Mr. McInnis to an old goat is quite a comedown
from the frequent association of him previously with a golden lion.

When, in farcical fashion, the women are shortly chased away by a
herd of goats, Welty undercuts further Mr. Don's glory, and she does
so in keeping with the symbolic association of him with Dionysus. If
one is to use the association at all, the most appropriate symbol for
Mr. Don would be a goat, since according to myth Dionysus himself
frequently appeared as a goat or as half-goat. His followers, the satyrs,
also were represented as half man and half goat. But of course goats
elicit negative connotations—stubbornness, stupidity, indiscriminate
eating habits, smelliness. To reflect the women's dreams about him,
Welty has earlier compared Mr. McInnis to a golden lion, king of the
jungle, and her allusions have associated him with the sensuous god
of wine rather than with the goat image of the god. The women have
for years been remembering Mr. Don as they wish; they have made
him into a defiant, godlike figure, and it is only the McInnis of their
legend that we have seen until now. But once Welty shows us Mr.
McInnis himself, she suggests that as a human being he resembles the
goat part of the myth more than the god part. While his sun-tanned
skin is golden as a lion's, he bears greater overall kinship to a lech-
erous old billy goat. The frenzied, stampeding goats that soon chase
the women away might be the rowdy, hedonistic satyrs or goat-men
who are Dionysus's followers.

Though all the women should now have experienced a rude awakening from their hero-making, as Cora seems to have, Phoebe, after

her initial shock, returns to her mythicizing: "Her voice was soft, and she seemed to be still in a tender dream and an unconscious celebration—as though the picnic were not already set rudely in the past, but were the enduring and intoxicating present, still the phenomenon, the golden day" (p. 113). In the small, static community in which excitement is rare, it is more pleasant to recall Mr. Don as a young, sensuous god figure than as an old man or old goat.

Whereas in "Livvie" and "At the Landing" the reader's concern is for the overly protected young women Livvie and Jenny Lockhart and the nature of the choice—Dionysian or Apollonian—which they suddenly confront, in "Asphodel" there is no young naive girl, and the reader experiences no real concern for the fate of the three middle-aged women, who are hardly individualized at all. The focus of the story is not on a choice or on individuals but on the nature of the society depicted in the women's reminiscence and the nature of the tale-telling process itself, a process which the author equates through her allusions with myth-making. She suggests that the convention-bound (Apollonian) community has romanticizing propensities. Its members choose as their hero a person who appears to be a sensuous defier of convention (Dionysian) whose exploits they can enjoy vicariously, and then they glamorize the figure in their tales.

With few exceptions, critics have seen "Asphodel" as a simple treatment of the Dionysian-Apollonian contrast that shows the Dionysian forces triumphant.[4] Many take the women's narrative as fact: Miss Sabina *did* set the time for births, deaths, and marriages, name all the town's children, cause the Maypoles to tangle, etc. Such interpretations overlook the significance of the role of the three women as narrators. ("Livvie" and "At the Landing" do not have narrators.) The very importance of "Asphodel" in Welty's canon is its revelation this early in her career of her interest in the romanticizing of Southerners. The story anticipates the role of allusions to myth in the author's subsequent, more-complex treatments of Southern romanticizing, and it introduces a motif in her choice of family or community heroes: by making the hero a living rather than a dead man, Welty is able implicitly to criticize and to poke fun not only at the romanticizer but also at the object of romance. For when the hero of legend is still alive, the reader can see him not only as his admirers see him (as indicated by their thoughts, conversations, and tales) but also as he appears in his ordinary flesh when he steps onto the stage. This striking juxtaposition

of the legendary version of a character with his unprepossessing physical presence can be immediately deflating and, in Welty's fiction,
wickedly comic. "Asphodel" is the first of several works in which
Welty explores and explodes the myths which we in general and the
Southern reminiscer in particular create. She turns the tables on the
romantic hero, and on those who make a human being into such a mythic
figure.

Like "Asphodel," three of Welty's longer works, *Delta Wedding,
The Golden Apples*, and *Losing Battles*, portray Southern hero-making
as myth-making. Whereas "Asphodel" has a playful impressionistic
surface as a result of its blatant mythic context and parody and its
colorful but shallowly developed characters, these later works are realistic. In each a legendary presence stands above the other characters,
exalted to that position by them. And Welty again draws on mythology both to suggest the exaltation and to undermine it. The allusions
are most extensive and most comic in *The Golden Apples*.

Many of the allusions to myth in *The Golden Apples* reflect Morgana, Mississippi's attitude toward King MacLain, Morgana's counterpart to Don McInnis. While "King" is a believable name for a Mis-
sissippian (names such as Prince, Lady, Duchess, Duke, Mann, and
Mister are not surprising in the South), it also is an emblem of Morgana's enchantment with the man. King represents the Dionysian side
of Welty's recurring contrast; Morgana's social code is the Apollonian
side, with Miss Lizzie Stark, community matriarch, and to some extent King's wife Snowdie MacLain as its chief embodiments.

The book's first story, "Shower of Gold," depicts the community's
myth-making about King through the storytelling of Katie Rainey. As
indicated in the mention of them in Chapter 3, the tales about King
multiply because he, like Don McInnis, is "willful and outrageous,"
apparently oblivious to social decorum. Anyone who takes a trip out
of town is sure to return with a tale of having seen him: "Somebody's
cousin saw King MacLain. Mr. Comus Stark . . . claimed three or
four times he saw his back, and once saw him getting a haircut in Texas"
(p. 9). Mr. Rainey, Katie's husband, vowed that he saw him in Jackson, in a prominent position at the governor's inauguration. Morgana's
admiration of King is tinged with hate, the citizens sometimes resent-
ing that he has escaped the small community's confines while they have
not had the courage to do likewise. Yet their admiring envy always

wins out. Even as Katie accuses King of being a conceited scoundrel, she creates myths about him: "I believe he's been to California. Don't ask me why. But I picture him there. I see King in the West, out where it's gold and all that" (p. 10).

Through Katie's tales King emerges as a Zeusian and a Dionysian figure, a traveler whose home ties are not binding, one who freely populates the countryside with his offspring and who treats his wife like just another of his mistresses, even arranging a secret and romantic meeting in the woods with her, during which she conceives twin sons. Section 1 of "Shower of Gold," then, presents King as Morgana sees him, and the allusions to myth reflect the community's attitude toward King: most of the citizens view him as decidedly special. Such an allusion appears in Katie's description of Snowdie following Snowdie's woodsy tryst with her wandering husband: "It was like a shower of something had struck her, like she had been caught out in something bright. It was more than the day. There with her eyes all crinkled up with always fighting the light, yet she was looking out bold as a lion that day under her brim . . . " (p. 6). As critics have observed, the title of the story is taken from this allusion to the myth of Zeus's visit to Danae, for sexual gratification, in a shower of gold.[5] Katie Rainey does not know the myth; *she* is not intentionally alluding to it. Rather, the author incorporates the allusion into Katie's narration; not, however, to elevate King and Snowdie's experience above the ordinary, as critics have contended,[6] but to suggest Katie's (and probably Snowdie's) view of King and the incident. To Katie, King is like a handsome, sensuous, and demanding god, sexual intercourse with whom would transform the lucky woman—much as Danae was transformed by the sexual experience with Zeus.

Even as it reveals the romantic status King has for Morganans, Section 1 of "Shower of Gold" begins to lead the reader to see King as a mock hero. The combination of the realistic (Katie's colloquial and concrete language) and the romantic (the aura she envelops King in) is so incongruous as to make King seem not heroic but comical and Katie's attitude seem absurd. To imagine a mysterious hero as having the power to transform a woman simply by having sexual intercourse with her yet also as doing something so ordinary and unmysterious as "getting a haircut in Texas" is to demonstrate the absurdity of the romantic view which exalts him above the human.

The elevation of King is further undermined in the second half of the story, and King comes tumbling ungracefully down—in the reader's eyes, but not in the narrator's or community's. Welty's method here is similar to that she had used in "Asphodel": she first introduces the hero as he appears to his admirers—through their tales—and she then allows a glimpse of him with the kingly mask removed. King's unmasking occurs, appropriately, through Katie's account of an episode that occurred "only last week," on Halloween.

While Katie and Snowdie were cutting out patterns in Snowdie's dining room, the MacLain twins, Eugene and Randell, wearing their Halloween masks, were skating in and around the house. According to Katie, King returns home unannounced, but before he can knock on the door his twin sons, whom he may never have seen before, begin skating circles around him and yelling "Boo!" King is briefly and confusedly imprisoned in his masked sons' noisy circle: "The minute come, when King just couldn't get out quick enough. Only he had a hard time, and took him more than one try. He gathered himself together . . . but he was confused, I take it. But he got aloose and up and out like the Devil was after him—or in him—finally" (p. 14).

In this episode Welty makes comic-realistic use of a familiar pattern in classical mythology: the wandering, warring King returns home after an absence of many years and is killed by his own child or children who do not recognize him.[7] However, this King, whose wanderings have just been imagined by Katie, returns home only to flee unheroically from his little masked boys. King emerges from the tale as a comic figure. If the children's masks and commotion are the cause of his fear, then he is a ridiculous coward. If, as is more likely, he is running from a renewed recognition of what home responsibilities would be, then he is an irresponsible slackard rather than a nonchalant defier of convention. In either case, he looks more like a buffoon than a godly, mysterious hero as he makes his frantic escape "over the bannister and the ferns, and down the yard and over the ditch and gone" (p. 14).

The comedy is heightened by the fact that it is only the author and the reader, not the community, who see King shed of his crown and glory. Katie and other Morganans have fantasized about him for so long that their vision is obstructed by blinders. Plez, an old Negro who observes King's flight and from whom Katie gets her information, says that King's fear of the masked twins was justified: "Plez said if those children had been black, he wouldn't hesitate to say they would remind a soul of little nigger cannibals in the jungle" (p. 14). Of course,

Plez may merely be saying what he knows the white lady would like to hear. But Katie takes the comment straight. And despite his frantic escape, she finds that King left a strange, supernatural influence behind. Though she remembers that the twins ran into the house with a tale of having just seen a booger and "chased him down the steps and run him off," in her interpretation she somehow makes the twins the ones who were frightened: "Well, then, the children, I reckon, just held open-mouth behind him, and then something got to mounting up after it was all over, and scared them." Katie even finds the weather different after King's presence, the air itself golden. Her description evokes a myth-like change of seasons: "Outdoors the leaves was rustling, different from when I'd went in. It was coming on a rain. The day had a two-way look, like a day will at change of the year—clouds dark and the gold air still in the road . . . " (pp. 15–16). Thus, through the tale-telling of Katie and others, King's visit home (if it really was King who appeared) becomes for Morgana another exciting episode in the body of legends about him. But while King remains an enchanting figure in the eyes of Morgana, he is rapidly becoming a mock hero in the eyes of the reader.

Welty uses the comic reversal repeatedly in *The Golden Apples* to separate the real King from Morgana's dreams and myth-making. "Sir Rabbit," like "Shower of Gold," is divided into two sections, with the first section introducing not King himself but the King of legend and the second section eventually providing the reversal as King in the flesh steps forth.

The story opens eight or ten years after "Shower of Gold." King has been away from Morgana so long that a fifteen-year-old girl, Mattie Will Sojourner, knows him only through the tales she has heard about him all her life. Thinking she spots the daring, impudent hero peeking at her from behind a tree, she cries out to him, " 'I know the way you do,' " and the authorial voice explains, "When it came down to it, scared or not, she wanted to show him she'd heard all about King MacLain and his way" (p. 86). Instead of King, his fifteen-year-old twin sons pop out from behind the tree and run a "tinkling circle around her," entrapping Mattie Will in their circle just as they had their father on Halloween many years before. Mattie submits to their love-making, although disappointed that they are not King come to carry her off.

In the second section of the story, set in the same woods a few years later, King himself arrives on the scene. Mattie Will, like other Morgana women, has through the years been fantasizing about being se-

duced by King, and now she gets her chance. She is out hunting with
Junior Holifield, her husband, when the real King peeks out from behind a tree. King is not hunting birds, as he claims, but a woman (any
woman). Junior warns Mattie to stay hidden, for he knows the legends: " 'You heard who he said he was and you done heard what he
was, all your life, or you ain't a girl. . . . He's the one gits ever-
'thing he wants shootin' from around trees, like the MacLains been
doing since Time. . . . And don't nobody know how many chirren
he has' " (p. 92). King peppers Junior's hat with buckshot, Junior faints,
and King has his way with the quite willing Mattie Will. As Ruth M.
Vande Kieft suggests, the love-making scene may echo the myth in
which Zeus, disguised as a swan, seduces Leda.[8] Mattie Will finds King
very grand despite, or perhaps because of, his rough, selfish love-making, and she is pleased that she has finally become part of his legend:
"She was Mr. MacLain's Doom, or Mr. MacLain's Weakness, like
the rest, and neither Mrs. Junior Holifield nor Mattie Will Sojourner;
now she was something she had always heard of" (p. 95).

The comic reversal comes as the reader realizes that King is in reality more akin to "Sir Rabbit" of the children's rhyme which runs
through Mattie's head than to a king of the gods. Initially, in fact, while
King appears glorious to Mattie Will, to the reader he may seem merely
a middle-aged lecher as he tries to entice the young wife away from
her husband and into the bushes with him: " 'Won't you come out and
explain something mysterious to me, young lady?' " (p. 91). The apparent allusion to the myth of Leda and the swan which occurs in the
account of the subsequent love-making reflects Mattie's view of King;
to Mattie, King is as wonderful as a god: "*When she laid eyes on Mr.
MacLain close*, she staggered, he had such grandeur, and then she was
caught by the hair and brought down as suddenly to earth as if whacked
by an unseen shillelagh" (p. 95, emphasis added). But the physical
description of King's attire, which seems an allusion to the white swan,
can apply equally well to a white rabbit, which, like King, has the
reputation for freely and abundantly populating the countryside: "Mr.
MacLain appeared on top of the gully, wearing a yellowy Panama hat
and a white linen suit with the sleeves as ridgy as two wash boards.
He looked like the preternatural month of June." Rabbit-like, he approaches "light of foot," hopping down the bank "in three or four
knee-deep steps." He has a "puckered face . . . like a little boy's"
(p. 94)—or like a rabbit's.

As is the case with Phoebe in her view of Don McInnis in "Asphodel," even when Mattie Will comes face to face with King's ordinariness, his legend dominates her mind. Before the love-making, he seems less splendid than she had expected: "To his back, he was not so very big, not so flashy and splendid as, for example, some brand-new evangelist come into the midst" (p. 94). Yet the fleeting observation has no effect on Mattie. In contrast, she takes more seriously her own husband's lack of splendor and mystery, which she notices after King makes love to her. As she looks at her sleeping husband, she thinks, "Fools could set foot on him, walk over him. . . . His old brown pants hung halfway up his legs and there in his poky middle pitifully gleamed the belt buckle anybody would know him by, even in a hundred years. J for Junior" (p. 96). Just as Katie Rainey finds King interesting because her own husband "ain't got a surprise in him, and proud of it" ("Shower," 6), so does Junior seem (like his name) ordinary, incapable of surprise, to his wife. Then Mattie unexpectedly walks up on King, now sleeping also after his strenuous love-making, and snoring with his mouth open. Junior's sleeping body curved over a fallen tree had struck Mattie as like "the bridge over little Chunky." Now the neck of King's sleeping body also calls up for her a commonplace image, "a little porch column in town." All the parts of King's body look "no more driven than her man's now, or of any more use than a heap of cane thrown up by the mill and left in the pit to dry" (p. 96). But despite all the concrete evidence of King's lack of mystery, the mythic version prevails in Mattie's mind. To her, Junior, not King, is ordinary. Though King's body parts look no more mysterious and special "than her man's," she hypothesizes that "they were, and would be."

Then, suddenly, like a rabbit rudely startled, King "leaped to his feet, bolt awake, with a flourish of legs," an action that evokes in Mattie's mind the Sir Rabbit ditty:

> In the night time,
> At the right time,
>   So I've understood,
>   'Tis the habit of Sir Rabbit
>   To dance in the wood—

Again, despite what she sees, for Mattie, as for Katie Rainey, King will always be the king of magnificent myth, not a comic rabbit figure: "He looked horrified—that he had been seen asleep? and by Mattie

Will? And he did not know that *there was nothing she could or would take away from him*—Mr. King MacLain?'' (p. 97, emphasis added).

The allusions to specific myths—here to Leda and the swan, there to Zeus and Danae—contribute to the comic contrast between the legendary King MacLain and the real MacLain whom Welty shows us. Or, rather, in order to deflate Morgana's inflation of King, Welty shows us less than a real man. She makes him a mock hero, a cartoon figure, a flat character. To produce caricature or burlesque, political cartoonists frequently associate human beings with animals. Welty achieves such an effect through her similar but more subtle treatment of King MacLain and, before him, of Don McInnis. Whereas on the one hand the allusions to myth reflect Morgana's exaltation of King, on the other hand the emphases which Welty gives certain aspects of the myths create analogies between the hero and subhuman figures or things. Welty does not compare King to a superhuman such as Odysseus who returns home in the disguise of a human, a beggar; rather, her allusions suggest that he is to be compared to a shower of gold and a swan, disguises assumed by Zeus in his love-making. But her allusions make specific reference to the unhuman disguise rather than to the god in the disguise, and the effect thus tends to be comic.

For example, to imagine a woman seduced by a great white swan is to imagine the preposterous, and Welty emphasizes the cartoon nature of the allusion by using the swan's unglamorous cousin, the goose, in her most explicit comparison of King to a swan: ''Mr. MacLain's linen shoulders, white as a goose's back in the sun, shrugged and twinkled in the glade'' (p. 94). In analogies, a swan is assumed to be stately and handsome, but a goose is considered a comic character; someone is ''silly as a goose,'' we say. And Welty is aware of this connotation. In her children's book, *The Shoe Bird*, Gloria the Goose is frequently referred to as ''the silly goose.'' This goose is vain as well as silly. King himself is vain, always wearing a stiffly starched white linen suit and confident of the admiration of women. In ''Sir Rabbit,'' the allusion to the myth of Leda and the swan becomes, through Welty's manipulation, Mattie and the goose.

Throughout *The Golden Apples*, King is repeatedly associated as well with a rabbit or Sir Rabbit, a comic figure from American ''mythology'' or folklore. As we have seen, the allusion is to a rabbit not as a soft, cuddly, graceful creature but as a promiscuous, rapidly multiplying, easily startled woods animal. King's propensity for choosing the woods as the setting for his frequent love-making aligns him as easily with a rabbit as with a wood spirit or satyr figure.

In "The Wanderers," the last unit in the cycle of *The Golden Apples*, King has returned to Snowdie and the Apollonian community in his old age, no longer the promiscuous, fast-moving, far-ranging rabbit, retaining only the rabbit's spirit and alertness: "He wore the stiffest-starched white suit Virgie ever saw on any old gentleman; it looked fierce too—the lapels as alert as ears" (p. 223). King has come home to roost, a little sorry that he has ended up at the wrong end of his travels, a shaking, elderly man with an old man's lapses in memory. His grandchildren, too young to have been influenced yet by the legends about him, see him without the romantic embellishments. One child says, " 'Grandaddy's almost a hundred. . . . When you get to be a hundred, you pop' " (p. 229). The comment is like that of Cora near the end of "Asphodel" when she sees Don McInnis stripped of the fantasy: " 'He must be old as the hills.' "

Yet despite his now-daily presence among them, to other Morganans King remains the glamorous figure of legend—just as Don McInnis remains to Phoebe. Watching the shaking man as he is led out of the house, like a child, by his wife Snowdie, Virgie Rainey somehow sees his back as a "mysterious, vulnerable back" whereas, at the same time, Snowdie appears "unmysterious" to her. And when Virgie sees King separate himself from the long-faced mourners present for her mother's funeral and begin nibbling greedily at the food, she sees an exciting nonconformist rather than an old man with a "wobbly head": "Then he made a hideous face at Virgie, like a silent yell. It was a yell at everything—including death, not leaving it out. . . . Then he cracked the little bone in his teeth. She felt refreshed all of a sudden at that tiny but sharp sound" (p. 227).

King's irreverent action does seem refreshing in contrast to the artificial reverence and false mourning of many other Morganans at the funeral, although it may not be a conscious act of defiance, as Virgie assumes, but simply the childish self-indulgence of an old man. Virgie sees King as having spent his life defying social convention, "butt[ing] like a goat against the wall he wouldn't agree to himself or recognize. What fortress indeed would ever come down, except before hard little horns, a rush and a stampede of the pure wish to live?" (p. 233). This passage clearly associates King with Dionysus, or with the uninhibited goat-men who are his attendants. King's free-spiritedness—if that is the quality he displays—is more attractive than Morgana's life-denying social conformity. Welty allows King the attractive quality of a gusto for life, an inclination to live rather than merely to exist according to the dictates of social custom.

But there is another side to the Dionysian allusions that applies equally well to King. King's irreverent attitude, his cracking "the little bone in his teeth," and the comparison of him to a butting, stampeding goat together evoke the image of Dionysus or his satyr followers on one of their self-indulgent, frenzied binges, an image similar to that evoked in the portrayal of Don McInnis at the end of "Asphodel." This association is actually uncomplimentary, for satyrs are ugly and entirely hedonistic. But they reflect one side of Dionysus, who, like the wine he celebrates, may inspire not only joy but also wild and heartless behavior. The Dionysian life may become an impulsive, hedonistic, self-centered life that rejects responsibilities. King's butting against the wall of social conformity has not been a responsible, deliberated action but the butting of a hard-headed, irrational goat. In enjoying his "pure wish to live," he has self-centeredly deserted his wife and children, who have waited longingly for his sporadic and unannounced visits. Both sons grow up to be men who face grave family problems without a father to turn to for sympathy and advice. Ran addresses his wayfaring father at the beginning of "The Whole World Knows," "Father, I wish I could talk to you, wherever you are right now"; and Eugene's one-day affair with the Spanish guitarist in "Music from Spain" is in part a search for a father figure.

Whereas the Greeks may have seen clearly the two sides of Dionysus,[9] most Morganans, unlike Welty, close their eyes to the double side of King's free-spiritedness. Charmed by his vitality, virility, and daring, they easily overlook or forgive the pain he causes others, even while they are protective toward his wife Snowdie. Indeed, the fact that he has deserted his family becomes a major element in his fascinating legend. There is a fondness, not condemnation, in Katie Rainey's observations that King is a "handsome devil" and "scoundrel." On the one hand, then, the Dionysian images reflect Morgana's view of King as an exciting, sensuous hero; and on the other hand, Welty undermines this glorification of a man with the reminder of the goat image in the myth.

The glorification of King is undermined further by one possible reading of another myth important to the book. As several critics have

pointed out, Welty may have taken the title of *The Golden Apples* from
a poem by William Butler Yeats about the Celtic myth of Aengus's
quest for a visionary girl, and she quotes or alludes to lines from that
poem several times. According to the poem, Aengus caught "a silver
trout" which changed into "a glimmering girl" who then slipped away.
Aengus spends his life dreaming of and searching for her, expecting
when he finds her to pluck "The silver apples of the moon/The golden
apples of the sun." Ruth M. Vande Kieft explains the application of
the poem to Welty's work:

> [T]he search of the passionate, tireless, wandering Aengus is the search of all
> the wanderers in *The Golden Apples*: a search for the glimmering vision which
> is love, adventure, art, through the achievement of which the golden apples
> may be plucked, or individual fulfillment realized. And yet, to any Morgana
> son or daughter, a dream of fulfillment may be only . . . a mirage, an illu-
> sion.[10]

Whereas Snowdie MacLain and most other Morganans never wander,
King is one of a handful of wanderers in the book and hence, according to Vande Kieft and others, is a searcher like Aengus. However, an
ironic application of the Aengus myth to *The Golden Apples* seems
equally, if not more, appropriate. Perhaps King MacLain himself should
be seen as the "glimmering vision" and Snowdie (and others) as the
one who desires and searches. For Snowdie is a dreamer who longs
for the return of her husband, the golden man whom she caught but
had only briefly before he slipped away. (She even set the Jupiter Detective Agency searching for him once.) In fact, to all Morgana, King
is like Aengus's "glimmering girl" who slips away and then becomes
a vision, a legend, a symbol of adventure. Katie Rainey, we recall,
imagines him in California, "out where it's gold and all that."
"Everybody to their own visioning," she says (p. 10).

Ironically, when King returns to her in her old age, Snowdie discovers that her dream has been only a mirage; she finds that possession
of her glimmering man, or the plucking of the golden apples of the
sun, is not so magical after all: " 'I don't know what to do with him,'
Miss Snowdie said. . . . When her flyaway husband had come home
a few years ago, at the age of sixty-odd, and stayed, they said she had
never gotten over it—first his running away, then his coming back to
her" (p. 217). Snowdie's confusion illuminates Morgana's illusions

about King. The King of people's dreams is no more real than are golden apples.

Morgana's mythicizing of King represents the hero-making of the restrictive, excitement-hungry community in its most extreme form. King throughout *The Golden Apples* is a flat, comic character, and those who dream about him, in particular Katie Rainey and Mattie Will Sojourner, appear ridiculous. Together, the excessive quantity of the myth-making and the comic quality of the author's allusions to myth effectively undercut the validity of the allusions. Furthermore, Morgana's lavish glorification of King and Welty's ironic portrayal of him as a cartoon figure create two hugely comic stories, "Shower of Gold" and "Sir Rabbit," which form counterpoints to the more subtle portrayals of hero-making-in-progress in other situations in *The Golden Apples*, such as in "Moon Lake." Whereas King MacLain is drawn broadly, the two "heroic" figures of "Moon Lake" are treated with complexity and subtle comedy, as are their admirers. "Moon Lake" is about childhood and adolescence and the discovery of the heroic by the young.

While from the beginning of *The Golden Apples* a whole body of legends exists about King MacLain, revealing to the reader his exalted position in the community, in "Moon Lake" no such body of legends exists about Easter and Loch. Rather, it is the thoughts and words of young girl campers at Moon Lake summer camp, along with, again, allusions to myth, which inform the reader that the orphan Easter and the Boy Scout lifeguard Loch Morrison are fascinating figures to the young campers. But this time, the comic reversals illustrate the heroic figures' ultimate falls from their pedestals in the eyes of their former worshippers. Myth-making about them is thus nipped in the bud. Nonetheless, like Morgana's myth-making about King, the girls' illusions about Loch and Easter reflect their desires for heroes and excitement. Moon Lake summer camp is Morgana in miniature, and its young inhabitants are miniature dreamers. At the same time, the disposition for hero-worship of these young, still-growing girls not only represents a Morganan or Southern inclination but also suggests the inclination to romanticize, or mythicize, inherent in human nature.

Like King, Easter and Loch deliberately separate themselves from the group, thus exhibiting an apparent individuality that fascinates Morgana youngsters accustomed to conformity. Their unusual names (like King's) may also make them appealing—certainly Easter's name is discussed by some of the children. And the two share with King a third distinction: each has a special role or background. King, of course, is a handsome and charming member of an old and important family in the Morgana-MacLain area. Easter is an orphan, an identity which could earn for her second-class citizenship and both pity and ridicule from Morgana girls were she humble rather than defiant. But as a defiant orphan, a loner, and the acknowledged leader of the other orphans, Easter inspires awe in the young observers. Loch seems special and mysterious to the pre-pubescent girls because he is the only boy (other than a Negro boy, son of the cook) at camp, because he is a few years older than the girls, and because he isolates himself from them.

Easter dispels the advances of Morgana girls, no doubt aware that their interest in her is mixed with condescension. Her rebukes of them and her apparent independence make her even more interesting to them: "Easter was dominant among the orphans. It was not that she was so bad. The one called Geneva stole, for example, but Easter was dominant for what she was in herself—for the way she held still, sometimes" (p. 104). Once she bit the hand of "Mr. Nesbitt, from the Bible Class." "It was wonderful to have with them someone dangerous but not, so far, or provenly, bad" (p. 105). She carries a jack-knife and plays a game called mumblety-peg.

The reader sees Easter primarily through Nina Carmichael's eyes, and to Nina, Easter seems ancient and mythical, her eyes the color "of metal, flat ancient metal," like the coins from Greece and Rome that Nina's grandfather has. "The color in Easter's eyes could have been found somewhere, away—away, under lost leaves—strange as the painted color of the ants. Instead of round black holes in the center of her eyes, there might have been women's heads, ancient" (p. 106).

Stretched out unconcernedly on an old boat which she, Nina, and Jinny Love Stark discover, Easter seems mysterious and distant to Nina. Her pose is like that of a marble goddess, and to Nina, "If this was their ship, she was their figurehead, turned on its back, sky-facing" (p. 117). Goddess-like, she inspires in Nina a desire to be different, not to be the same old, unexciting Nina. Imitating what she sees as Easter's daring and leadership, "Nina, taking a strange and heady initiative," decides that they will go floating in the boat out on the lake, three young girls courageously and excitingly alone (p. 115). As in the later scene in the cabin when Nina explicitly thinks about and wishes to change into Easter, here Nina wishes both to serve and to become her heroine.

Throughout the story, the allusions related to Easter—allusions not always evoking specific myths but often only enveloping Easter in an aura of myth—suggest the children's awe of her. She appears foreign, distant, and mysterious. After her near-drowning, with mud in her mouth and seaweed in her hair and Loch working over her, she seems vulnerable for the first time but also remains separate and strong.

> Easter's body lay up on the table to receive anything that was done to it. If *he* was brutal, her self, her body, the withheld life, was brutal too. While the Boy Scout as if he rode a runaway horse clung momently to her and arched himself off her back, dug his knees and fists into her and was flung back careening by his own tactics, she lay there.
>
> Let him try and try! (p. 129)

The two mysterious and separate souls, Loch and Easter, are joined together in a symbolic sex act, performed on a statue base or pedestal (the picnic table), and the children stand by, staring hypnotically. Only Jinny Love Stark, self-possessed always, is unawed; she tries to become part of the center of attention by grabbing a white towel and fanning the two, and thus symbolically becomes a servant to them.

But the children's hypnotism is soon ended with the arrival from their everyday world of Miss Lizzie Stark, prim Morgana matriarch, Apollonian figure, and Jinny Love's mother. She scolds rather than praises or encourages Loch for his life-saving tactics, which seem implicitly sexual to her, and thus converts the scene from the wondrous and somewhat frightening to the improper but ordinary: "Her presence made this whole happening seem more in the nature of things. They were glad Miss Lizzie had come! It was somehow for this that they had given those yells for Miss Lizzie as Camp Mother" (p. 130). Miss Lizzie hugs the little girls, and they cling to her. Her belittling remarks rob Easter and Loch of their heroism and return them to childhood. Now the girls' admiration has switched from the mysterious, sensuous figures to the familiar mother figure, proponent of order, who issues commands and slaps even the counselors when they become hysterical. "Several of the little girls looked up at Miss Lizzie instead of at what was on the table. Her powdered lips flickered, her eyelids hooded her gaze, but she was there" (p. 131).

To the girls, Easter now seems weak rather than defiant as she lies limp and dirty on the picnic table. They become tender and protective toward her: "Easter had come among them and had held herself untouchable and intact. Of course, for one little touch could smirch her, make her fall so far, so deep. . . . 'Don't touch her,' they said tenderly to one another" (pp. 131–32). After a while, the children actually become bored with the life-saving scene; there's nothing thrilling or strange there any more. Their attention wanders. Some begin to nod. They desert the once-domineering Easter. Now they are just tired little girls, and Easter is delaying their supper.

"I'm so tired!" Gertrude Bowles said. "And hot. Ain't you tired of Easter, laying up there on that table?"
"My arms are about to break, you all," and Jinny Love stood and hugged them to her.
"I'm so tired of Easter," Gertrude said.
"Wish she'd go ahead and die and get it over with," said Little Sister Spights. . . . (p. 134)

When Easter returns from "the dead," she has changed and so have they. She is no longer dominant and apart, and they are no longer awed by her. She begs softly to be carried—to be included and pitied and protected: " 'Carry me.' Easter's words had no inflection. Again, 'Carry me.' She held out her arms to them, stupidly" (p. 135).

The myth-like enlargement of Easter earlier in the story reflected only the children's attitude toward her. She is in fact a little girl with the conflicting and changing needs of a little girl, not a strong, strange, and mysterious supergirl with affinities to a Greek goddess. This reversal, unlike the toppling of Don McInnis and King MacLain, is not, overall, comic, since it involves Easter's near-death. And the comic irony present in the situations involving McInnis and MacLain is lacking here, for the men do not fall from their pedestals in the eyes of their admirers, whereas Easter does.

But "Moon Lake" does not end with Easter's return to life and her diminishment. The last section of the story extends the reversal to involve Loch Morrison—he suffers a comedown in the girls' eyes also, and his is quite humorous.

Even more so than Easter, Loch is an enchanting, heroic figure to the girls. He holds himself so much apart from them and so much above them that they can only dream over him: "From the beginning his martyred presence seriously affected them.'' They know he despises them and is there only through pressure from his mother: "He hardly spoke; he never spoke first. Sometimes he swung in the trees; Nina Carmichael in particular would hear him crashing in the foliage somewhere when she was lying rigid in siesta.'' Of course, the girls have never *seen* him swinging in the trees, like a wood spirit or Tarzan, but they fantasize that he does. While they endure silly little-girl wading periods in "Mr. Dip, Dip, Dip,'' the lifeguard stands "against a tree with his arms folded, jacked up one-legged, sitting on his heel, as absolutely tolerant as an old fellow waiting for the store to open, being held up by the wall'' (p. 99), a description that recalls Katie Rainey's vision of King MacLain waiting for Snowdie to meet him in the woods: "Can't you just see King MacLain leaning his length against that tree by the light of the moon as you come walking through Morgan's Woods and you hadn't seen him in three years?'' ("Shower,'' 5). It is the self-centered pose of a loner, of one oblivious to what is going on around him. Katie sees King's pose as conceited yet no less charming. The children see Loch's as charming and his isolation as romantic. His every action charms them: "In early evening, in moonlight sings, the Boy Scout and Life Saver kept far away. They would sing 'When all the little ships come sailing home,' and he would be roaming off; they could tell about where he was. He played taps for them, invisibly then, and so beautifully they wept together, whole tentfuls some nights'' (p. 100). They imagine him, like King, free and roaming, while they are confined to dull organized activities. He had pitched his tent way off in the depths of the woods among the birds and animals, like some mythic god of the woods. While he stands as disinterested guard over them during their daily dips, they spy on him.

Not even Easter earns his respect, as his rough, impersonal life-saving of her indicates, and at first the manner of his life-saving makes him seem all the more fierce and independent to the girls: "They saw him snatch the hair of Easter's head, the way a boy will snatch anything he wants, as if he won't have invisible opponents snatching first'' (p. 126). Not until Miss Lizzie arrives with her belittling, little-boy treatment of him does their awe lessen. Nina understands that Miss Lizzie thinks Loch is "odious,'' and she recalls the first thing Miss Lizzie had said to Loch on the first day of camp: " 'You little rascal, I bet you run down and pollute the spring, don't you?' '' (p. 130). Now, through Miss Lizzie's influence, Loch is transformed from the heroic to the insignificant: "Under her gaze the Boy Scout's actions seemed to lose a good deal of significance. He was reduced almost to a nuisance—a mosquito, with a mosquito's proboscis. 'Get him off her,' Miss Lizzie repeated . . . " (p. 131).

The last section of the story, employing allusions to myth, shows the great change in the girls' attitude toward Loch; and this comic turn-about is paralleled by a second one: Loch's own attitude toward his position as lifeguard changes drastically.

After Easter is revived and Miss Lizzie has departed, Nina and Jinny Love wander down toward the Boy Scout's isolated tent. Still swayed by Miss Lizzie's derision of him, they see "little old Loch Morrison . . . undressing in his tent for the whole world to see. He took his time wrenching off each garment; then he threw it to the floor as hard as he would throw a ball; yet that seemed, in him, meditative." They see him standing naked, "and there was his little tickling thing hung on him like the last drop on the pitcher's lip." But while they from their hidden position mock Loch, the Boy Scout is pleased with himself because of his life-saving performance of that day. He studies his sunburned back in a mirror and then comes "to the tent opening again and stood leaning on one raised arm, with his weight on one foot— just looking out into the night" (pp. 137–38). He feels proud and even heroic, as his careless, naked pose in the tent opening suggests—and it is a pose very similar to King's in the woods as imagined by Katie Rainey, and to Loch's earlier one as he leaned with apparent indifference against a tree while guarding the swimming girls. However, Loch's first pose of indifference actually expressed his hatred of his position as lifeguard to a bunch of little girls; he was sullen and defiant. This later pose is a much more casual, self-satisfied, conceited one, a much more King MacLain one.

It is a vaunting stance, much like the vaunting pose of Perseus after he beheaded Medusa, a myth alluded to frequently in *The Golden Apples*, including now in relation to Loch. With seaweed in her hair and mud in her mouth, Easter herself could be the beheaded Medusa as Loch rises from the lake pulling her by the hair. When Virgie Rainey thinks of the picture of Perseus in Miss Eckhart's room, "The vaunting was what she remembered, that lifted arm" ("The Wanderers," *GA*, 243). Loch's arm, too, is raised as he stands in the tent opening, and like the Perseus of the famous statues and pictures, he is naked. The pose suggests not only Perseus but also Dionysus, in that Loch here is a golden (sunburned) woods figure much like the Dionysian Don McInnis of "Asphodel," who also appeared nude and motionless, posed and poised with his weight on one foot: "Out into the radiant light with one foot forward had stepped a bearded man. He stood motionless as one of the columns. . . . He was as rude and golden as a lion. He did nothing, and he said nothing while the birds sang on. But he was naked" (*WN*, 109). Loch is observed by two formerly admiring females, Mr. McInnis by three as yet admiring ones. Loch, who once found his role as lifeguard to a bunch of little girls dreadful, now finds the role significant and his fulfillment of it heroic, as his vaunting Perseus stance suggests.

On the other hand, the little girls who earlier considered Loch mysterious, romantic, and heroic now, following Miss Lizzie's influence, find him silly and conceited. They belittle the naked "little old Loch Morrison" with "his little tickling thing" and accuse him of bravado:

Hadn't he surely, just before they caught him, been pounding his chest with his fists? Bragging on himself? It seemed to them they could still hear in the beating air of night the wild tattoo of pride he must have struck off. His silly, brief, overriding little show they could well imagine there in his tent of separation in the middle of the woods, in the night. Minnowy thing that matched his candle flame, naked as he was with that, he thought he shown forth too. Didn't he? (p. 138)

His isolation, which formerly seemed romantic and mysterious to them, is now ridiculed. They imagine him exhibiting "in his tent of separation" as much pride as a Greek god or hero—as much as a vaunting Perseus or a warring Achilles or Odysseus—as much as the conceited Mr. Don McInnis, who had stepped out into the "radiant" sunlight and shone "golden as a lion." Just as earlier they let their imaginations have free reign in their romanticizing about Loch—they thought that he, Tarzan-like, swung through the trees—so now they exaggerate his display of pride. It would not be surprising if they returned to Morgana with a tale of Loch's pounding his chest and bragging on himself. Jinny Love says, " 'I'll tell on him, in Morgana tomorrow. He's the most conceited Boy Scout in the whole troop; and's bow-legged' " (p. 138).

Welty uses allusions to the Perseus myth to suggest both Loch's pride in himself and the extravagant belittling of him by the little girls. The comic reversal here in regard to Loch is double: Loch does an about-

Benvenuto Cellini's sculpture of Perseus. Reprinted courtesy of Alinari/Art Resource, N.Y.

face in his attitude toward his role as lifeguard to little girls, and the girls' view of Loch as a mysterious hero is reversed. Moreover, Loch's pride in his action is comically undercut through the contrast between his view of himself and the girls' view of him.

In this story about illusions and the birth of myth-making, Jinny Love's final remark shows her forming a new illusion based on having seen earlier that day a girl and boy in brutal physical contact, sexually suggestive, and now seeing the same boy nude. She says to Nina, " 'You and I will always be old maids.' " Jinny Love's comment provides a final humorous touch to the story as it emphasizes that the girls no longer fantasize romantically about Loch. Furthermore, such a prediction about the future coming from the mouth of a pre-pubescent girl is comic in itself since it is obviously illusionary, susceptible to change overnight. The comedy is enhanced when we see in the very next story that Jinny Love not only does get married but, according to rumor, has an extra-marital affair.

Ironically, the tales the girls will now take home from camp will be as untrue as the ones they would have told had Loch and Easter not suffered downfalls, only now the tales will not be about the heroic. Instead, the tales will be malicious and sensational. The focus of their tale about Easter's near-drowning is likely to be not the once-glorious Easter but the little Negro boy who allegedly pushed her off the diving board: "Except that by that time they were all saying the nigger deliberately poked her off in the water, meant her to drown" (p. 132). And, as Jinny Love indicates, the once-heroic Loch will be described as behaving scandalously in the life-saving and showing off afterwards in his tent of separation.

Repeatedly in *The Golden Apples* and in several other works, Welty uses allusions to mythology to suggest characters' illusions about themselves or others. But allusions aside, the legends and dreams of Welty's Southern characters have kinships to classical mythology. Without exalting the local figures of legend, Welty appears to have drawn on the subject matter of, and the comedy inherent in, much mythology. In their stories about the gods, the Greeks and Romans imagined them as frequently engaged in sexual exploits with both mortals and other immortals, and many of the gods' problems resulted from their lust and promiscuity. Zeus, rather a slave to his lust, often stirred the jealousy and wrath of his wife Hera. Such is alleged to be true too of Don McInnis, whose extra-marital sex, according to legend, led his wife to throw him out of her house and to burn his house down. King MacLain is similarly promiscuous, and his success with females is due to the legends about him which the women all know, legends that depict him as a sensuous, exciting god or hero. Mortal women welcome him to their arms. Mattie Will Sojourner submits to the love play of two fifteen-year-old twin boys because they are MacLains and later to seduction by King for the same reason. And the tales about King's son Ran derive from his separation from his wife and his subsequent brief affair with a country girl who afterwards commits suicide. The love-making tends to occur outside civilization, outside the Apollonian community and in or near the Dionysian woods. Ran's affair with Maideen apparently occurs in a cabin on the edge of a woods near the Mississippi levee. In the episode involving Loch and Easter, the sexual act, symbolic rather than actual, is set in a clearing in a woods. Welty's comic allusions imply that Loch, after rescuing a damsel in distress, then takes the reward which the mythic god or hero usually takes, sexual intercourse. And if Loch and Easter are among King's illegitimate children, as some critics believe, then we see in Morgana, Mississippi, as in Greek mythology, "immortality" descending through a family line: from King to his children, "known and unknown." [11]

In alluding to the sexual promiscuity of mythic gods and showing sensuous men and their sexual acts to be the frequent subject of her characters' dreams, Welty is indirectly suggesting the Apollonian or restrictive social code of the small, provincial community. In convention-bound communities, in the South or elsewhere, defiers of convention are likely to ignite the imagination of the less daring. Especially are sexual actions, real or fantasized, likely to be a matter of interest. To the conformers in Welty's stories, the hero's sensuality seems to be an expression of forbidden liberty and becomes a symbol of freedom; and for the reader, the dreams and tales about the sensuality serve as emblems of the repressive society. The rigid social code of the traditional community is made comically explicit when Miss Lizzie Stark, herself representative of the code, is infuriated by a mere intimation of sex in an action which in fact is the saving of a life. So, not only do the author's allusions to mythology reflect her characters' mythicizing of local heroes and also mock both the heroes and the romanticizers; in addition, the nature of the allusions and of the characters' tales indirectly characterizes the Apollonian community.

In depicting living, contemporary figures as the objects of the romanticizing, Welty does not confine her implications to traditional
suggestions about a South that mythologizes its past. Rather, she hints
that in the small closed community, myth-making inheres in storytelling itself and in the romantic attitudes of the citizens. Or, further, especially since children are among her dreamers, she seems to imply
that myth-making is inherent in the human spirit itself. But the implications do not stop there. The similarities in form and subject matter
between the myths of ancient civilization and those of Welty's characters might suggest that the process of myth-making remains much
the same through the centuries. The ancient patterns of myth are also
contemporary patterns, the subjects of people's dreams changing little
through the ages. Hence, Morgana comments on the past just as the
past comments on Morgana.

6
HEROES OF SOUTHERN MYTH

Eudora Welty has borrowed from many simple story traditions which have romantic characteristics and oral roots: fairy tales, folklore, children's stories, ancient mythology. She has also written directly in some of these veins and has created variations on others. A versatile and talented storyteller fully aware of what she is about, she appreciates a romance as a romance (or fantasy as fantasy) but never confuses it with life. She recognizes, however, that many people do take the romantic for the real, and she delights in exposing their romanticizing.[1] In doing so, she has made use not only of ancient mythology but also of another narrative tradition and body of mythology. Whereas the allusions to ancient mythology suggest that the tendency to romanticize is universal, this second band of allusions, operating with the first, particularizes the myth-making.

This thesis was introduced in the preceding chapter in the discussion of ''Asphodel'' as a parody of Southern romanticizing and romantic Southern literature. Welty weaves in ''Asphodel'' two strands of allusions, allusions to classical mythology and allusions to sentimental Southern storytelling. In the three women's tale, Miss Sabina, the Apollonian figure, is depicted first as a Southern belle and then as a powerful and eccentric matriarch, and Don McInnis, the Dionysian figure, as a sensuous defier of convention, a brother to such characters as Rhett Butler. This combination of allusions to two bodies of narrative in ''Asphodel'' anticipates the author's frequent combination of two strands of allusions or images in subsequent works. For, like Don McInnis, the mythicized figures of local legend in other works also are

familiar Southern types. They are "classical" Southern heroes immortalized in oral legend originally but familiar to most of us through
Southern literature. Welty thus implies, as she did in "Asphodel," that
these conventional heroes are products of the romantic attitude and the
myth-making of the Southern community and writer. Indeed, she demonstrates that, just as there is a classical mythology, so is there an established "Southern mythology" with distinct hero types and values,
and she draws on this Southern mythology as naturally as she draws
on fairy tales, folklore, and ancient mythology. It is yet another narrative source which she has acquired through her lifelong love of reading stories and hearing stories told.

The allusions to ancient myth revealing the family's excessive romanticizing of the hero and the Southern allusions linking him to a
conventional character type are perfectly blended in *Delta Wedding*.

Since Denis Fairchild is dead from the beginning of the novel, the
reader sees him only through the Fairchilds' tales and thoughts about
him. Hence, this time Welty cannot allow the hero suddenly to appear
in the flesh as a comic counterpoint to his family's exaltation of him.
Yet there is no doubt that the real Denis since his death has been enlarged to a mythic figure. His exploits have been narrated so frequently that even quite young children mimic their elders' words about
him, speaking as though they know him. Nine-year-old India, for example, in reproving her Uncle George for an action which he proposes, says, " 'Uncle Denis would never do this,' " and is reminded
by her mother, " 'India, you don't even remember your Uncle Denis' "
(p. 245).

According to family lore, Denis exceeded everyone else in everything he did, and he could do the impossible.

Denis was the one that looked like a Greek God, Denis who squandered away
his life loving people too much, was too kind to his family, was torn to pieces
by other people's misfortune, married beneath him, threw himself away in drink,
got himself killed in the war. It was Denis who gambled the highest, who fell
the hardest when thrown by the most dangerous horse, who was the most de-
lirious in his fevers, who went the farthest on his travels, who was the most
beset. It was Denis who had read everything in the world and had the prodigious memory—not a word ever left him. Denis knew law, and could have
told you the way Mississippi could be made the fairest place on earth to live,
all of it like the Delta. It was Denis that was ahead of his time and it was
Denis that was out of the pages of a book too. (p. 116)

This passage, which represents the thoughts of seventeen-year-old Dabney Fairchild as she suddenly realizes that "it was Denis and always would be Denis that they gave the family honor to," shows that the family not only remembers Denis as looking "like a Greek God" but has elevated him to the status of one. The allusions associating him with wood spirits such as Dionysus, youthful and sensuous god of wine and revelry, clearly reflect the family's exaltation of him. Like Dionysus, Denis allegedly drank very heavily, traveled great distances, was intense and driven and full of "tender mischief [and] marvelous cavorting," and was at home in Dionysus's habitat, the fields and woods: " 'These fields and woods are still full of Denis, full of Denis,' Tempe said firmly. 'If I were to set foot out there by myself, though catch me!—I'd meet the spirit of Denis Fairchild first thing, I know it' " (pp. 116–17). Like Dionysus, who celebrates the fertility of nature, "Denis could have planted the world, and made it grow." But not only that; according to Dabney's summation of the legends, Denis had an answer for everything: "Denis knew what to do about high water, could have told you everything about the Mississippi River from one end to the other. Denis could have been anything and done anything . . . " (p. 116).

In its extravagance, the Fairchild mythology about Denis seems to encompass all romantic heroes of all time. Yet it also evokes the outline of a particular romantic figure, the glamorous hero of Southern family legend. Through their reminiscing, the Fairchilds honor Denis in much the way Southern families in literature have honored their heroes since at least the time of Thomas Nelson Page.[2] The typical legendary hero of such reminiscences is handsome, impulsive, spirited, dutiful, daring, exciting. Sometimes, he is reputed to be sweet as well— as is Denis Fairchild. A statement by Emily Cutrer to her nephew in Walker Percy's *The Moviegoer* provides in effect a brief synopsis of this family favorite: " 'More than anything I wanted to pass on to you the one heritage of the men of our family, a certain quality of spirit, a gaiety, a sense of duty, a nobility worn lightly, a sweetness, a gentleness with women—the only good things the South ever had and the only things that really matter in this life' " (p. 224). She loves to tell a tale of a sudden decision by several of the handsome young Bolling men to take off for a hunting trip in Europe, a tale which illustrates for her the men's impulsive, charming, carefree spirits (p. 49).

According to the legends about Denis, he would seem to have all the virtues which the Southern family hero has ever been claimed to possess, and additional ones besides. In fact, in presenting the mythicized Denis as the personification of romantic extremes, Welty seems to be parodying the legendary hero and certainly mocking the creators of such legends. Nothing the Fairchilds ever say provides evidence of Denis's specialness; they say he could do the impossible, was "the sweetest man on earth," and was devoted to his family exclusively, but their tales do not show this to be true. Rather, the tales indicate that he probably disappointed them, for the Fairchilds disapproved of his heavy drinking, of his marriage beneath himself, and of his travels away from the family circle. His exaltation, the reader suspects, is a consequence not so much of his actions and his personality but rather of what happened to him.

Besides being handsome, well born, impulsive, and charming, Denis and the typical beloved hero of family reminiscences in Southern literature have something else in common: they died young, in war. Other dashing young men who died in war and continued to live in the tales of their families and communities include Marse Chan and Marse Phil of Page's stories, Stark Young's Edward McGehee and several Confederate officers, Carolina Bayard Sartoris and the young John Sartoris (like Denis, noted for their "tender mischief [and] marvelous cavorting"), several Bolling men. Yet none of Denis's war exploits (apparently in World War I) are ever given. Welty implies that his heroism is the product of nostalgic exaggeration and that it is his early death that leads his family to make a godlike figure of him. This suggestion arises in the passage in which Dabney ponders Denis's legend: "Denis was the one that . . . got himself killed in the war"; "Denis could have been anything and done anything, *but he was cut off before his time*" (p. 116, emphasis added). Indeed, Denis's death has become part of his identity, his name being linked with the death every time he is remembered: Ellen "thought yet of the other brother Denis who was dead in France" (p. 23); in remembering an incident she observed as a child, Dabney recalls Denis as the uncle "who was killed the next year in the war" (p. 35); Shelley identifies Maureen's father as " 'Uncle Denis and he was killed in the war, don't you remember?' " (p. 62); Aunt Shannon "had torn herself to pieces over Denis's drinking and Denis's getting killed" (p. 63); and Aunt Mac remembers Denis as "dead young Denis she had loved best" (p. 67).

After his death, even the things the family viewed as flaws in him while he was alive become parts of his romantic legend, just as in Porter's "Old Mortality" Aunt Amy's shocking behavior becomes, after her death, the fond subject of legend. In contrast to Denis, the Fairchilds' living family hero, George, who was only wounded in the war in which Denis was killed, is viewed as less nearly perfect than Denis: "How in his family's eyes George could lie like a fallen tower as easily as he could be raised to extravagant heights! . . . The slightest pressure of his actions would modify the wonder, lower or raise it." George's marriage beneath himself is not romanticized; it receives the Fairchilds' unmitigated disapproval. On the other hand, "the daily presence of Maureen [Denis's retarded daughter] and the shadowy nearness of Virgie Lee [Denis's insane wife] had never taken anything away from the pure, unvarying glory of Denis" (p. 63). Thus it seems to be death that causes the uncompromised glorification of a loved one.

Welty links the Fairchilds' romantic attitude toward Denis with the older aunts' romantic attitude toward another generation of Fairchilds killed in war, the Civil War. It is significant that, unlike many other Southern writers, Welty depicts the grief and devotion of the aunts toward the Civil War dead as neither noble nor simply romantic but as funny, ridiculous, and even petty. Aunt Mac still dresses "herself in mourning for her husband Duncan Laws, killed in the Battle of Corinth sixty years ago" (p. 67). And Aunt Mac and Aunt Shannon have for sixty years carried on a rivalry over who mourns more for their men killed in the war.

Far back in Civil War days, Ellen had been told or had gathered, some ineradicable coolness had come between them—it seemed to have sprung from a jealousy between the sisters over which one agonized the more or the more abandonedly, over the fighting brothers and husbands. With the brothers and husbands every man killed in the end, the jealousy did not seem canceled by death, but extended by it. . . . (pp. 118–19)

Through deaths in duels as well as in wars, Aunt Shannon has over the years accumulated a greater number of brave men to grieve over, and now she is "dwelling without shame in happiness and superiority over her sister" (p. 119). In Aunt Shannon's mind, no separation exists between soldiers of two different wars. Senile as she is, she sometimes speaks to all the dead young men, Denis included, as though they were still alive.

The circumstance of Denis's death during the war is never given. There is no evidence that he was a war hero, just as there is no evi-

dence to support the other parts of his legend. Welty's implication is
that his family remembers him as heroic because of his early death,
and since Denis is a parody of the traditional war hero of family legend in Southern literature, the implication seems to be directed not at
Denis and his family alone. According to Edgar Allan Poe, the most
nearly perfect subject for poetry is the death of a beautiful young woman.
Welty might say that Southern reminiscers have found the early death
of a handsome young man or soldier the perfect subject for their myth-
making. Her suggestion depends on implication, while fifteen years after
Delta Wedding Walker Percy makes the suggestion more directly. In
The Moviegoer, Binx's uncle, Alex Bolling, "an astonishingly handsome young man," becomes a legendary hero following his death in
World War I: "His death in the Argonne . . . was held to be fitting
since the original Alex Bolling was killed with Roberdeaux Wheat in
the Hood breakthrough at Gaines Mill in 1862" (pp. 24–25). Binx's
father, killed in World War II, is similarly enveloped in myth by his
wife and sister. Binx thinks that his father, Jack, by going to war, had
found a way to please himself and his family also, to "carry off the
grandest coup of all: to die. To win the big prize for them and for
himself" (pp. 156–57).

    Whereas Jack Bolling, through the reflections of Binx and the tales
of others about him, emerges as a complex being who puzzles and dis-
turbs both Binx and the reader, Denis Fairchild exists for the reader
only in the realm of legend. The reader is not interested in Denis himself but only in the nature of his family's romanticization of him.

    As discussed in the preceding chapter, Welty uses allusions to Greek
and Celtic mythology in *The Golden Apples* to reflect Morgana's mythicizing of King MacLain. Like Don McInnis and Denis Fairchild,
King emerges as an exaggerated version of a recognizable character
type from Southern literature. Or, rather, he seems a parodic version
of a combination of types.

    On the one hand, he exhibits superficial characteristics of the South-
ern gentleman, being well-born, well-dressed, generous, and mannerly. A handsome and charming member of an old plantation family
with a town named after it, he dresses in a spotless white linen suit,
wears a panama hat, has impeccable manners ("Mr. King even *whis-
tled* with manners," according to Mattie Will Sojourner in "Sir Rabbit," p. 89), and likes to give people gifts. (He returns periodically

from his wanderings with gifts for his wife; he supposedly gave a chair, which he calls a throne, to Katie Rainey; he promised Loch Morrison a talking bird.)

On the other hand, King's behavior, unlike that of the typical Southern gentleman, such as Major Buchan of Allen Tate's *The Fathers* or Virginius Littlepage of Ellen Glasgow's *They Stooped to Folly*, arouses both indignation and envy in the folk of Morgana. Indeed, like the newly rich, nonaristocratic Thomas Sutpen of *Absalom, Absalom!* (who also marries the daughter of a pious and staid local family), King frequently violates his community's moral and social conventions, and Morgana feels pressed to disapprove. Morgana nonetheless regards King largely as heroic, whereas Sutpen seems foreboding to Jefferson. In each case, however, it is the man's very departures from the norm which fascinate his observers. King bemuses and bewitches Morgana with his travelling, his desertion of his family, and his promiscuity, just as Sutpen bemuses and bewitches Jefferson with his wild, French-speaking Negroes and his attempts to build a name and an empire almost overnight. To Morgana and Jefferson, King and Sutpen seem to stand apart and alone; they are challenging and mysterious. Such is the attraction of a host of other handsome Southern characters as well—Rhett Butler of *Gone With the Wind*, George Posey of *The Fathers*, Charles Bon (as well as Sutpen) of *Absalom, Absalom!*, Charles Taliaferro of Stark Young's *So Red the Rose*, Wesley Beavers of Reynolds Price's *A Long and Happy Life*, Don McInnis of "Asphodel," and, to some extent, George Birdsong of Glasgow's *The Sheltered Life*. Like them, King is a handsome scoundrel, a fascinating defier of convention.

As Welty suggests through the myth-making of Morgana and, earlier, through that of the three women who romanticize Don McInnis, such men become awesome figures in the rigidly structured community because they seem exciting and perhaps threatening contrasts to the usual sameness of life in that community. Proper and prim Narcissa Benbow of *Sartoris*, for example, becomes enamored with young Bayard Sartoris largely because he seems different, strange, mysterious, and violent, in contrast to her brother and other men she knows (such as the doctor who courts her). Similarly, Lucy and Edward McGehee of *So Red the Rose* find Charles Taliaferro appealing as well as unsettling because of his differences from them and their orderly life. Charles is "reckless, headstrong, dashing, . . . forever after women, oblivious and willful"—a description which would fit King

MacLain also, if the tales about him are to be believed. Charles is described further as "a perfect example of a certain Southern type, planters' and lawyers' sons, who knew horses, rode well, hunted—were fine shots, had manners, a certain code of their own, and would not have been afraid of the devil himself. . . . Life with its powers and magnetisms came to him easily . . . " (p. 127). King is a caricature of such a "Southern type," reputedly handsome, dashing, and willful, mannerly and independent, yet a comic coward rather than a brave man unafraid even of the devil: he runs from his two young masked sons, or from the responsibilities they represent, "like the Devil was after him—or in him" ("Shower," 14). And although he is a womanizer who easily reaps life's rewards, his success with women can be more accurately credited to the well-known legends about him than to any qualities which he exhibits for the reader to see.

What is important about King and the other mysterious defiers, Eudora Welty seems to say, is that they furnish their communities with subject matter for tales or dreams. Viewed realistically, the legends about Thomas Sutpen, like those about King and Don McInnis, might be seen to be in part the mythological enlargements of an excitement-hungry people, especially the legends as handed down by Mr. Compson, whose role is close to that of the traditional Southern reminiscer, and even those of Rosa Coldfield, who initially found Sutpen both attractive and repulsive because he seemed so strange. Yet King, in spite of his deviation from the social code, is accepted socially by the community, unlike Sutpen, for he, like violent young Bayard Sartoris, is descended from one of the area's oldest and most prominent families and hence is part of the "inside" group, whereas Sutpen is on the outside hoping to get in. Because he is a Southern gentleman by name and manners, King's disreputable behavior is excused, allowed, and even envied.

The fact that King *is* a MacLain is essential to the extensiveness of the myth-making about him. The MacLain name has itself been enveloped in myth by Morgana. It is from this fact that we can trace some striking and comic similarities between *The Golden Apples* and *Sartoris*.

Through the tales which Morganans tell, King MacLain and his male ancestors, in particular his father Virgil, who served in the Confederate Army, are depicted as ruthless empire builders on the order of such Southern characters as Colonel John Sartoris before them. We remember Junior Holifield's remark on the MacLain mystique in "Sir Rabbit": " '[King's] the one gits ever'thing he wants shooting' from around trees, like the MacLains been doing since Time. Killed folks trespassin' when he was growin' up, or his pa did, if it so pleased him. MacLains begun killin' when they begun settlin' ' " (p. 92). Junior's description could be a comic version of Sartoris history, or rather, a vague and reduced version of a similar family history as it might appear many years later in the tales of non-family members. Virgie Rainey, in reminiscing about King's family in "The Wanderers," has an even dimmer recollection of MacLain history, and in her version, it was not King or his father but his grandfather who did the killing: "Didn't he [King's grandfather] kill a man, or have to, and what would be the long story behind it, the vaunting and the wandering from it?" (p. 241).

Implicit in the passages above are revelations about the nature of storytelling. With the passage of time, the specific legends about father and son become intermixed, indistinct, so that finally the individual MacLains all become one person and their stories one story. The reader has no way of knowing whether the legends have any factual accuracy—whether one of the men (which one?), or all of them, or none of them ever killed anyone. The motives for the killing or killings have also become blurred. The reader can anticipate that, with the passage of time, King-the-charming-scoundrel-and-free-spirit, who is so much a concrete personality in people's dreams and tales throughout *The Golden Apples*, will also lose his individuality—a forewarning that is perhaps one of Welty's jokes on the hero and his fans. What survives and will survive is a mythic concept of the MacLain name; to Morgana, the name connotes mystery, glamor, daring, authority, self-centeredness, and aristocracy.

We can see the influence of the MacLain name in Morgana's attitude toward King's sons. As is the case with the twin Sartoris boys of *Sartoris*, the MacLain twins are expected to live up to the legends about their forebears. Once the townspeople discover in Ran MacLain something of his father's excitement and glamor, in their view he forever after exudes those qualities:

And didn't it show on Ran, that once he had taken advantage of a country girl who had died a suicide? It showed at election time as it showed now, and he won the election for mayor over Mr. Carmichael, for all was remembered in his middle-age when he stood on the platform. . . . *They had voted for him for that—for his glamour and his story, for being a MacLain and the bad twin,* for marrying a Stark and then for ruining a girl and the thing she did. . . . They voted for the revelation; it had made their hearts faint, and they would assert it again. ("The Wanderers," 210, emphasis added)

Clearly, like the Sartoris name, the MacLain name, through Morgana's years of tale-telling and dreaming, has become embellished with a glamorous aura of myth. But there is a significant difference in the aura of the two names, a difference traceable to the difference between Faulkner's tragic-romantic vision here and Welty's comic-realistic one. In a well-known passage near the end of *Sartoris*, the Sartoris name is said to be joined inseparably with glamor and disaster, the Sartorises being "pawns" in a game perhaps itself named Sartoris: "a game outmoded and played with pawns shaped too late and to an old dead pattern, and of which the Player Himself is a little wearied. For there is death in the sound of it [the name], and a glamorous fatality, like silver pennons downrushing at sunset . . . " (p. 380). The Player is Fate, and his game of Sartoris heroism is past its time. The passage is about the end of an era, the passing of the old glamor and heroism. Fate, in this sense, has no role in *The Golden Apples* at all; it is Morgana, not Fate or time, that makes glamorous figures of MacLain men. Ran and his twin Eugene grow up to be very different from one another and very different from their father (Ran never wandering from Morgana and suffering anguish when he and his wife separate briefly), yet Morgana wills that Ran be a true son of his father. In "The Wanderers" Ran is, in truth, a fat, middle-aged, long-married, conventional man, mayor of Morgana, leading two fat women to a ceremony at a graveside, yet Morgana sees him always through the misty lens of MacLain legends. He is seen not as he actually appears but as he is remembered because of his one moment of glamor many years ago—a man who ruined a girl who afterwards committed suicide, "for all was remembered in his middle age." Even Virgie Rainey, though in spirit an individualist, sees Ran as other Morganans see him, as a "passionate" and independent man, like his father and all other MacLains, and she feels an alliance with them ("The Wanderers," 225).

In *The Golden Apples*, lives are not ruled by fate, except in an ordinary and obvious way: people are "fated" to be male or female, to bear a certain last name, and to have certain parents. This ordinary element of fate does, admittedly, have considerable consequences since Morgana judges everyone according to who his or her parents are. The MacLains "fate," then, is simply to *be* MacLains, and so being, to be romanticized in myth. And other Morganans are "fated" to be bewitched by the MacLain name. These consequences, however, develop because of human nature, not because of the existence of an ominous, powerful outside force.

The inconspicuous role that fate plays in Morgana is humorously suggested through the irony of a name Welty gives a character. Katie Rainey's husband is Fate Rainey, yet this Fate in no way reigns in Morgana, just as the other does not. A hard-working milkman and peddler, he is all but ignored by everyone; even his wife finds King more interesting than him. Fate Rainey's role in *The Golden Apples* and in Morgana is small. He dies inconspicuously in middle age, never having really affected anyone. Young Loch Morrison thought that the song Fate sang as he peddled his milk sounded like the last call "of somebody seeking about in a deep cave, 'Here—here! Oh, here am I!' " ("June Recital," 22). But nobody paid heed.

Despite Katie Rainey's funeral and King's old age in "The Wanderers," then, death and fate do not color the atmosphere of this the last section of *The Golden Apples*. Welty is not writing about the end of a glamorous era, for the glamor of the MacLain name is not the product of a passing romantic age but of a romanticizing people, and people's dreams are unmarked by time. The youngest MacLains, Ran's children little King and little Jinny, will inherit the MacLain legend. Spoiled and flattered, they already seem "magnetic MacLains" (p. 222). But there "is death in the sound of [the Sartoris name], and a glamorous fatality," not only because the "game" may be drawing to an end, but also because the Sartoris men, and especially the present embodiment of the name, young Bayard, survivor of World War I, seem to seek death. In contrast, despite the legends about MacLain killings in years past and the suicide of a girl who fell vainly in love with Ran, there can be no "death in the sound of" the MacLain name, for the still-living perpetrator of the name, King MacLain, is reputed to be a promiscuous *creator* of life and to demonstrate in his every action "the pure wish to live" (p. 233). In the last paragraph of *The Golden Apples*, Virgie Rainey smiles as she recalls "the hideous and delectable

face Mr. King MacLain had made" at her mother's funeral—a face
which had seemed, when she observed it, "like a silent yell. It was a
yell at everything—including death, not leaving it out . . . " (p. 227).

And finally, for the reader, there can be no death in the sound of
the MacLain name because King throughout *The Golden Apples* has
been presented as a comic rather than a tragic figure, and a comic version of a traditional Southern hero.

After *The Golden Apples*, Welty depicts not just comically but farc-
ically her characters' legendary heroes as conventional Southern types.
In *The Ponder Heart*, rather than linking allusions to classical mythology with allusions to Southern mythology in depicting a legendary figure, as she had done previously, she links tall tale conventions with a
character type from Southern mythology. Whereas the allusions to
classical mythology only subtly and ironically undercut a group's myth-
making, the tall tale context serves to deflate Edna Earle's outright. In
Welty's tall tale and Edna Earle's reminiscence, the hero Uncle Daniel
Ponder seems a caricature of the Southern gentleman Edna Earle considers him. He wears a red bow tie and Stetson hat—"always just swept
it off to somebody. He dresses fit to kill, you know, in a snow-white
suit. . . . He has the nicest, politest manners. . . . If he ever did a
thing to be sorry for, it's more than he intended" (p. 11). Uncle Daniel has completely respectable origins; is so generous that he gives
something away every day, be it money, a dog, or a hotel—and often
gives the same thing away more than once, to different people; is so
polite that he is exceedingly shy; and is so pure that he apparently never
sleeps with his wife. His merits exaggerated to the extreme, the Southern gentleman appears a gentle man-child and buffoon.

Sam Dale Beecham, the idolized legendary hero of *Losing Battles*,
is also a tall tale version of a conventional character type. Like Denis
Fairchild and Uncle Daniel, he exists for the reader only in his family's tales; and like Denis, he is the dead romanticized war hero, but in
more comic dress. While the traits he allegedly possessed are conventional ones of the dead young hero of family reminiscence, the clan's
exaggerations of them evoke images of a tall tale hero rather than a
radiant and transcendent figure of myth. Using the concrete, hyper-
bolic, boasting language of the tall tale, his sister compares him to his
brothers: " 'Handsomer than Dolphus ever was, sunnier than Noah
Webster, smarter than Percy, more home-loving than Curtis, more quiet-

spoken than Nathan, and could let you have a tune quicker and truer than all the rest put together,' " a description that leads Cleo, the new aunt in the family, to say, " 'He sounds like he's dead' " (p. 221). And of course Cleo is right. Like Denis Fairchild, Sam Dale died as a young soldier during World War I and as a result was immortalized and made perfect in his family's tales. Yet Sam Dale never got to war— he died of unspecified causes at his army base in Georgia. But his heroic feats *are* specified, and again the tall tale tradition rather than classical mythology lies behind the tales. Compared to the feats of a Greek hero or the alleged ones of Denis, Sam Dale's would seem silly and mundane, those of a superpowerful commoner rather than of an exalted noble being. One tale has him engaged in an all-day berry-picking contest with a girl: " 'They filled the tub and every bucket on the farm, and Sam Dale finally had to hollow him out a poplar log and fill that and come carrying it over his shoulder.' " The contest ended in a tie but only because, according to the storytellers, Sam Dale, like a Southern gentleman, *let* Rachael catch him (p. 259).

Don McInnis, Denis Fairchild, King MacLain, Daniel Ponder, and Sam Dale Beecham, then, are all parodic simplifications of Southern hero types. Of the men in Welty's fiction who are glorified in legend by their admirers, only Jack Renfro of *Losing Battles* and George Fairchild of *Delta Wedding* transcend legend to become completely realistic and round characters.[3] And George alone is a complex individual, full of ambiguities. Yet the Fairchilds do not see George for what he is. They try to force him to fit a mold which they have created, that of his dead older brother Denis. They expect him to be the proponent of cherished family values, a typical handsome, self-sacrificing, family-devoted hero. His wife Robbie understands that, to the Fairchilds, "He was to be all in one their lover and protector and dreaming, forgetful conscience. . . . If anything tried to happen to them, let it happen to him!" (pp. 212–13).

Of the legendary favorites of Welty's fiction, only George Fairchild is not a humorous figure. In fact, George is probably the closest representative of Welty's own concept of heroism, although King MacLain and even moreso Jack Renfro surely have some qualities which she esteems, just as George has some which would make her smile. Yet, paradoxically, George does not exhibit the qualities of heroism which his family sees in him. This time, Welty uses mythological allusions to suggest both Fairchild illusions about George and his actual qualities which she, and we, respect. The allusions simultaneously undermine the family's view of George as Family Hero (that is, family-devoted hero) and help reveal his reality and true heroism.

The Dionysian allusions related to Denis Fairchild, as indicated earlier in this chapter, reflect the family's embroidering of Denis's personality. The Fairchilds like to recall him as a passionate free spirit. It is a romantic view of Denis without any implication that he was in fact a free spirit on the order of his mythic counterpart or of the promiscuous Dionysian figures King MacLain and Don McInnis; for, as discussed in Chapter 4, the Fairchilds try to exclude sexuality from their world. Although the Apollonian *community* may find sensuous, uninhibited men who go against community mores exciting and may embroider their adventures in tales, the Apollonian *family* cannot similarly exalt members for defying family mores since to do so would amount to an attack on personal and parental values. Instead, Denis is remembered as having been totally devoted to his family. The Fairchilds' concept of Denis encompasses an impossibility; he is supposed to have been both the most exciting and daring man on earth and also the personification of narrow Fairchild values.

George Fairchild, whom the family tries to make a second Denis (p. 196), is presumed also to combine the contradictory traits. But as with Denis, the Fairchilds would grant him only superficial free-spiritedness. Imagining him as an uninhibited man, similar to a mythic god of wild unrestraint, is only part of their game of titillation. For example, George's sisters Primrose and Jim Allen playfully exaggerate and feel titillated by George's sensuousness, imagining that he might create a revelry befitting a Roman god:

"Uncle George's coming from Memphis today. He's bringing champagne!" said Dabney over her shoulder.
"Mercy!" said both aunts. They smiled, looking faintly pink. . . . "I declare!" "George—wait till I get hold of him!" "He'll bring all the champagne in Memphis! We'll be tipsy Primrose! He'll make this little family wedding into a Saturnalian feast! *That* will show people," Aunt Jim Allen said without hearing herself. (p. 47)

Yet were the wedding to turn into a Saturnalian feast, Primrose and Jim Allen, the most decorous of the Fairchilds, would be the most embarrassed.

Similarly, Ellen is stirred when she remembers George as *looking* like a Dionysian figure after he had fought a fire, standing there "with his shirt torn back and his shoulders as bare . . . as a Greek god's, his hair on his forehead as if he were intoxicated, unconscious of the leaf caught there, looking joyous" (p. 166). Yet Ellen is hurt and offended, we recall, when George later tells her of an action that such a sensuous, intoxicated Greek god might have performed: en route to Dabney's wedding, he had stopped in the woods to make love to a beautiful stranger.

George is, by constricted Fairchild standards anyway, indeed a free-spirited man, and Welty uses allusions to myth to correspond both to the Fairchilds' playful romanticizations of him as such a figure and to his real sensuousness and independence. The incident which produced the family's protectively comic "Rape of the Sabines" tale—George and Robbie's teasing romp during a family picnic on the edge of a woods—could be an allusion to the myth of Dionysus. And in an incident from her childhood which Dabney remembers, George again seems a Dionysian figure. George and his older brother Denis were swimming in a bayou on the edge of the woods when two little Negro boys began a knife fight nearby. The handsome and nude George, like a wood god or Greek hero, jumped between the boys, catching the knife in midair as it was thrown. Then he hugged the little boys to him. Just as the "Rape of the Sabines" incident and the incident of sex with the beautiful stranger he met in the woods reveal aspects of George's individuality which the family finds offensive, so does this one. But it is less his nudity that offends Dabney than his seeming actually to care for the little boys. The family forms the center and the circumference of the world for the Fairchilds, and George as family hero is expected to devote his heroism exclusively to them. To Dabney, he suddenly seems not like a Fairchild: "He stood looking not like a boy close kin to them, but out by himself, like a man who had stepped outside—done something. But it had not been anything Dabney wanted to see him do. She almost ran away. . . . [A]ll the Fairchild in her had screamed at his interfering—at his taking part—*caring* about anything in the world but them" (p. 36). In this incident, as in the others, George has stepped outside the family code of behavior.

Welty thus turns the tables on the myth-makers by revealing that while George is a very special person, he is not a hero by their standards, his Dionysianism and individuality being real rather than only

symbolic and playful. But whereas King MacLain exhibits primarily
the hedonistic or irresponsible side of the double-natured god Dionysus, George represents the Dionysian spirit at its best: he makes his
worshippers merry and inspires in them courage to act unconvention-
ally. Following his example of marrying beneath himself, Dabney defies family tradition by marrying the plantation overseer; and Shelley,
remembering his daring on the railroad trestle, impulsively drives across
the track as a train approaches—a reckless action, as she later admits.
But Dionysus's followers, too, when they drank too much wine, acted
unwisely.

George's most significant departure from the Fairchild code of behavior, his real "godlike" quality, however, is to be found in the
largeness of his sympathy and love. Dabney had recognized the nature
of George's love when she saw him "care" about the two little Negro
boys: "And George loved the *world*, something told her suddenly. Not
them [the Fairchilds]! Not them in particular" (p. 37). In contrast, the
Fairchilds (except for a few growing and aware ones) love only themselves, as Robbie, George's lower-class wife, comes to realize. Conscious of their hypocritical attitude toward her, she flings at them,
" 'You're just loving yourselves in each other—yourselves over and
over again! . . . You don't need to know how to love anybody else.
Why, you couldn't love *me!*' " (p. 165). Shelley observes that George
differs from the family in the way he loves: "I think Uncle George
takes us one by one. That is love—I think. He takes us one by one
but Papa takes us all together and loves us by the bunch . . . " (p. 84).
George loves individuals, not the Fairchilds simply because they are
family.

In their narrowness, most of the Fairchilds want to close their eyes
to George's broad and unselfish love. They assume that when he risked
his life on the railroad trestle " 'he did it for Denis,' " his dead brother,
whose child had caught her foot under a railroad tie (p. 115). But George
did not necessarily take the risk for Denis. His heroism is a "quality
of his heart's intensity and his mind's" (p. 189), not a fulfillment of
the code of family devotion and sacrifice. " 'I don't think it matters
what *happens* to a person, or what comes,' " he says, and then adds,
" 'Only, . . . I'm damned if I wasn't going to stand on that track if
I wanted to! Or will again' " (p. 187).

The reader suspects that Dr. Murdoch is right: George is not a family-oriented man, although he answers every beck and call from his

relatives. ("He took that part, but it was the way he was made, too, to be like that," p. 213). He frequently tramples on Fairchild values, having married beneath himself, moved away to Memphis, and repeatedly violated the Fairchild sense of decorum. George "single[s] himself from the Fairchilds" (p. 157). His love is expansive rather than limited. But the Fairchilds usually see in him only what they wish, just as they remember Denis only as they wish. Shelley's anger at Dr. Murdoch's comment is an example of Fairchild defensiveness.

"[George] . . . doesn't strike me as a family man."
"He is so!" flashed Shelley.
"Nope, no more than Denis. I grew up with Denis and knew him like a book, and George's a second edition." (p. 135)

Because Welty portrays George from so many different angles, as he is seen by many different people, and never through his own thoughts, his character remains ambiguous. He cannot be pinned down so surely as King MacLain and Don McInnis can be. He shares with his family a sense of the romantic and dramatic, which Welty would probably smile over: " 'I'm damned if I wasn't going to stand on that track if I wanted to! Or will again,' " he says; and, dressed in white and carrying a gold flask, he arrives at Shellmound plantation on horseback, having ridden his niece Dabney's wedding present all the way from Memphis, over a hundred miles away, across the fields and through the woods. But he rises above his family in the largeness of the love which he displays, and in this respect, he is a hero by Welty's standards. Paradoxically, he is a hero in the Fairchilds' eyes yet in reality not a hero by their narrow standards. Their concept of him as a handsome, innocently tempestuous, family-oriented hero (a familiar type in Southern narrative) is an illusion. Unlike King MacLain, however, he is not less than he seems to his admirers; he is more than he seems.

7
LOSING BATTLES: *TALL TALE AND COMIC EPIC*

I think we have a native love of the tale. I remember once Robert Penn Warren was at my house, and there were a lot of us sitting around talking. And he laughed so hard, and he stayed so late. And when he left he said, "I had a perfectly wonderful time—not a serious word was spoken all evening." (Eudora Welty[1])

Published in 1970 after fifteen years of near-silence from Eudora Welty, *Losing Battles* came as a surprise and a treat. It is a highly original and imaginative novel, some might say unique in American fiction. Yet in the context of the author's previous work, it was almost inevitable. Welty's delight in Southern talk and her increasing revelations about the oral culture reach a hilarious climax here, as does the effect on her fiction of her ready familiarity with multiple narrative traditions. Linking Southern reminiscing to the tall tale, myth, and the folk epic and simultaneously parodying conventions common to Southern literature, *Losing Battles* represents Welty's most critical yet most amusing evaluation of standard interpretations of Southern life and values. It is a tall tale and comic epic about the rural South.

Evidence of the society's oral culture pervades the novel, appearing on every page. Twenty-five or more tales, many in several versions, are repeated during the day-long reunion of the extended Vaughn clan, the front yard of the old family home being the scene of this storytelling marathon. The characters seem unable to hush; not only does Granny talk in her sleep, but casual conversation continues even as a human chain struggles in the mud and rain to pull Judge Moody's car back

off the edge of a cliff, leading the exasperated judge to exclaim,
" 'We're all holding on here now by the skin of our teeth! Can't conversation ever cease?' " (p. 390).

The oral culture encompasses more than conversation and tale-telling. A religious people, the Vaughn-Beecham-Renfros take for granted
prayers, sermons, and parables as part of their daily lives. Folk songs
as well as hymns are sung during the reunion, and children's rhymes
are recited—by children and adults. Political oratory is represented in
Uncle Homer Champion, a candidate for local office, who has to desert the reunion for hand-shaking and speech-making. And Miss Pet
Hanks, lone telephone operator for this rural area, supplies the latest
local news with every call she connects.

In this novel, Welty throws everything in—every trait of the oral
tradition which she had depicted earlier—and adds some new ones. She
borrows from herself, even seems to parody herself, making previous
observations explicit through the dramatic means of farcical action. Yet
the portrayal of the culture remains realistic. The major action of the
novel, in fact, is the rambling, often trivial conversations of the people, through which characters take shape and family values are unveiled. The oral tradition shows itself to be a bond that holds the family together.

That the narrators of tales often mold rather than report reality was
repeatedly suggested in earlier works; now Welty adds incidental and
comical insights into the molding process. While Southern writers have
frequently shown characters to romanticize poignant events and heroic
persons from their pasts, Welty suggests that some embroidering occurs in almost all oral narration. Without it, many tales about the distant past or about events which the narrators know only by second-
hand would be brief and general and hence less interesting.

One of the more amusing examples of such innocent embroidering
appears in Uncle Curtis's tale about the original settlement of the family at Banner Top. " 'Granny's granddaddy built this house. Built it
the year the stars fell,' " he begins. As the reunion is celebrating
Granny's ninetieth birthday, he thinks it fitting to end the story with
an account of her birth, and he does so in a quaint and effective dénouement: " 'And after Captain Jordan's son settled for a Carolina bride,
Granny herself was born squalling in that very room by the licking
fire.' " However, this ending is Uncle Curtis's own imaginative

rounding-out of the narration, as Welty makes clear through the resulting exchange between Uncle Percy and seven-year-old Elvie, who
is justifiably astounded by a licking fire in Mississippi on the day Granny
was born:

> "In August?" Elvie cried. "On the first Sunday in August?"
> Granny studied her through the long narrow slits of her eyes.
> "Winter used to come early around these parts," said Uncle Percy. "Lots
> of old tales about those winters. I believe 'em." (p. 180)

Uncle Curtis has apparently tried to give a favorite family tale a likely
and compact conclusion, a habit that comes naturally to any experienced tale-teller.

Through this and similar incidents, Welty demonstrates that the unconscious embellishing of minor details to make the tales fuller and
more entertaining may be inherent in the process of nostalgic reminiscing. And by doing so, she foreshadows and makes more believable
the family's significant reshaping of events through subsequent tale-
telling—such as their remolding of the past to hide the unpleasant, as
discussed in Chapter 4.

Even after Elvie exclaims over the absurdity in Uncle Curtis's tale,
the family's belief in the tale remains unshaken. The Beechams and
Renfros have heard and enjoyed the same tales retold, with small variations, so many times that thinking as they listen is not necessary or
possible. But a young child like Elvie, who may never before have
listened to this story, has yet to acquire the family's practice of listening with an approving mind. So when such a tale falls on her untrained
ears, it elicits an interested but amazed response rather than the expected satisfied one. Elvie has yet to realize that the sentiment which
the tale expresses is more important than its individual facts. The stories give the family a sense of pride in themselves and their past. They
accept the stories contentedly, without thought or question, just as they
accept the cycle of the seasons.

In other comparatively minor episodes, the family's innocent color-
ing of past incidents is outrageous—though still believable, given their
propensity for exaggeration and their love of play, both of which the
author has well established by this time. The Beechams tell—and accept as true—stories that could pass for tall tales. Frontier humor is
laden with stories about men's prowess; one man is reputed to be the
strongest of all, another the meanest, another the dirtiest, another the

most foul-mouthed, still another the biggest eater. Welty borrows from this tradition with Mr. Renfro's tale about Aycock Comfort's consumption of fourteen squirrels at one meal (p. 228), an exaggeration reflecting the family's view of the Comforts as lazy and greedy. Also borrowed from folklore, or from mythological tradition, is the family's tale about the bois d'arc tree in Granny Vaughn's front yard. Like those ancient myths deriving from a primitive people's efforts to account for natural phenomena, this tale explains, agreeably but unscientifically, the origin of the huge old tree. And like many tales in American folklore, it supposes that a tree sprang from the discarded riding crop or walking stick of a legendary or much-admired person.[2] Uncle Curtis tells the tale: " 'Yes sir, old-timers used to call that tree Billy Vaughn's Switch. . . . He'd stick it in the ground when he got down from his horse, trotting up here to court Granny, and one night he forgot it. Come up a hard rain, and the next thing they knew, it'd sprouted' " (p. 181).

Though this tale seems preposterous, it is again little Elvie alone who expresses disbelief. She points out that " 'there's bodocks and bodocks' " extending all the way from the house to the road.

"They couldn't *all* be Grandpa Vaughn's horse switches from when he came riding to see Granny and get her to marry 'im."
"Who says they couldn't?" Granny said swiftly. (p. 182)

In "Old Mortality," published thirty years before *Losing Battles*, Katherine Anne Porter had used the objective view of children to reveal their elders' unconscious romanticizing of family history. Young Maria and Miranda are surprised when they hear their father say, " 'There were never any fat women in the family, thank God,' " for they themselves know of two very fat great-aunts.[3] Welty makes a similar scene farcical by showing Elvie's elders vouching for what seems to be a tall tale. Yet while the Beechams are sincere, there is at the same time a degree of playfulness in both the telling and the accepting of such tales, which Elvie in her youthfulness does not recognize. The adults are, after all, entertaining themselves with these tales.

Welty thus shows the Southern nostalgic tradition to include traits usually associated with other oral patterns. However, not all the tall tale episodes occur within the characters' narrations. On one level, *Losing Battles* is itself a tall tale, and its author exaggerates as fabulously as do the characters. According to family legend, Aycock ate fourteen squirrels one night for supper, but Jack puts away even more food at the family reunion. In Welty's description (pp. 190–92), he starts with a dozen pieces of chicken, moves on to "the pickled peaches and the pear relish, the five kinds of bread, the sausages and ham— fried and boiled—and the four or five kinds of salad," and Aunt Beck's chicken pie. One plateful is only a beginning, his mother being attentive to his needs: " 'Elvie! Buttermilk! This time bring him the whole pitcher!' " He finishes up with three servings of watermelon, half a melon per serving. Here, Welty exaggerates the South's reputation for extravagant hospitality expressed through the custom of serving and eating much food at family gatherings.

Exaggerations themselves are a custom for which Southerners are famous—we recall the Fairchilds' and Ponders' numerous exaggerated threats—so Welty's own embroiderings seem doubly fitting in her tall tale about Southern life. The dandiest tale in the book, in fact, is not one of the many told by the characters—grand as they are—but the long one told, with gusto, by the author: her narration of the events occurring on the day of the reunion and the next morning, the action-packed, uproarious tale of Judge Moody's car dangling over the cliff— how it gets there and how the hero Jack Renfro rescues it. When the Beechams tell this story at the next reunion, as they are already planning to do, they will surely embroider it, but they won't be able to improve on it.

Losing Battles is far more than a humorous folk tale about Southerners and their customs. It is a complex work which points to an established tradition of literature. In a review for *The New Republic*, Jonathan Yardley ventured that *Losing Battles* may be the last good " 'Southern novel,' " ending a tradition "that began when Faulkner sat down to write *Sartoris*"; and M. E. Bradford has written that the novel is itself "an allusion to the corpus of Renaissance fiction," its action familiar to readers of "William Faulkner, Caroline Gordon, Katherine Anne Porter, Andrew Lytle, and Allen Tate."[4] *Losing Battles*'s relationship to this tradition of Southern literature is significant and needs fuller exploration.

Yardley's suggestion that the novel is motivated by nostalgia for a lost South and a lost Southern literature indicates that he is taking the characters' nostalgia for the past to be the author's nostalgic view as well, a mistake critics frequently have made in regard to Welty's fiction. The corpus of Welty's fiction would suggest a different answer. Just as the novel climaxes hilariously the author's comprehensive portrayal of the South's oral culture, so does it climax deliciously her subtle exposure of the romantic view of the South and her parodic use of conventions and motifs of Southern literature. Behind *Losing Battles* lies a narrative tradition that originated after the Civil War in oral storytelling and was carried over into written literature; this tradition is a resource Welty draws on, much as she has drawn on other narrative resources acquired through her insatiable love of oral and written storytelling.

That Welty should come to parody a tradition of Southern literature which not only was firmly established but, according to some critics, even dying by the time she began *Losing Battles* should not be surprising. She has always had a parodic streak,[5] a consequence in part of her thorough acquaintance with and enjoyment of many narrative and literary traditions. Conscious of the conventions of a particular tradition as conventions, the realist cannot easily take them seriously— much as the filmmaker of the 1970's could seldom take seriously the conventions of the Western, although he might have been a fan of the genre since childhood. As a result, the writer, like the filmmaker, plays with the conventions, draws on them as a resource, but creates a new and different work. The *Robber Bridegroom* is, as Marilyn Arnold has argued, a parody: Welty actually parodies conventions and characters from fairy tales in borrowing them for a story set on the American frontier.[6] Written straight, the story would have been a children's story, but written tongue-in-cheek, it reflects an adult's memory of and enjoyment of children's stories—and a realist's awareness that the conventions are contrived and the ideas romantic. "Asphodel," as we have seen, is a parody of conventions of another narrative tradition, but this time with satiric effect. It satirizes the romantic attitudes of a people and the romantic conventions of a literature. Like "Asphodel," "Clytie" and "The Burning" also draw on the Old South tradition, and perhaps the best way to read them is as parodies as well. As in "Asphodel," the characters in both stories have names taken from classical mythology or classical literature, indicative of the society's romantic identification of itself with a golden age of the past. "Clytie" seems to parody the degenerate Southern aristocratic family, and "The Burning" the refined, sheltered, helpless Southern lady, these being familiar character types in Southern literature. And, as the preceding chapter demonstrates, parodies of conventional Southern heroes underlie the portrayals of legendary heroes in several Welty works.

In *Losing Battles*, however, the parody is not limited to the legends about the dead Sam Dale Beecham; it underlies the work as a whole. While the novel is first and foremost a convincing and amusing story about a particular family, on a second and subtler level it is a parody of values often called Southern and of conventional literary incidents which depict them. And since the characters express these values chiefly through their conversations and tales, the parody is subtly developed as the oral culture is portrayed.

The characters of *Losing Battles* are not from the plantation South. Neither are they descendants of old aristocratic families. Nonetheless, the social order they compose, the family and community relationships they exhibit, and the values they hold to are similar to those commonly associated with the Old South and the plantation region. The cast of characters is, as M. E. Bradford has observed, "a yeoman, hill-country version of the familiar order that *was the South*" (his emphasis).[7] It is a transformation that a comic-realist might think to make. The "familiar order" *is* familiar largely in the form of the plantation South; however, the plantation region has always represented only part of the South, and the sometimes-idealistic portrayal of it represents little of the South. But the system of relationships, customs, and values linked to it are, or have been (in the abstract), true to much of the South. Set on a Mississippi plantation, *Delta Wedding* offers an unconventional and realistic picture of the familiar order—and an indirect corrective to conventional portraits of the plantation family. *Losing Battles*, in contrast, depicts a similar social fabric but locates it in a different setting: the red clay hills of northeast Mississippi during the early 1930's. This is Welty's realism; it is also her comedy, for as represented in a poor, hill-country family and community, the traditional values and customs seem caricatures of the sacred traditions lauded by the Agrarians of *I'll Take My Stand* and assigned to the wealthy big landowners of many Southern novels.

Two objects of parody are the values of family devotion and unity. Beulah Renfro specifically claims these virtues for her family in a comment she makes to the new aunt by marriage, Aunt Cleo. " 'By now you ought to know this is a strict, law-abiding, God-fearing, close-knit family, and everybody in it has always struggled the best he knew

how and we've all just tried to last as long as we can by sticking together' '' (pp. 343–44). Yet the family's actions demonstrating these
sacred values often seem ridiculous rather than conventionally noble.
Family pride and unity are promoted in petty ways, such as through a
condescending attitude toward poorer neighbors and a sense of com-
petitiveness with people of other religions and other values. In a determination to prove themselves better than Julia Mortimer, the Beechams insist that their family reunion has brought together more food
and more people than has Julia's death, which is being mourned across
the way on the same day.

The parody implicitly questions the purity of these cherished virtues. In fact, some of the tales told at the reunion (and discussed in
Chapter 4) make mockeries of them. The reader learns that this "law-
abiding" and "close-knit" family has a murderer in its midst and a
couple of deserting parents in its history. With the bald assertion that
Nathan " 'did it for Sam Dale,' '' Granny remolds a horrendous story
about murder, the hanging of an innocent man, and self-mutilation into
a mysterious but conventional tale of brotherly devotion and sacrifice.
These conventional values are thus asserted through a tale that is a
grotesque parody of romantic reminiscences and incidents in Southern
literature which show local heroes exhibiting these virtues. And if Nathan did, in fact, "do it for Sam Dale," as subsequent ambiguous revelations hint, the grotesqueness of this incident as an example of
brotherly love is increased rather than diminished. Earlier, in *Delta
Wedding*, a family had sentimentally misinterpreted a brother's daring
on a railroad track as deriving from brotherly love and sacrifice (George
" 'did it for Denis,' '' says Aunt Tempe), yet this situation lacked the
grotesquery—and the parody. With another tale, Beulah outrageously
converts an incident of deserting parents into a conventional tale about
romantic and tragic love. The tale, about two handsome and tempestuous lovers who die one dark night when their "runaway horse" falls
into the swirling rush of a flooding river, is a satirical parody of a mul-
titude of tales in Southern literature through which either the author or
the reminiscers exalt romantic love and the tragic death of beautiful,
intense lovers. Forerunners of the tale range from Page's "Unc Edinburg's Drowndin'," in which the handsome lover-hero, after leaving
a dance in a fit of jealous despondency, drowns tragically but beautifully one dark stormy night in a flooded river while trying to save his
faithful slave, to a Southern family's romantic tales about tempestuous

Aunt Amy, a much-beloved and radiant beauty who dies an early and tragic death in Porter's "Old Mortality."

Despite Granny's and Beulah's whitewashing of the incidents from the past, Welty succeeds in impressing the reader with the pain and horror they embodied, a pain and horror often lacking in occasions of family sacrifice or tragic love as recorded in other Southern fiction. Faulkner seems to depict romantically rather than ironically an episode vaguely similar to that of Nathan's tale. Whereas Nathan killed a man, allowed a Negro to hang in his place, and cut off his own hand in penance, adolescent Bayard Sartoris in *The Unvanquished* tracked down and killed his grandmother's murderer, cut off the murderer's hand and placed it at his grandmother's grave, and, years later, in penance, swore off violence. Yet Bayard's bloody act of vengeance, which derived also from family devotion and honor, appears less horrible than it does heroic.

By making clear the dishonorable behavior which Beulah's tale conveniently ignores and Granny's comment covers up, Welty calls into question the real truth behind other, seemingly more innocent romanticizations. In addition, the apparent desertion of their children by Beulah's parents punctures the extended Vaughn clan's self-image in particular and the Southern image in general of family togetherness and sacrifice. In the same way, the explanation that Nathan, out of brotherly love, killed a man and allowed a Negro to hang for his crime undermines the very morality of family devotion as a sacred virtue.

Losing Battles surely presents the Southerner's dedication to the past with the tone and exaggeration of parody. The mere fact that Miss Beulah *asks* her husband if he ever thinks of the future emphasizes their lack of thought for it (p. 348). Like Southern families in any respectable novel about the Old South, the Beechams have their tales about the heroics of family members during the Civil War. One such briefly told tale appears to be a parody of tales of such incidents, in that family bravery is claimed so simply and broadly, and without illustration. Uncle Curtis tells a child that Granny's grandfather Captain Jordon " 'Died brave. His son died brave. And there's one of those Jordans, Jack Jordan, they had to starve to death to kill him' " (p. 180).

Aunt Beck would insist that such old stories are reliable because the feelings experienced when the events from the past occurred are lasting and hence reliable (p. 346). This trust in emotions is often said to be typical of the Southerner. Literature frequently contrasts the so-called

Southern intuitive mind with the (often Northern) scientific mind. In Young's *So Red the Rose*, a New Jersey professor who has come South after the Civil War to collect statistics tries to explain to the McGehees that Southerners live by a false ideal, their notion of the Old South being " 'pure romance,' " to which Hugh McGehee replies, " 'That's incidental,' " for " '[t]he point turns on what we believe in and desire, and want to find embodied somewhere' " (pp. 383–84). Like the McGehees, the Vaughn-Beecham-Renfros of *Losing Battles* are guided by their hearts rather than by logic.

Rather than implicitly approving or glorifying such faith in feelings, Welty discovers comic possibilities in it by imagining the consequences if a family should actually live absolutely by feelings and opinions. And, as other Southern writers have done, she emphasizes the family's intuitive approach by setting the group in contrast to representatives of institutionalism and rationality. However, she does not portray these representatives derogatorily. Moreover, her proponents of rationality—Julia Mortimer, a school teacher, and Judge Moody—are "representatives" only incidentally, being fully developed characters. And they are Southerners born and reared, not Northerners who have migrated South. The contrast between Judge Moody and the clan is demonstrated in the judge's initial response to the clan's tales about Gloria's parentage. He attacks the tales on objective and legal grounds as hearsay. On the other hand, Gloria's response is based on personal feelings, as are the Beechams' tales about her parentage; she does not want to have been born a Beecham and thus simply insists stubbornly that she was not. Another explicit example of the contrast occurs as Judge Moody and Jack Renfro cling to a rope from which a car dangles: Moody wants to plan how to solve their problem while Jack relies simply and absurdly on faith in himself.

> "I still believe I can handle trouble just taking it as it comes," he gasped.
> "It takes thinking! We've got to think!" Judge Moody broke out. (p. 390)

The corrective to the Beecham-Renfros' blind faith in themselves as well as to their blind dedication to the past is Julia Mortimer's lesson that through education the people could improve themselves and their region. " 'She wanted us to quit worshipping ourselves quite so wholehearted!' " Miss Beulah says of Julia (p. 236).

Welty draws on still another familiar literary convention: a contrast

between the Southern family rooted in the past and the land, whose
values exemplify humanity, and an upstart aggressor or outsider who
is materialistic, a rootless American Adam figure with no respect for
tradition or the past. By developing this contrast with realism, Welty
parodies the convention.

Besides being selfish and money-oriented, the upstart or outsider
usually does not respect nature. Samuel Mack, a Northerner who comes
to the South following the Civil War, is such a figure in *So Red the
Rose*. According to Hugh McGehee, Mr. Mack " 'buys land, exploits
it, ruins it—what's the difference? is the way he sees the case—and
sells it. In sum, . . . to Mr. Mack the land's no more than stocks and
bonds' " (p. 395). Faulkner's Thomas Sutpen and the Snopeses are
more familiar versions of the type. According to the Beechams' tales,
Dearman was also such a man.

> "Dearman is who showed up full-grown around here, took over some of the
> country, brought niggers in here, cut down every tree within forty miles, and
> run it shrieking through a sawmill." (p. 341)

> "Yes'm, he put up a sawmill where he found the prettiest trees on earth. Lived
> with men in a boxcar and drank liquor. Pretty soon the tallest trees was all
> gone." (p. 341)

Dearman's similarities to such forerunners as Sutpen are striking. Sutpen arrived in Jefferson, Mississippi, in 1833 with apparently no past
and no possessions except a wagon-load of French-speaking Negroes,
and he set about carving a one-hundred-square-mile plantation out of
former Indian territory. Dearman, like Sutpen before him, emerges from
the characters' tales as a cold, calculating man who sees land and people not as valuable in themselves but as means to an end he has set
himself. " 'It was a tearing ambition he had to make all he could out
of us,' " says Uncle Percy. " 'That's him!' said Miss Beulah. 'Just a
great big grabber, that's what Dearman was' " (pp. 341–42). Dearman, like Sutpen, seemed to have a dream, big ambitions, and to know
where he was going.

As the Beechams portray him, Curly Stovall, who acquired Dear-
man's store after his death, could be a descendant of Flem Snopes.
The Stovalls' entry into Banner, as described in a tale told by Mr.
Renfro, is a concise parallel to the Snopeses' entry into Frenchman's
Bend, described at the beginning of *The Hamlet*: " 'The first Stovalls

around here walked into Banner barefooted—three of 'em, and one of
'em's wife. I don't know what description of hog-wallow they come
from,' said Mr. Renfro . . . 'but the storekeeper then alive put the
one in long pants to work for him. Stovalls is with us and bury with
us' " (p. 23). Like Flem, Curly started working for the storekeeper
and eventually had the store. He has no dream; in the Beecham-Renfros' opinion, he is a low-class manipulator motivated only by self-
aggrandizement. Just as Flem as store manager charged the store owners themselves for every item they took, so is Curly careful of every
penny: " 'Curly don't let even a Baptist preacher have anything free,' "
says Uncle Percy (p. 35). He charges the Moodys two dollars for his
part in rescuing their car from the cliff's edge whereas the Renfros
practice the hospitality and humanity associated with members of the
Old South tradition in inviting the stranded Moodys home for dinner,
putting them up for the night, and generously helping them rescue their
car from Banner Top.

Welty's portrait of the upstart aggressor seems, then, to be quite
conventional. This synopsis of Dearman and Stovall is drawn, however, from biased sources: largely from the uncles' and aunts' stories
about them. Having been killed by Uncle Nathan some time before the
present action, Dearman is seen only through such tales, and then only
briefly. Curly, on the other hand, appears both in person and in many
tales, and the total picture of him reveals sharp contrasts to the typical
cold aggressor type—contrasts reflective of Welty's comic-realistic vision. Curly emerges as a round character not without humanity and a
sense of humor. Physically, he is the opposite of the short, gaunt, silent Flem Snopes:

"He's great big and has little bitty eyes!" came the voice of Ella Fay. . . .
"Baseball cap and sideburns." (p. 23)

"Listen, Sister Cleo, here's what Curly Stovall is: big and broad as the kitchen
stove, red in the face as Tom Turkey, and ugly as sin all over . . . " said
Uncle Dolphus. (p. 25)

The enmity between Curly and Jack Renfro is as good-humored as it
is serious. Though it is Curly's testimony that sends Jack to prison,
the two greet each other upon Jack's return like long-separated bosom
friends, slapping each other on the back and sizing each other up with
affection. Political rival to Jack's Uncle Homer Champion, Curly can-

not resist showing off in front of Homer when the latter arrives at the
scene of the car rescue. Curly hops out of his truck "into the naked
air, and heavy-shouldered as if doubled over in knots of laughter, he
cut a short caper, his face beaming from side to side, and then he was
back inside again" (p. 388).

Unlike the cold-mannered Flem, Curly is actively interested in women.
" 'Better Friendship Methodist is where he worships, and at pro-
tracted meetings, or so I'm told, every girl younger'n forty-five runs
from him,' said Uncle Percy primly" (p. 24). In one of the family's
tales, Ella Fay Renfro, at age fourteen, is described as an earthy country girl whom Curly chases when she comes into his store. Like Faulkner's Eula Varner, Ella Fay is an early bloomer, ripe for the picking.
At age sixteen, she announces that she may marry Curly, and it is clear
the marriage will be a lively one based on mutual attraction. Hence
the enmity between the Renfros and the Stovalls is drawing to an end,
and the resolution is happier than the lifeless arranged marriage of Eula
to Flem. Jack's only complaint is that the marriage will mean an end
to his playful battles with Curly.

Thus Curly, the capitalist in comic mask, shows himself to be more
human than his literary predecessors, not so cold and unfeeling, a jolly,
fun-loving fellow. Whereas Flem leaves his cousin Mink Snopes to rot
in jail, Curly himself had put up bail money for Jack, although Curly
was the victim of Jack's "crime." Even so, Jack's family passes Curly's
action off as one of pure greed: " 'How else did he think Renfros was
going to live? How else did he figure he stood a chance of getting a
penny out of 'em?' " (p. 45). This apparently spiteful interpretation
of Curly's action may suggest that the family's remembrance of Dearman is also one-sided. Curly is a round character (both physically and
theoretically), a money-hungry manipulator who can be humane, a
"good ole boy" who loves fun, a contest, and girls, whereas Flem is
a flat character (and a skinny runt), representing an idea rather than
flesh-and-blood humanity.

> . . . he cried, "Do you know me?"
> "It's Odysseus!" I called, to spoil the moment. But with a shout he had
> already sprung to their damp embrace.
> Reunions, it seems, are to be celebrated. . . . All of us feasted together on
> meat and bread, honey and wine, and the fire roared. We heard out the flute
> player, we heard out the story, and the fair-haired sailor . . . danced on the
> table. . . . (Welty, "Circe," *BI*, 106)

Southern literature and the tall tale are not the only narrative traditions which lie back of *Losing Battles*. Welty weaves into the novel borrowings from still another tradition. Whereas in *Delta Wedding* and *The Golden Apples* she alludes to classical mythology in suggesting the myth-making which storytelling about heroes often amounts to, in *Losing Battles* she adds allusions to epic patterns, borrows epic conventions, and occasionally evokes the visage of Odysseus. As early reviewers noted, *Losing Battles* is, like *The Odyssey*, the story of the homecoming of a tribal hero. The association is no accident. Welty has drawn on *The Odyssey* before, most explicitly for "Circe," in which appear motifs and incidental actions that reappear in *Losing Battles*. But though its epic framework is extensive and purposeful, *Losing Battles* is no epic and Jack Renfro not the superhero his relatives think him. Rather, the novel is a comic epic or mock epic about the rural South, and Jack Renfro is the comic epic hero, in reality more akin to Joseph Andrews and Don Quixote than to Odysseus.[8] The parody of Southern literary conventions and Southern ideals as well as the tall tale exaggerations are consistent with the comic epic context—just as the comic epic context contributes to the parody and tall tale.

In fact, given its implicit parody of a tradition in Southern literature and its comic epic design, *Losing Battles* might suggest an ironic parallel between two times in which oral storytelling produced a written literature. Just as oral tales about national or tribal history and heroes lie behind the great folk epics of the past, so does the oral storytelling about family heroes and regional history which followed the Civil War lie back of much Southern literature, not as verbatim source necessarily but as influence on the writers who are the recognized bards of the South. In both cases, oral storytelling and myth-making led to a written mythology or epic literature about a people. *Losing Battles* might reflect this oral-to-written pattern, the bards of the Beecham family creating a folk epic and Welty acting as epic poet to record it.

A folk epic is the oral history of a people passed down through the years by successive generations of experienced storytellers. *Losing Battles* portrays such oral history in progress. The ancestral happenings of the extended Vaughn family have been and are now being passed down by word of mouth from one generation to the next. On grand occasions which draw the clan together, such as the present annual reunion celebrating the ninetieth birthday of the head of the clan and the homecoming of the tribal hero, such tales are told. Like the stories of the bards of old, these stories are a major form of entertainment, they preserve and mythicize tribal history, and they typically focus on the deeds of heroes. Invited to the reunion specifically to entertain the clan with a long saga of its history, Brother Bethune, a Baptist preacher, is the professional bard, but more popular ones are the uncles and aunts who tell their stories throughout the day.

Welty plays the role of the epic poet who collects the oral tales and weaves them into a written record, dividing her uncharacteristically long novel into five major "Parts," just as lengthy epics are often divided into "Books." And she plays the role straight, self-effacingly, spotlighting neither the epic conventions nor the irony behind them. However, her style in descriptive or narrative passages, which has perplexed and displeased some critics, is a clue to the role she has assumed. The novel begins this way:

When the rooster crowed, the moon had still not left the world but was going down on flushed cheek, one day short of the full. A long thin cloud crossed it slowly, drawing itself out like a name being called. The air changed, as if a mile or so away a wooden door had swung open, and a smell, more of warmth than wet, from a river at low stage, moved upward into the clay hills that stood in darkness.

Then a house appeared on its ridge, like an old man's silver watch pulled once more out of its pocket. (p. 3)

A departure from the short, unadorned factual statements with which Welty's works often begin, the flowing, melodious style of this passage would seem lofty were its fecund poetic images not homey and its vocabulary not simple. Yet some critics have found this descriptive style falsely poetic and inorganic to the work. The profusion of metaphors and similes is, one has said, "a gentle overkill."[9] Once we recognize *Losing Battles* as the long epic poem it pretends to be, and this passage as part of its prologue, however, the images and style seem exactly right. Not as long or elaborate as the famous Homeric similes, Welty's numerous similes are adapted to the unsophisticated nation or clan being described. For her comic epic, she has designed a style which suggests, without mirroring, the conventional epic style of "grand simplicity."

Indeed, in introducing dawn through the personification of the moon, the opening sentence of her prologue—"When the rooster crowed, the moon had still not left the world but was going down on flushed cheek, one day short of the full''—might seem a quaint imitation of Homer, an allusion to the epic style of *The Odyssey*, in which several books begin with a personification of dawn ("When primal Dawn spread on the eastern sky/ her fingers of pink light . . . "[10]). Welty's version is poetic without being elevated, a perfectly conceived style for a comic epic about the rural South.

This poetic style adopted by the epic poet is pronouncedly different from the energetic, conversational style of the local storytellers (or bards), whose voices are heard much of the time, and the contrast intensifies the distinctiveness of the former. Even while choosing homey images and simple language to describe a poor farm setting, Welty maintains the epic poet's tone of high seriousness. Furthermore, the contrast in styles represents the difference between the artistic and literate style of the poet, writing in a later century, and the oral style of a pre-writing society, preserving its history in tribal tales. For although she sets the story in the 1930's, Welty emphasizes that the gregarious Vaughn descendants consider reading and writing esoteric activities. Rather than writing to Jack in the many months he is away, his parents and uncles save up tales to tell him. And when Judge Moody reads a letter aloud during the reunion, Aunt Birdie complains, " 'I can't understand it when he reads it to us. Can't he just tell it?' " (p. 298).

It is easy to see that the novel's numerous Biblical allusions (for example, Jack is called "a Good Samaritan" and "the Prodigal Son") are organic to the work, consistent with the characters' ready familiarity with Bible stories. But recognition of the novel's epic framework makes the allusions newly suggestive. Like the allusions to epic patterns, they appear to amplify the action of the story by associating it with an antecedent of great seriousness and cosmic significance. Like *The Bible* and *The Odyssey, Losing Battles* is a long poetic narrative which records the adventures and history of a people as the people themselves view them.

But a story of great seriousness and cosmic significance? Certainly not. The melodious rhythm, Biblical references, and epic allusions belie the true nature of this work. Despite the epic poet's dignified tone, *Losing Battles* has neither the epic's solemnity nor characters of heroic proportions. After all, an epic hero is a hero who struggles but wins battles, whereas in Welty's story, battles are continually lost. Moreover, whereas the conventional epic hero faces such superpowerful foes as sorceresses, angry gods, and warriors of other nations, Jack Renfro's chief opponent is a fat, red-headed "good ole boy" who owns the local general store; and the family's long-time enemy, whom they oppose ferociously, is a lonely school teacher who wages a single-handed war against ignorance and complacency.

This discrepancy recalls, of course, the difference between the serious epic and the comic one. Welty has written a "comic-epic-poem-in-prose" which, like Henry Fielding's, exposes romantic attitudes. Hers, like his, is a parody, though not of a specific literary work but of conventions of a storytelling and literary tradition. The comic epic's distinctions from "the serious romance," as described by Fielding, can be seen in *Losing Battles*: its "fable and action" are not "grave and solemn" but largely "light and ridiculous"; its characters, poverty-stricken, uneducated dirt farmers of Mississippi hill country, are of "inferior rank and consequently of inferior manners," having neither the exalted positions of the characters of classical epics nor the alleged graces of the upper-crust Southerners of plantation society; and its "sentiments and diction" are "not of the sublime" but often of the "ludicrous."[11] Indeed, the comedy of the book's sentiments and diction is illustrated by the incongruity between the epic poet's tone of high seriousness and the small world of often trivial actions which she describes.

In this comic epic about the rural South, then, characteristics of the traditional epic are rendered comic by being given a rural flavor. The serious epic has catalogues of warriors and armies. *Losing Battles* has "catalogues" of domestic things, such as a "catalogue" sixteen-items-long of the birthday presents given a beloved grandmother (ranging from "a pillow of new goose feathers" to a "nine-month-old, already treeing, long-eared Blue-tick coonhound pup," p. 287). The serious epic has a setting broad in scope, its hero travelling far from home, across seas and into unfamiliar countries. *Losing Battles*'s setting is a small Mississippi farm and the nearby dirt and gravel roads, along which the whole county spins on the day of the reunion, bringing adventures *to* the hero. But first the hero returns from a long sojourn in foreign territory. Whereas Odysseus returns home after eighteen years of glorious war and adventure on the other side of the sea, Jack Renfro returns home after eighteen months in prison on the other side of the state. Yet to the isolated rural Southerner, the state penitentiary at Parchman could be the other side of the world.

Aunt Birdie suddenly asked, "Where *is* Parchman?" . . .

Uncle Curtis said, "Well, only our brother Nathan's ever seen for himself where it is. . . . "

Vaughn . . . pointed straight through them. "Go clean across Mississippi from here, go till you get ready to fall in the Mississippi River."

"Is he in *Arkansas*?" cried a boy cousin. . . . (pp. 69–70)

Not quite. Parchman is in the Delta area of Mississippi, a fertile farming region viewed by the Beechams and Renfros of the red clay hills as a land flowing with milk and honey and peopled by a foreign race, a paradise that Odysseus might have encountered during his travels. " 'Jack's in the Delta,' said Uncle Curtis. 'Clear out of the hills and into the good land. . . . Where it's running with riches and swarming with niggers everywhere you look' " (p. 74).

In all her works in which there is a living legendary hero, Welty has had a group tell tales about him before she presents him in the flesh. The approach is ideally suited to the comic-epic context of *Losing Battles*. Faithful to the traditional epic pattern, *Losing Battles* begins *in medias res*, with the day of the hero's homecoming rather than with the "Trojan" battle with Curly Stovall that precipitated his leave, and past action is recounted by the Beecham bards, who sing of Jack's previous adventures for seventy-five pages before he himself suddenly bursts upon the scene.

In one tale, Uncle Percy praises Jack for his heroic feats on the first day of school two years ago, when Jack was seventeen. Upon arriving at school, Jack " 'ran and shot two or three dozen basketball goals without a miss, hung on the oak branch while Vaughn counted to a hundred out loud, and when it's time to pledge allegiance he run up the flag and led the salute, and then come in and killed all the summer flies while the teacher was still getting started' " (p. 28). The tale illuminates the mock-heroic nature of the epic, epic heroes usually shooting without a miss three dozen arrows rather than three dozen basketball goals and killing all the tribe's enemies rather than all the summer flies. That is, unless they are local heroes of rural America. And they become comic heroes when their feats are viewed as of more than local significance. While Jack is a hero of epic proportions to his family, and ancestral history is appreciated by the family as much as if it were of national importance, the family's view of its importance and his heroism seems absurd to the reader.

And thus we arrive at the effect and an apparent purpose of the comic-epic design of the work. The epic pattern and epic allusions serve as reflections of the family's glorification of its heroes and its way of life. Welty mocks, good-naturedly, the insulation of life in the rural South. The Vaughn descendants have such an exaggerated notion of their own importance and the glory of their favorite sons because they know so little of the larger world. Hostile to education and books, expressed explicitly through their rejection of school teacher Julia Mortimer, they have little knowledge of or interest in the world outside their county. To most of them, their immediate environment is the whole world, and they themselves are at its center. At one point after his return, Jack carries his baby to the top of Banner Top Cliff, a few hundred yards from the family home, and "show[s] her the world." He points out all the familiar landmarks, as though he is a god looking down on his kingdom from on high. " 'Right here in the world is where I call it plain beautiful,' said Jack. 'That way is Banner.' He pointed. 'And that's the other way' " (pp. 101–2). And Welty, in the objective, dignified voice of the epic poet, describes this setting as it would appear to a local chronicler. In the prologue, she equates the Vaughn farm with the world at large: "the moon had still not left the world" and chickens are let "loose on the world."

In particular, Welty's account of the homecoming of the hero—when Jack finally arrives after much anticipation—demonstrates the role of the mock-heroic effects. She uses images to suggest the high importance that the homecoming has for the family. It could be the Second Coming—" 'Might as well be coming back from the dead,' " says Miss Lexie—or the triumphant return of a knight of old. Yet the colorful procession, the blowing trumpets, the beating drums, the waving flags, and the cheering throngs which one would expect to greet a returning warrior, or the thunder and earthquake linked to the return of the Biblical hero, are rendered through rural counterparts:

There came a sound like a pistol shot from out in the yard. All heads turned front. Ella Fay had cracked the first starched tablecloth out of its folds—it waved like a flag. Then she dropped it on the ground and came running toward them, screaming. Dogs little and big set up a tenor barking. Dogs ran from all corners of the yard and from around the house and through the passage, streaking for the front gate.

The floor "drum[s] and sway[s]" as family members rush out in response to the commotion, and the new tin roof seems "to quiver with a sound like all the family spoons set jingling in their glass." Then suddenly, out of the "whirlwind of dust" created by the dogs, a smiling nineteen-year-old boy materializes: Jack Jordan Renfro, home at last (p. 71).

It is a mock-heroic, comic rural description of the hero's return, yet to the gathered family Jack is a knight in shining armor. The contrast between their certainty of his magnificence and the ragged, sweating nineteen-year-old boy who appears is humorous. He has cockleburs on his pants legs, June bugs on his torn sleeve, and split, worn-out shoes on his feet. Although Jack is returning from prison, the imagery and welcome suggest that he is returning from war. His torn sleeve "flowed free from his shoulder like some old flag carried home from far-off battle." Like the noble warrior Odysseus returning home disguised as a beggar and riding in on the waves of the sea, Jack arrives in shabby attire, "[r]iding a wave of dogs" (p. 71). However, to Jack's poverty-stricken family, such shabbiness is no disguise.

After being fondled by the womenfolk, Jack faces the first task often awaiting the long-absent warrior or king. He must re-establish his authority in the homeland and banish pretenders to the throne. Though Jack's place in the hearts of his people has never been challenged, in his absence his twelve-year-old brother Vaughn has, by necessity, assumed Jack's responsibilities on the farm, just as he has usurped his big brother's one pair of pants. A playful duel ensues between Jack as the returning king who had seemed to have forsaken his homeland and Vaughn as the son who had to try to play a man's role in his father's absence—a duel fought with cornstalks rather than swords! (p. 72).

This play-duel is hardly distinguishable from Jack's real battles, though the latter have graver consequences. Whereas a serious epic records challenging deeds requiring superhuman valor from the hero, Welty's comic epic records ludicrous deeds executed with extraordinary earnestness but foolhardiness by Jack. His combats display the country boy's love of rough competitions fought determinedly but light-heartedly. They are initiated for a reason common to epic battles: in defense of pride and honor. The conventional epic hero may act in defense of his own; Jack more often acts in defense of the family's. Exemplifying an American—especially a Southern—heroic ideal, Jack is the champion of the weak, the protector of the family.

His first battle, with his bosom enemy the burly Curly Stovall, took place two years earlier and got him sent to prison. The fight had a goal appropriate to mythic adventures, possession of a gold ring, a Renfro family heirloom which Curly had confiscated as payment for past-due Renfro bills. According to the storytelling of the Beecham bards, this rip-roaring fist fight ended with Curly tied in a coffin in his general store and the hero staggering home with Curly's huge safe on his back, the ring presumably inside. The tale is a farcical version of nostalgic tales Southern characters narrate about the heroic efforts of devoted sons and brothers to defend the family and its honor.

Heroic though Jack appears in the tale to his family, to the impartial observer—the reader and the new Beecham aunt, Aunt Cleo—he is more like the buffoon of a tall tale, a giant-killer by reputation only. Aunt Cleo wonders, " 'How come he didn't just crack open that safe and try carrying home nothing but the ring?' " And Aunt Birdie explains (or exclaims), " 'Do you think he had all day?' " After the panting hero dropped it a few times, the old safe cracked open on its own, and whatever was inside fell out and was lost in the dust. Jack's mother stresses the size and weight of the safe (" 'big as a house and twice as heavy!' ") and hence Jack's superstrength in being able to carry it at all. Aunt Cleo, on the other hand, puts the emphasis on Jack's fool-ishness: " 'And just to think of an ignorant boy walking along this hilly old part of the world, dropping out pennies and nickels and dimes and quarters behind him!' " (pp. 30–31).

Beulah and the uncles elevate Jack's sportive battle and his foolish incompetence afterwards to heroic action while Aunt Cleo trims the glitter from the tale, baring the seventeen-year-old boy's ignorance and foolhardiness. Nonetheless, the family is not deterred from seeing Jack as a shining and noble hero, the embodiment of sacred family values. " 'To me and the majority,' Uncle Curtis said, 'Jack had acted the only way a brother and son could act, and done what any other good Mississippi boy would have done in his place' " (p. 43).

The second adventure, also the product of family pride, occurs on the day of the reunion. Outraged that Jack has played the Good Samaritan to a way-laid traveler discovered afterwards to be the very judge who had sentenced him to prison, Jack's family now orders him to push Judge Moody's car right back into a ditch where it belongs. Jack himself spells out for his wife the purpose of his errand: " 'Family duty' " (p. 103). Like Jack's earlier battle with Curly, the silly errand on which his family sends him surely parodies conventional romantic incidents through which Southern heroes fulfill family duty—incidents such as knightly duels over insults, challenges to unsuitable suitors of sisters, and revenge against murderers of grandmothers and fathers. And Jack is just as incompetent at accomplishing this task as he was at regaining the gold ring from Curly. Rather than pushing the car into a ditch, he ends up trying to rescue it from the edge of a cliff.

A third battle comes near the end of the epic. In a fist fight again, the hero is knocked out by Curly, who then cuts off Jack's shirt-tail. The latter action appears a rustic symbol for defeating an opponent, a ludicrous but harmless counterpart to the Indian warrior's scalping his enemy and the Greek warrior's taking the armor and mistresses of his enemy. Curly nails his shirt-tail trophy up in his store for display, just as frontier hunters displayed their coon-tail trophies.

All these adventures reveal Jack to be in reality not the hero of extraordinary powers that his family thinks he is but instead an eager and noble-hearted son who more often causes than remedies family problems. In comic-epic fashion, Jack's ignorance and innocence contrast sharply with Odysseus's prodigious cunning. Always acting on impulse rather than from forethought, Jack is no Odysseus "skilled in all ways of contending." [12] On the contrary, he is very like another mock hero, the good-intentioned but bumbling Don Quixote, also an impulsive romantic who over-rates his abilities. And like Don Quixote, Jack loses one laughable battle after another yet remains undaunted, never recognizing defeat.

The heroine of the epic, Jack's wife Gloria, [13] fights her battles as relentlessly and often as naively as does he. A red-headed country girl, she fights her in-laws for possession of Jack and for an identity separate from them. During the reunion she consciously establishes two things as emblems of her superiority to the clan: the dress she wears, a large-skirted, white dress made of store-bought lace and satin; and her refusal to eat or to allow her child to eat common Beecham food. Both emblems figure in symbolic defeats which Gloria experiences during the day.

Her humiliation begins with a mock-heroic battle featuring women as warriors and watermelon as the weapon. To Gloria, watermelon, which the otherwise barren land produces in bushel-basket size, is representative of Beechanism—common and low-class. Thus, when the Beecham aunts half playfully wrestle her to the ground and roughly force watermelon down her throat in an attempt to make her admit she too is a Beecham, they have symbolically beaten her. Somewhat subdued by this indignity, Gloria afterwards submits passively to criticism of her dress and to the scissors of Aunt Lexie Renfro. Wearing dresses probably made from feed sacks, the aunts scorn Gloria's white, wide-skirted, satin dress as impractical and frivolous—a waste of money and many yards of material. And they resent its implicit defiance of them, its capacity for singling Gloria out from the rest. So when Lexie Renfro begins to cut away much of the skirt, with Gloria still wearing it, Gloria's defeat is symbolically assured: Lexie is remaking the dress to fit the family's image of correctness, just as they would like to remake Gloria. Lexie's paring away of Gloria's skirt-tail is a parallel to Curly's cutting of Jack's shirt-tail as a mock-heroic, rural emblem of the heroine's defeat.

Just as Jack never recognizes defeat, Gloria, who is aware of both her own and her husband's losses of individual battles, will never give up the field. These warriors' illusions about their abilities to win appear preposterous. In one moment, Jack, clinging stubbornly to a rope from which a car dangles, cries " 'I ain't never licked!,' " and in the next, the rope breaks and both he and the car go plummeting over the cliff. Similarly, Gloria, rising from her humiliating defeat by the Beecham aunts, denies that she is licked. And despite the preponderance of evidence that Jack will continue to serve his whole family, Gloria holds onto the illusion that she can separate him from them: " 'I still believe I can do it, if I live long enough' " (p. 356). She dreams of their moving to a " 'little two-room house, where nobody in the world could find us—' " (p. 431). Jack's notion of the ideal home is the direct opposite of Gloria's. He imagines himself out plowing and fence-mending while his wife helps his mother in the kitchen, tutors his little brother, and gives his little sisters " 'ladylike examples of behavior' " (p. 360).

At novel's end, Jack's and Gloria's individual dreams remain unchanged. The last glimpse of Jack is of him as the ideal Beecham-Renfro hero, planning to farm for his whole family—" 'My wife and girl baby and all of 'em at home' "—and singing the harvest hymn "Bringing in the Sheaves." And "all Banner could hear him and know who he was": Jack Jordan Renfro of the Vaughn-Beecham-Renfro clan. Gloria has illusions about separating Jack from his family; Jack has illusions about pulling the whole family out of poverty through simple faith, will power, and muscle power. " 'And I've got my strength,' " he says. " 'I can provide. Don't you ever fear' " (p. 434).

Though Jack is looked to as the champion and savior in the battle

against poverty and the deterioration of the farms, this battle belongs
to the whole clan, the whole county. It is the major battle of the small
farmer of the 1930's—or of almost any time. A one-sided war, it requires continuous heroic effort from its human participants but seldom
rewards them with success or heroic stature. The Beecham-Renfros have
been fighting "General Green" for years but year by year have lost
ground in the struggle. Nonetheless, they remain optimistic about the
future, the uncles vowing they are " 'Farmers still and ever more will
be' " (p. 194). Like Gloria and Jack, these other warriors are winners
in their hearts if not in fact. Welty admires their determination to fight
on, yet she, like Julia Mortimer (who is short-sighted in other ways),
is aware too of the foolishness of such a blind and extreme optimism
which leads them to rely for victory on little more than human will.

Ironically, they are losing the battle against poverty partly because
they have won that against Julia. Though the many politicians, teachers, lawyers, and doctors among her former students who show up for
Julia's funeral are evidence that her struggle to educate local children
was not entirely in vain, most of these successes settled outside the
impoverished rural area, making Boone County the loser. Moreover,
the majority of Julia's students resisted her efforts. Content with doing
things the way they always have, the extended Vaughn clan win in the
struggle against Julia—and hence face more likely defeat in the dire
battle with the land. By insulating themselves in their small and narrow world, they make certain that their world will remain small.

That defeat is so often the outcome of the characters' battles is consistent with the realism of the novel and the character of a comic epic.
Moreover, defeat is the appropriate solution in a comic epic about
Southern life and its traditional values in that the Old South out of which
those values supposedly grew experienced a never-forgotten defeat in
the Civil War. Just as that South fought a battle of national importance
in an attempt to preserve "its way of life," the extended Vaughn clan
fights civil wars of great tribal importance with many local forces
(Gloria, Julia Mortimer, Dearman, Curly Stovall, encroaching poverty) in an attempt to preserve its values and way of life. Furthermore,
the Beecham-Renfros' illusions about themselves, their battles, and their
favorite son recall the Southern sense of romance which turned a war
of defeat into a glorious mythology full of brave, faultless heroes and
stubborn, virtuous heroines.

Thus, in parodying values and conventions made familiar through a mass of Southern literature, *Losing Battles* good-naturedly mocks Southerners for their illusions about themselves and their history. The ironic epic framework and epic allusions give form and unity to the novel while also serving as a comic reflection of Southerners' sense of grandeur in their small world.

Despite the characters' poverty, despite their defeats in battle, despite the author's exposure of their many human flaws, *Losing Battles* has a spirit that soars. The book's spirited life derives not from any one factor but from the combination of ingredients that compose it: the highly amusing tall tale told by the author, her exhaustive comic-realistic portrayal of the clan's oral culture, the underlying parody and comic-epic design, and the clan's own very evident joy in living. Also, it has—as any epic or comic epic must—a captivating hero. Jack Jordan Renfro is a wonderfully conceived hero who deserves another word.

Jack lacks the conventional epic hero's awesome superior abilities. At the same time, he is not a comic epic's broadly drawn farcical fool whose only identity derives from repetitive foolish adventures. Rather, he transcends the level of parody. He is a simple fellow who breathes and feels and shines and stumbles, a supreme product of Welty's comic-realism. Though we laugh at his impulsive, bumbling antics and smile at his exaggerated confidence in himself, we love and even admire him. In his loyalty, devotion to the family, love of the past, and self-sacrifice, he exhibits the traditional Southern values at their best, without the meanness of some of the rest of his family. And in his determination to win, his genuine effort, and his extensive love and generosity—even toward the family's enemies, Judge Moody and Julia Mortimer—he exhibits the heroic spirit at its very best. Though he loses his battles, he more than survives; he triumphs as a human being.

The magic of his portrait emanates from the conjunction of realistic detail with an evoking of archetypes from various literary and oral traditions. For Jack is a comic yet realistic version not only of the mythic Southern hero but also of, for example, a related hero type, the clean-cut All-American boy. Like the mythic All-American boy, Jack is a commoner who excels in sports (basketball) and who loves not only his family but also his buddy (Aycock Comfort, whom Jack remains loyal to, despite his wife's disapproval), his dog (Sid, who is the first to greet Jack upon his return from prison and who accompanies him on his day-long adventures), his horse (Dan, whose alleged death moves

Jack to tears, as does the eventual discovery that Dan is still alive),
his truck (a do-all contraption which Jack has built lovingly from
wrecked parts and which his wife Gloria labels " 'just a play-pretty
. . . a man's something-to-play with' "), and his religion. At novel's
end, Jack is singing a hymn as he follows Sid and escorts his wife
toward home. Jack is the self-confident, clean-cut, dutiful, athletic All-
American boy, loved by and lover of the old and the young. He is the
mythical male of rural America: the boy with his dog, the Westerner
with his horse, the twentieth-century teenager with his car or pickup
truck.

Jack's relation to Aycock Comfort also evokes a familiar archetype,
that of a hero with a sidekick of lower station or of comic appearance.
Aycock, considered white trash by Jack's family, plays a hillbilly Smiley
Burnette to Jack's undignified Gene Autry; or, for a Southern parallel,
he plays the faithful black servant to Jack's Southern hero role. Like
Thomas Nelson Page's Unc Edinburg and such Western sidekicks as
Smiley, Aycock is frightened where the hero is brave, and selfish where
the hero is self-sacrificing. But he is also practical and realistic where
the hero is romantic: whereas Jack thinks that if he hangs onto the rope
from which the car dangles long enough, he will surely win the absurd
tug of war with the car, Aycock refuses to join the human chain stretched
out in the mud but, right before the rope breaks, offers advice: " 'You
could cut that rope,' suggested Aycock. 'Save time' " (p. 390). Hence
another and older forerunner of Jack and Aycock's relationship is that
of the romanticizing Don Quixote and his faithful but practical retainer
Sancho Panza.

And here we are back at the earlier similarity noted between Jack
and Don Quixote: they are mock-heroic figures who refuse to acknowledge defeat. Jack's heroic cry, " 'I ain't never licked,' " echoes
through time, an idiomatic expression of the battle cry of all mythical
heroes. Yet it is also a peculiarly American battle cry, and most particularly the cry of the mythical hero of the South, where—paradoxically—a great war admittedly was lost . . . yet no heroes were ever
licked.

8

THE OPTIMIST'S
DAUGHTER: *REWRITING*
THE SOUTHERN NOVEL

In creating a great fiction which has become synonymous with Southern literature, William Faulkner also created a problem for other Southern
writers, a problem described by Louis D. Rubin, Jr., in 1967 in his
essay "The Difficulties of Being a Southern Writer Today: Or, Getting
Out from Under William Faulkner":

So far as literature goes, the South of the period between 1925 and 1950 is
most importantly William Faulkner's South. Compsons, Sutpens, Sartorises,
Snopes, de Spains, Beauchamps, McCaslins—the image is accurate, inevitable, unforgettable. It is safe to say, I think, that few Southern writers coming
after Faulkner can fail to respond to him.[1]

Rubin gives evidence that some writers respond to the master with poor
imitations of him; they succumb to his influence. Lifelong resident of
the same state as Faulkner, Eudora Welty might have been especially
susceptible to his influence. She has said that living in the same realm
as Faulkner was "like living near a big mountain, something majes-
tic."[2] Yet Welty has managed, while admiring the mountain, to create
an admirable art of her own.

  She has, however, responded to Faulkner, or, rather, to the larger
Southern literary tradition of which he is the dominant force. She has
drawn on elements of this tradition as spontaneously as she has drawn
on her broad familiarity with other narrative resources such as fairy
tales and ancient mythology. But as her career has progressed and the
tradition has become more clearly definable, her response seems to have
become increasingly more conscious. In an interview in 1972 she her-

self commented on the Southern writer's dilemma: "I mean the art of writing as a Southerner would now be a self-conscious thing to do. . . . It never used to be. When we were coming along we just wrote because this is where we lived and what we knew. But to write strictly a Southern book now—I think you are quite conscious that you are seeing a segment and that people are going to look at it—." [3]

Her two most recent novels, *Losing Battles* and *The Optimist's Daughter*, published in 1970 and 1972, reveal a continual acknowledgment of the Southern literary tradition. With *Losing Battles* Welty does not follow the tradition but instead uses and parodies many of its conventions in a work distinctively her own. *The Optimist's Daughter's* relation to the tradition is not so ironic. In it Welty creates a strikingly original character in Laurel McKelva Hand, yet she also echoes motifs common to much Southern literature. The novel evokes the popular theme of the changing South, an "Old South" with a strong sense of tradition and community giving way to a "New South" with little regard for either. Just as *The Shoe Bird* is Welty's children's book and "The Purple Hat" her ghost story, *The Optimist's Daughter* might be her traditional Southern novel.

Welty brings freshness and even originality to the tradition, however. She subtly modifies recognizable character types, techniques, and themes, thus avoiding a nostalgic lament for dying or lost values, the direction in which the novel initially seems to be heading. This time, the oral culture does not have the boisterously comic and central role that it has in *The Ponder Heart* and *Losing Battles* but, in a more inconspicuous way, contributes to the characterization of the amenities of the Old Tradition and the vulgarity of the New—and to the new insight that Welty brings to established territory.

In taking up the familiar theme of the changing South in this novel, Welty introduces a standard character contrast: New South representatives versus Old South ones. [4] In the conflicts between characters in her preceding novels, there is never the implication that a character or a group represents a rising class whose vulgar values threaten the old, sacred values. In *Losing Battles*, Gloria Short Renfro may want " 'to live for the future,' " but she is not an emblem of the future. Similarly, Curly Stovall and Dearman pose no serious threat to the traditional values. Rather than representing a new South, Gloria, Curly, and Dearman, like the Beechams and the Moodys and Julia Mortimer, are part of the total composition of The South. In *The Optimist's Daughter*, on the other hand, while the two opposing groups again belong to The South, at the same time the Old-Family McKelvas represent a tradition that seems to be passing away while the Chisoms are part of the new Southern mechanization and consumerism. The former are explicitly associated with the past, the latter with the future.

The initial portrait of the small, stable community, Mount Salus, Mississippi, is fairly conventional. This old town has many stately homes still occupied by descendants of their original owners. Its citizens follow leisurely community traditions, the women enjoying a gardening club, the men a hunting and fishing club, and the whole community partaking in the funeral activities constituting much of the novel's action. The town's leading family, the McKelvas, are descendants of the area's earliest settlers and plantation owners. As a young man, Clinton McKelva went to college in Virginia and brought back home a West Virginia bride. Like his ancestors, he spent his life quietly pouring money and influence back into the community to help it improve itself. He became a lawyer and then a judge and served as town mayor. At his death at age seventy-one, his house is full of relics of the past. In his honor, the courthouse lowers its flag and the businesses close on the day of his funeral.

The comedy of Welty's previous portraits of members of old respectable families is lacking here. Neither exuberant Fairchild talkers, obsessive Ponder gabbers, nor tireless Beecham tale-tellers, the McKelvas enjoy quiet conversations and occasional warm reminiscences. Laurel McKelva Hand remembers stories from her childhood which her mother told her about the mother's own happy girlhood in West Virginia. In addition, the McKelvas are Welty's first aristocrats (aristocrats by local standards) to display a high regard for such intellectual or cultural activities as reading books. They have a well-stocked and well-used family library and a long-practiced custom of reading. The parents read to their daughter when she was a child and to one another when she was put to bed, and Laurel rereads to her father one of his favorite books, *Nicholas Nickleby*, while he is hospitalized. By contrast, in the author's earlier portraits of prominent local families, the oral tradition and nonintellectualism go hand in hand, talking and bustle being valued over any intellectual or solitary pursuit. One of many examples appears in *Delta Wedding* in Battle Fairchild's refusal to allow his daughter Shelley to have a reading lamp in her room; he prefers that she read in the lower part of the house amidst family flurry. In respecting the written equally with the oral word, the McKelvas of *The Optimist's Daughter* are more typical of aristocrats portrayed in many other Southern novels and of the Southerners described in *I'll Take My Stand*.

This time, it is the upstart Chisoms who scorn books and talk constantly, and these characteristics now become points of satire rather than of good-natured humor. Whereas in *The Ponder Heart* Edna Earle Ponder's warning to her visitor that reading will "put your eyes out" (p. 11) reveals amusingly how desperate Edna is to talk to someone, Wanda Fay Chisom McKelva's similar comment in the later work illustrates not only anti-intellectualism but ignorance and insensitivity as well. As her husband recuperates from a critical eye operation, she blames his trouble on the years he spent " 'putting [his] eyes out' " reading " 'dusty old books' " (p. 25). The Chisoms' incessant, unimaginative talking recalls the triteness of shallow-minded characters satirized in some of Welty's early short stories. At the gathering preceding Judge McKelva's funeral, they repeatedly voice commonplace platitudes. Sis says to Mrs. Chisom when the latter bemoans the long-past death of her son Roscoe, " 'He's better off, Mama. . . . Better off, just like Judge McKelva laying yonder. Tell yourself the same thing I do' " (p. 76).

The Chisoms and their twins, the Dalzells, "never let the conversation die" (p. 36), and they are never inhibited by place or audience. Their subjects of conversation differ from those of old Mount Salus. In times of illness and death, they do not, like Mount Salus, romanticize away the reality of these with pretty or comic tales. Instead, their conversation turns directly to the details of illness and death. As the elderly head of the clan lies dying in a room nearby, the huge Dalzell family sit in the waiting room of the hospital swapping tales of trouble and gore. Each person tries to tell the most gruesome tale, and someone brags about the direness of their kinsman's condition: " 'He's been in intensive care ever since they got through with him. His chances are a hundred to one against' " (p. 36). At Judge McKelva's house before his funeral, the Chisoms do the same thing. Whereas Mount Salus turns attention away from McKelva's death by telling romantic tales allegedly about his life, Mrs. Chisom vies for attention with a detailed account of her son Roscoe's suicide. Such tales offend Mount Salus's sense of polite conversation; they seem crude, out of place, and too personal.

The Chisoms are unambiguously portrayed in the role of the growing mechanical and commercial culture of the South, a lower but rising class with vulgar tastes and shallow values. They are both products
of and producers of the new mechanism. No respecter of nature, DeWitt
Chisom has " 'folks' appliances stacked over ever' blooming inch of
space' " in his yard back in Texas. He is, appropriately, a machine
repairman—" 'vacuum cleaners and power mowers and bathroom
heaters and old window fans' " (p. 98). And what could be more
symbolic than Bubba Chisom's occupation? He operates " 'a wreck-
ing concern,' " tearing down the old so that it can be replaced by the
new. The Chisoms assess things according to their cost, showiness,
and newness. Fay chooses a fancy casket for her husband and vouches,
" 'It was no bargain, and I think that showed' " (p. 95). She shocks
Mount Salus by burying the old community leader in the new, bare
part of the cemetery near the new interstate highway, and no doubt on
top of Clint's grave will soon be an "indestructible plastic Christmas
poinsettia" identical to those on the graves nearby. In pronounced
contrast, Clint himself had planted his favorite camellia on top of his
first wife's grave, in the old part of the cemetery, and the plant is in
bloom during his own burial.

The Chisoms' unconcern for tradition is suggested through several
overtly symbolic incidents. Fay has frivolously allowed her nail polish
to stain a carefully preserved desk which had belonged to Judge
McKelva's great-grandfather, and she has thoughtlessly scarred a pre-
cious hand-made breadboard which had belonged to Judge McKelva's
first wife and Laurel's mother, Becky. The conflict between Laurel and
Fay represents a conflict between the traditions of the past and the
crassness of the future, as is demonstrated by the breadboard incident.
To Laurel, the breadboard is a sacred remnant of the past, lovingly
hand-carved by her husband for her mother, while to Fay the breadboard is " 'just an old board.' " To Laurel, Fay's mutilation of the
board is a desecration of the past.

"What do you see in that thing?" asked Fay.
 "The whole story, Fay. The whole solid past," said Laurel.
 "Whose story? Whose past? Not mine," said Fay. "The past isn't a thing
to me. I belong to the future, didn't you know that?" (pp. 178–79)

Through such character contrasts and the characters' actions, Welty
encourages the reader to suspect that with the onset of the upstart Chi-

soms, led by Fay, the values and possessions of Old Mount Salus will gradually be corrupted or destroyed. Fay's mother even proposes turning the old McKelva home into a boarding house. The proposal might be a forewarning that Mount Salus is en route to changes that have already hit old New Orleans. During Judge McKelva's hospitalization there, Laurel and Fay had gotten rooms in the Hibiscus, "a decayed mansion on a changing street," next door to which stood "its twin," half demolished (p. 17).

Boarding houses and decaying mansions are legion in Southern fiction, but they also are true to the region. The symbolic use of the clock is another convention of Southern fiction.[5] Frequently it is used to suggest the passing of the old way of life. The old family clock on the mantel in the McKelva living room has stopped running with the death of Judge McKelva, who embodies the civility of the old tradition. The symbol seems to indicate that the judge's death parallels the ending of an era; the old time, the old pleasures and values, the tasteful and leisurely traditions are dying away—including the smooth New Orleans-to-Chicago train which McKelva "had always so enjoyed traveling on": "he had taken full pleasure in the starched white damask tablecloths, the real rosebud in the silver vase, the celery crisp on ice. . . . The days of the train itself were numbered now" (p. 44). As Laurel rides that train with her father's body, she notices a seagull "hanging with wings fixed, like a stopped clock on a wall" (p. 45). Laurel, clinging to the orderly and consistent past, wishes to set the mantel clock going again, as though it had never stopped: "it had not been wound, she supposed, since the last time her father had done duty by it, and its hands pointed to some remote three o'clock, as motionless as the time in the Chinese prints. She wanted to . . . wind the clock and set it going at the right time" (p. 73). On the other hand, McKelva's widow, Fay, agent of the New South, remarks that the first thing she will get rid of is " 'that old striking clock!' " (p. 100). Fay, to whom the past means nothing, does not appreciate the instrument and symbol of time marching steadily and changelessly onward.

Issues related to time are central to much Southern fiction, and the symbolic role of the clock is only one reflection of this interest in *The Optimist's Daughter*. The old tradition respects time, is in no race against it (unlike Bubba Chisom, who, the minute he arrives for the funeral, is already talking about needing to hurry back home), and measures it out in leisurely traditions that give order and continuity to time's passing.

Through the words and actions of the Chisoms, disrespect for the past and tradition emerges as only part of a general obliviousness to the thoughts and feelings of others. The direct opposite of her self-effacing husband, Fay constantly thinks in terms of "me" and deliberately draws attention to herself. Much of her action in this regard is merely silly, a vulgar way of showing strong feeling—as when she cries into the coffin, " 'Oh, Judge, how could you go off and leave me this way? Why did you want to treat me so unfair?' " (p. 85). This emphasis on "me" is set off against the old tradition's submersion of the individual in community and family. The funeral rituals, for example, submerge personal grief in a formalized community expression of grief that presumably brings order and dignity to strong emotion. Fay's most emphatic dramatizing of the isolated "me" is also an emphatic violation of the old tradition's sacred value of family: she denies that she has one. She does so not in shame of her family but through a childish desire to depict herself as a poor little waif all alone in the world.

Like Bonnie Dee of *The Ponder Heart*, whom she resembles, Fay is a comic character, yet Bonnie Dee's self-concern is merely silly whereas Wanda Fay's is also unintentionally destructive. Her husband, who is supposed to remain immobile as his eye heals, dies after she shakes him in an effort, she says, to get him to pay more attention to her and to scare him into living. Thus, Wanda Fay, chief embodiment of Chisom shallowness, may be the immediate cause of the death of Judge McKelva, her husband of less than two years and chief representative of the old tradition.

With such characters and symbols, *The Optimist's Daughter* appears to be a conventional Southern novel that treats the familiar theme of a South undergoing change and on the threshold of decline. Indeed, Welty leads the reader to expect this theme by her uncharacteristic lack of subtlety in the use of the symbols and contrasts. The comic bumper sticker on the Chisoms' pickup truck—"Do Unto Others Before They Do Unto You"—epitomizes the reversal of traditional values. Nonetheless, a careful reading of the novel reveals that Welty has, characteristically, brought individual insight to a common literary concern.

For one thing, *The Optimist's Daughter* subtly alters a character type that often appears in conjunction with this theme: the gentle, elderly community patriarch, a representative of the Old Order. Rather than bold and imperious demons in the Colonel John Sartoris pattern, those of the gentle patriarch lineage are usually kind, sensitive, intelligent,

and rather soft gentlemen—General Archbald of *The Sheltered Life* by
Ellen Glasgow, Fontaine Allard of Caroline Gordon's *None Shall Look
Back*, old Bayard Sartoris of *Sartoris*, perhaps Judge Irwin of *All the
King's Men*. Blair Rouse has described David Archbald as Glasgow's
"most perfect embodiment" of "that rarest creature, whether gentleman or commoner, the civilized man."[6] The gentle patriarchs are, first
and foremost, civilized men; they usually have large libraries of well-
read books, abhor violence, and put the comfort and well-being of their
friends and families above their own desires. Judge Clinton McKelva
is such a man in *The Optimist's Daughter*. Perceptive family friend
Adele Courtland answers Laurel McKelva Hand's assertion that her
father " 'never would have stood for lies being told about him' " with
the comment, " 'Yes he would. . . . If the truth might hurt the wrong
person' " (p. 83). Such civilized, gentle men are the real Southern
gentlemen.

Though not flagrantly bold, the gentle patriarchs conventionally
possess, beneath their mildness, the courage and daring necessary for
special circumstances. At some point in their lives, they *have* acted
boldly and dramatically. As a young boy in *The Unvanquished*, Bayard during the Civil War had hunted down and killed the murderer of
his grandmother and years later had, unarmed, faced and overcome the
armed man who had killed his father. David Archbald, though a shy
and unaggressive youth, nonetheless daringly assisted a slave in escap-
ing. And just as Archbald became a Confederate general, Judge Irwin
of *All the King's Men* is a decorated hero of a later war. Irwin is "a
man" and "won't scare," even when threatened with blackmail by a
powerful politician.

Welty's Judge McKelva breaks the pattern of the gentle patriarch
who has performed conventionally heroic action. Although a perfect
example of the type in other respects, he has no particularly daring or
sensational performance in his past. A quiet man living a civilized but
ordinary life, he wrote touching letters to his first wife when she was
away from home, attempted to prune rose bushes, married a second
time because of loneliness, and was hesitant to worry his daughter with
news of his eye trouble. After his death (which is itself neither romantic nor noble, occurring in old age during his recuperation from an eye
operation), his friends try to honor him by glamorizing his life, but
Welty exposes the falsity of their tales. She reverses here a procedure
she had previously used to reveal a group's hero-making: rather than

first introducing the legends about a character and then undermining the romance by allowing the real man to step forward, this time she first introduces Judge McKelva himself, at some length, and then with his death, shows a mythic version beginning to develop already. Major Bullock, an elderly friend of the dead man, exclaims, " 'And under that cloak of modesty he wore, a fearless man! Fearless man!' " (p. 79). While that exclamation perfectly describes the typical gentle patriarch of Southern literature, it does not provide an accurate image of the Judge McKelva whom the reader has come to know. Major Bullock follows his comment with a tale in which McKelva, unarmed, single-handedly turns away an armed and angry "White Cap" mob which tries to remove from jail a man McKelva has sentenced for murder.

The tale is Bullock's effort to create a flattering eulogy for his dear friend, and it speaks more about Bullock's own personality and about storytelling as funeral custom than it does about McKelva's history. But it may have other implications as well. Welty may be parodying with the false tale the romantic acts of heroism of many literary characters and satirizing common concepts of heroic behavior, for it is clear that (as Laurel says) Bullock is trying to make Judge McKelva a hero such as he would like to be himself. In fact, McKelva's actions in the tale, though they could be the mythic exploits of a cowboy hero, bear remarkable similarities to acts of bravery from the pasts of two other gentle patriarchs. In *The Unvanquished*, Bayard refuses to abide by the Sartoris code which demands that he kill his father's murderer. Instead, he faces Redmond unarmed, walks deliberately toward Redmond as the latter fires twice, and then calmly disarms his enemy. It is a heroic act, a romantic act, and it wins the respect, if not the understanding, of the supporters of the Sartoris code. In *All the King's Men*, the narrator Jack Burden reports a similar incident from Judge Irvin's past. Threatened by a man whom he had sent to prison, Irvin merely laughed and walked away. When the man then drew a pistol and called menacingly, the Judge "walked straight at the man, not saying a word," and "took the pistol away from him." [7]

In portraying Judge McKelva as facing down an armed mob all alone, Major Bullock's false tale is close to these presumably true accounts of acts of bravery of other gentle patriarchs. But there is a difference. Although Bullock begins his tale by making of his friend a modest but "fearless man!" on the order of the Bayards, the Archbalds, and the Irvins, by the end of his tale *his* gentle, fearless man has lost any sense of reserve or humility. Through Bullock's embroidering, Judge Mc-Kelva acquires a keen sense of daring, a vivacious recklessness, and a charming wit.

"But Clint, Clint all by himself, he walked out on the front steps of the Courthouse and stood there and he said, 'Come right on in! The jail is up-stairs, on the second floor!' "
"I don't think that was Father," Laurel said low to Tish. . . .
Major Bullock was going irrepressibly on. " 'Come in!' said he. 'But be-fore you enter, you take those damn white hoods off, and every last one of you give me a look at who you are!' "

Bullock has turned the shyest, most modest of the gentle patriarchs into a witty, bold, dashing, forceful figure—a figure close to the leg-endary Sartoris brothers, John and Carolina Bayard.

"Father really was modest," Laurel said to him.
"Honey, what do you mean? Honey you were away. You were sitting up yonder in Chicago, drawing pictures," Major Bullock told her. "I saw him! He stood up and dared those rascals to shoot him! Baring his breast!" (pp. 79–80)

"Baring his breast" indeed! The action would be that of a swaggerer. But though less extravagant, aren't the supposedly factual acts of her-oism of the other civilized, gentle men nonetheless romantically bold? With only a little embroidering, the standard modest but heroic patri-arch can be turned into his more glamorous kinsman, the flashy, ro-mantic hero of family legend.

Frequently Southern writers of this century (or characters in their fiction) have implied that an unfortunate result of the changing times is the loss of heroism. In the frontier South, the Civil War South, and the post-war South, so the theory goes, heroism was possible and nec-essary—acts of dashing bravery by ancestors of the books' contem-porary characters are recalled. Yet for the present-day characters them-selves no chance for such nobility arises; it is as though honor and bravery were possible only in the golden past, not in the machine-ori-ented present. Eudora Welty never makes such a suggestion. There is no implication that the absence of real deeds of thrilling heroism in Judge McKelva's life is a consequence of his times. Instead, it is a consequence of his character and personality. As Laurel says, " 'He hadn't any use for what he called theatrics' ''; and she thinks, "It was my mother who *might* have done that! She's the only one I know who had it in her" (p. 80).

Yet even Laurel's mother did not demonstrate such theatrical daring in the act of bravery about which Laurel later reminisces. At age fifteen, Becky had, with a neighbor, accompanied her sick father on a raft, at night, down an ice-filled river to seek medical help. Though her action required daring, it was not romantic or reckless. Rather, it was born purely of necessity and love, being the only course open to her if her father were to live. It contrasts sharply with Bayard Sartoris's teenaged vengeance against his grandmother's murderer, with teenager David Archbald's defiance of his society by assisting a fleeing slave, and with teenager Mattie Ross's vengeance against the murderer of her father in Charles Portis's more recent *True Grit* (1968).

Though there is no stunning act of bravery in his past, Clinton McKelva is not without his nobility. He served his family and region generously and faithfully. Laurel wonders why the eulogizers did not honor him for his considerable achievements in flood control. And McKelva's long years of devotion to his first wife after she became a blind invalid who berated him with hostile accusations was heroic, though he failed, because of his personality, to become the partner in her desperate rage against death and fate that she desired. McKelva's heroism was like Becky's own brave assistance to her ill father, born also of love and necessity and requiring much giving. It is a type of nobility observable in the lives of ordinary men and women, yet it remains unsung and often unappreciated because it lacks melodrama. It is not a sensational attempt to fulfill—or to defy—a code of behavior sanctioned by society.

Simple as this nobility seems, Wanda Fay Chisom McKelva is not capable of it. She cannot endure her husband's short recuperation from a critical operation. The contrast between McKelva's patient and compassionate devotion to his first wife as she experiences a prolonged illness and Fay's selfish impatience toward her husband as he experiences a two-week one is significant. But also significant is the contrast between Welty's realistic concept of heroism as expressed through Clinton and Becky McKelva and the romantic concept often glorified in literature and legend.

Welty's most conventional Southern novel is unconventional also in another way. While the contrast between the old civilized values and the multiplying vulgar ones is bluntly spelled out, and Fay, the chief illustration of the latter, is portrayed unfavorably, Welty does not treat the conflict and the rise of the Chisoms tragically. For, despite the sharpness of the contrast and conflict between the two groups of characters, their differences turn out to be rather superficial.

The representatives of the growing commercial culture are not portrayed as Northern, New Adam outsiders, like Mr. Mack of *So Red the Rose*, nor as noncommunicative, exploitative, money-hungry Snopeses. The Chisoms as a group are poor, native Southerners, talkative and family-loving, who migrate around the South in search of better opportunities. Their main flaws are not avarice or coldness or an absence of family feeling but ignorance and a satisfaction with ignorance, complete self-absorption, and a tendency to think and speak in clichés. As Laurel observes, the Chisoms are "the great, interrelated family of those who never know the meaning of what has happened to them" (p. 84). The Dalzells, whom Laurel encounters in the lobby of the New Orleans hospital, are much like the Chisoms and elicit from Laurel a similar judgment. Listening to them compete with each other as they swap tales of their troubles, Laurel thinks that they (unlike her father) are "all as unaware of the passing of the minutes" as the man drunk on a couch nearby (p. 38). The Chisoms and Dalzells are ordinary people leading their simple, vulgar lives.

When viewed closely, the people of Mount Salus, descendants of the Old South, seem only marginally more admirable than Fay and her clan. Both groups do have favorably presented members—little Wendell and Grandpa on the Chisom side, and Laurel, elderly family friend Adele Courtland, the maid Missouri, and the dead judge and his first wife Becky on the Mount Salus side. Except for these few, Mount Salus people appear trivial and childish, although also "civilized" rather than vulgar. Old aristocrat Major Bullock is a sentimental old fool, and a tipsy fool to boot. His daughter Tish still gives the girlish wink of comradeship which has long been an unconscious habit. Tish and Laurel's other girlhood friends, now middle-aged women, still call themselves bridesmaids though Laurel's wedding was some twenty years ago. The Presbyterian preacher's wife talks too much about the ham she is providing the bereaved household. And old friends of the judge and his first wife Becky carry on a subtle defensive rivalry with the Chisoms when the latter arrive unexpectedly for McKelva's funeral and don't stay in their "place." Adele Courtland afterwards concludes that the Mount Salus crew behaved as badly as the Chisoms, only the Chisoms " 'were a trifle more inelegant' " (p. 109).

Is the novel, after all, a nostalgic lament about the corruption of old traditions by new values? Not at all. In the first place, by bringing the community together to mourn a respected leader, Welty makes evident that the small town is composed of multi-levels, not just the rich and the poor and the old aristocracy and the upstarts. Yet the descendants of the old tradition still have status at the top, and their manners and customs are emulated by others, who may lack real understanding of the values behind the customs and thus achieve only surface reflections of that which they copy. But the superficiality of those who defer to the Old Order does not explain the flaws of descendants themselves of the Old Order. And though Fay may be responsible for the defacement of some McKelva prized material possessions, she and her kin have not been in Mount Salus long enough to have influenced similar changes in human character. The point is that, until now, change has hardly touched Mount Salus at all except through occasional deaths, births, and a bit of physical expansion. For example, all Laurel's childhood friends married high school sweethearts and remain in Mount Salus, raising families in what is called "the new part of town." Apparently only a few people from the middle generation, including Laurel, moved away. Most of the significant changes are yet to come and will probably be wrought not by new inhabitants but by the younger generation of established families, such as high school students like Tish Bullock's son, who enjoys a privacy with the opposite sex that would have been deemed scandalous in his mother's youth. So, unlike *The Sound and the Fury, Lie Down in Darkness*, and many other novels, *The Optimist's Daughter* does not suppose that the weaknesses observable in members of the Old Order are products of the changing times, nor does it suggest that once upon a time people were better. Saccharine Major Bullock and his rather fatuous daughter Tish are not contrasted with ancestors who were more admirable. We can only assume that in any time, even in the South, there might be within the same class sentimental, tipsy fools and sensible, sensitive McKelvas.

But might not the very stability of the small community over the years have led to a degeneration in values and customs?

What makes little Wendell Chisom and the loner old Grandpa Chisom more attractive than their kin is that their behavior and comments, unlike those of the others, are natural and honest. Wendell has not yet learned, and Grandpa has somehow avoided, the standard formats of their class. In a moment of tenderness for Wendell, Laurel sees in him "a young, undriven, unfalsifying, unvindictive Fay" (p. 76). Grandpa breaks the Chisom pattern of clichés with his simple but delightful response to a question from his daughter-in-law:

"Out of curiosity, who does he remind you of?" Mrs. Chisom asked him as he gazed down [at Judge McKelva in his coffin].
The old man reflected for a minute. "Nobody," he said. (p. 77)

Grandpa "reflects" before he speaks whereas the other Chisoms rely on pat expressions, requiring no thought, which they suppose appropriate for the occasion.

And therein lies an interesting and informative similarity between Mount Salus folk, on the one hand, and the Chisoms and Dalzells, on the other. The latter may be ignorant of revered old traditions, but they are not without their conventions. At Judge McKelva's house, the Chisoms' actions, like those of the Mount Salus community, are predicated on their interpretation of funeral proprieties. They too are following a code of behavior learned through the years. As Miss Adele realizes, Fay's melodramatic demonstration of sorrow was her " 'idea of giving a sad occasion its due' " (p. 109), and Mrs. Chisom heartily seconds her daughter's performance: " 'Like mother, like daughter. Though when I had to give up her dad, they couldn't hold me half so easy. I tore up the whole house, I did' " (p. 86). Fay does her best for her husband, buying him an expensive coffin and burying him in the newest part of the cemetery, and her relatives are favorably impressed. And if the Chisoms are discovered, like Mount Salus, to act according to their society's standards, the behavior of Mount Salus folk, like that of the Chisoms, is discovered to be patterned and unreflective. As practiced by most of them, the customs and amenities inherited from previous generations are not vital but merely habitual. Indeed, Welty shows the Mount Salus triviality to be the result not of change but, paradoxically, of a lack of change.

After years of use, the funeral customs have become rigidly ritualized. Their role as a social event for the community has become primary; as comfort to the most bereaved, secondary. Tennyson Bullock insists that the judge's coffin remain open for all to peer into, despite

Laurel's objections: " 'But honey, your father's a Mount Salus man. He's a McKelva. A public figure. You can't deprive the public, can you?' " (p. 63). The mourners in general seem more curious about who will be the next to arrive—and how that person will act—than genuinely grieved by McKelva's death. Dot Daggett, McKelva's former secretary, scores this funeral highly: " 'I want to tell you, Laurel, what a beautiful funeral it was. . . . I saw everybody I know and everybody I used to know. It was old Mount Salus personified' " (p. 92). Old Mrs. Pease, on the other hand, feels it fell short of expectation: " 'The whole day left something to be desired, if you want to hear me come right out with it' " (p. 108).

In particular, the conversational amenities which are part of funeral etiquette appear cut to formula, and as sentimental and false as those of the Chisoms. Tennyson looks at the rouged and powdered corpse and says, " 'Oh, he's lovely' " (p. 63), words echoed by Mrs. Chisom, who recalls that her son was " 'pretty as a girl' " in his coffin (p. 75). The little speech the mayor of Mount Salus makes over the coffin seems just as mawkish: " 'Oh, I've modeled myself on this noble Roman. . . . And when I reach higher office—' " (p. 72). As custom requires, some of McKelva's old cronies attempt to eulogize him, but their tale-telling, being self-consciously undertaken, does not flow naturally. Moreover, some of the tales—such as Major Bullock's—well-intended though they may be, gratify the narrators' fantasies about themselves more than they honor the dead or please McKelva's daughter. Furthermore, an impetus for the general embroidering (" 'They said he was a humorist. And a crusader. And an angel on the face of the earth,' said Laurel") is, as Adele Courtland explains, as much the present rivalry with the Chisoms—" 'they thought they had their side, too' " (p. 82)—as the desire to eulogize McKelva. The noble purpose of the tale-telling, then, has been diffused and, in some cases, displaced, while the form has ossified.

Personal habits, such as Tish's now-automatic wink, have become just as petrified. In their self-absorption, the people have quit growing: middle-aged women still see themselves as bridesmaids. And no one expresses any interest in Laurel's designing career in Chicago. Instead, most assume that she should wish to return to Mount Salus and spend her afternoons playing bridge with the women who have been meeting together for half a lifetime.

So Mount Salus comes off little better than the invading Chisoms

not because the community's old way of life has been contaminated
by the changing times but because in the changeless community the
customs have become stale and rigid habits. Allen Tate makes a similar suggestion in *The Fathers* but in relation to an individual character
rather than a community. Yet while Tate's Major Buchan follows too
inflexibly a once more-viable code of behavior, he also appears to remember the values behind the customs which express the code. Many
of the Mount Salus folk, however, seem as unconscious of the values
which once underlined the customs as is Tish of her wink. Tish's wink
is like Fay's over-dramatizing her grief, or vice versa, as Laurel indicates: "Fay didn't know what she was doing—it was like Tish wink-
ing—and she never will know" (p. 131). If the Chisoms are "the great
interrelated family of those who never know the meaning of what has
happened to them" (p. 84), Mount Salus is the small, interrelated
community which is unaware of what has happened to it. The community has become in-grown, feeding on itself (like Grandmother's pi-
geons) and rejecting other nourishment. Indeed, Fay's continual assertion of herself, her silly claim for attention, is in part defensive; by
word and deed Mount Salus excludes her, and she is fighting back in
the only way she knows how.

Because Fay is so easy to dislike, Mount Salus's unkind treatment
of her might easily be overlooked; but very subtly, from the beginning, Welty exposes it through the medium of the oral culture. In the
first scene, at the hospital, as Dr. Nate Courtland examines Clinton
McKelva, Fay is made to feel the outsider—though, as Welty says,
"New Orleans was out-of-town for all of them." The examining room
is in New Orleans, but the atmosphere is Mount Salus, thanks to the
presence there of Clint, his daughter Laurel, and Nate. Unconsciously,
the three Mount Salus natives erect an invisible circle which excludes
Fay and naturally ruffles her feathers. Speaking as old friends, they
discuss Clint's eye problem with many references to a past to which
they, but not Fay, belong, and they mention Fay's predecessor casually and fondly. Clint even refers to the rose bush he was pruning when
he discovered his eye trouble as "Becky's bush." Nate Courtland, in
turn, addresses his diagnosis specifically to Clint and Laurel, and to
Laurel alone when Clint is absent, ignoring Fay until she stridently reminds him of her existence.[8]

Back in Mount Salus, when Fay and Laurel arrive with McKelva's
body, the community, understandably, rallies around Laurel, one of its

own, but in doing so it makes Fay feel like an outsider, though she now lives in Mount Salus while Laurel has lived in Chicago for over twenty years. As Laurel and four of her mother's old friends visit together the day after the funeral, the pure snobbishness of the women toward Fay becomes clear, and the reader can imagine what Fay has gone through in the past eighteen months as second wife to Judge McKelva. The women tell Laurel tales about the horrors of Fay. They are scorning Fay's differences from them; her ways are not theirs. (She doesn't know how to cook and doesn't seem to care. She "bills and coos" in public with her husband.) They happily hypothesize that Fay will leave Mount Salus now that her husband is dead: " 'No, she won't last long,' " says Mrs. Bolt (pp. 105–6). The chimney swift that later gets inside the McKelva house might symbolically parallel Fay's position in Mount Salus. Closed up inside the house with Laurel, who dislikes and fears it (as she does Fay), the bird slams blindly around the house soiling everything it touches, much as Fay blindly scars the fine McKelva antiques. The bird wants out—knows it is in the wrong environment and is unwanted—yet even when Laurel and Missouri try to " '*make* it go free' " it struggles blindly "against rescue."

"Look," said Missouri. "He ain't got no business in your room."
" . . . It's got a perfectly clear way out now," Laurel called. "Why won't it just fly free of its own accord?"
"They just ain't got no sense like we have." (p. 167)

Although Mount Salus, including Laurel, considers Fay foolish and insensitive, she reveals that she is very much sensitive to the community's attitude toward her. She knows that under the mask of politeness is disdain. In fact, Fay recognizes in the people's words some of the very things that Welty is showing about the oral culture and has shown before. When Laurel accuses her of lying about not having any family, Fay replies that that lie is " 'better than some lies I've heard around here,' " a comment that seems to refer to the false tales about McKelva as well as to the politeness that etiquette requires the community show Fay. " 'Well, at least my family's not hypocrites,' said Fay. 'If they didn't want me, they'd tell me to my face' " (p. 99). The role the oral tradition plays in putting Fay in her place—keeping her isolated from the community and making her feel that separation—is pinpointed in something Fay says soon after the funeral, when she has been made most aware of the community's disapproval of her and her

family. She suddenly decides to go back to Texas with her family for
a few days because " 'I'd just like to see somebody that can talk my
language' " (p. 97).

Welty's attitude toward what has happened to the Southern community is significant. Although she presents Dalzell and Chisom (and,
later, Cheek) crudeness bluntly but Mount Salus staleness and hypoc-
risy subtly, the two sides end up fairly well balanced. Welty is not
lamenting lost values but showing what has become of those values.
While Fay fights with shrill words for acknowledgment and with mean
little fists to hold onto the material gains she thinks are hers by right
of marriage, Mount Salus misuses a tradition of polite words to keep
her in her place and has blindly allowed itself to grow stagnant. By
shaking her husband, Fay might in ignorance have hastened his death,
but even without her action, he was fading away on his own. The same
can be said for the strength of the Old Order. With one eye bandaged,
Clint McKelva was half blind, but as he lay in his hospital bed just
counting the passing of time, he day by day grew more passive. Soon,
he did not bother to open the good eye either.

Finally, despite its explicit and extensive portrayal of the changing—or changeless—South theme, the novel's major thematic statement is about a different sense of the past, one not commonly associated with Southern literature. Ultimately, the emphasis is on Laurel's
adjustment to changes in her personal past. Laurel is a rarity in Southern fiction, a Southerner born and reared who has adjusted well to the
replacement of native soil with foreign asphalt. She has spent all her
adult life pursuing a designing career in the North yet apparently has
not been haunted by her Mississippi heritage; she has not felt anger
toward it, been in flight from it, or sensed that she "can't go home
again." Nonetheless, Laurel does have a problem with the past that is
unveiled in the last third of the novel.

The first two-thirds of the novel, relying heavily on dialogue and
divided into scenes, is a comedy of manners which stages the contrast
between Old Mount Salus and the Chisom class. During this part of
the novel, Laurel is primarily an observer quietly reacting to the action
around her. She distinguishes herself from the other characters as she
tries to protect her dead parents from the romanticizing of their friends,
adherents to the past and the status quo, and from the destructiveness
of Fay, omen of change. In thus laying claim to her parents, she keeps

others who love them at arm's length. The amusing comedy of manners of the first two-thirds of the novel raises two serious questions: How are we to understand Laurel? And why on earth did Clinton McKelva marry Wanda Fay Chisom? This latter question plagues Laurel as well; her father's second marriage is at the heart of her problem.

At first the union of Clinton and Fay seems unbelievable, a flaw in the novel. We can understand that the simple-minded Daniel Ponder might marry the childish, selfish Bonnie Dee (*The Ponder Heart*), but not that the intelligent, sensitive Clinton McKelva would marry Bonnie Dee's fictional descendant Wanda Fay. Moreover, the methods of characterization seem inconsistent. Clinton is a round, complex character while Wanda Fay seems a flat, comic one. Slowly, however, we realize that Welty is showing us Fay as Laurel sees her. Fay *is* a shallow being, but in Laurel's prejudiced view, she is without any depth at all. In the preceding section, we have seen that Welty does allow Fay some sensitivity. Even so, the marriage is astounding, until Laurel leads us to understand it as she comes to terms with it herself.

When she returns to the South for her father's hospitalization and then his funeral, Laurel becomes entangled in her family's past. She was last home a year and a half ago, for her father's second wedding. At that time, the marriage must have shocked her, but she soon returned to her work in Chicago and thus escaped constant awareness of it. Now, being around Fay at length and under tragic circumstances, she is very much bothered by the marriage on two counts. First, the marriage seems a betrayal of her mother, Becky. And second, she fears that she is to blame for the marriage, and hence indirectly for her father's death since she blames Fay for the latter.

While Laurel is a very private person, resisting the curiosity as well as the genuine concern of the community, she has a strong attachment to family.[9] She was raised in a loving household, an only child doted on by her father and treated as a friend by her mother. Her resentment of Fay derives from this family love. Laurel remembers her family as always having been a harmonious whole. This idealistic picture is betrayed, she thinks, by her father's second marriage; how *could* her father have permitted Fay to usurp her mother's place? (Especially offensive to her must be the pink satin love nest Fay has made of her parents' bedroom.)

Moreover, her father's second marriage seems to Laurel a denial of her own concept of life and love. Laurel "had to believe" that any

life is "nothing but the continuity of its love." This concept is sym-
bolized for her in an image she encountered at a portentous moment,
and what soon followed explains why "she had to believe" in this
concept. On their way from Chicago to Mississippi to be married, Laurel
and Phil Hand had seen, as the train crossed a bridge south of Cairo,
"the confluence of the waters, the Ohio and the Mississippi." Everything in the scene—the rivers, the trees lining the banks, the birds flying
high in a V—seemed "at the point of coming together." And she and
Phil seemed "a part of the confluence. Their own joint act of faith had
brought them here at the very moment and matched its occur-
rence. . . . They were riding as one with it. . . . It's our turn! she'd
thought exultantly. And we're going to live forever" (pp. 159–60).
But Phil died in war the next year, and his body was never recovered.

Unlike other characters in Welty's fiction, Laurel has never romanticized her dead young war hero in glamorous tales; and, being the
private individual she is, she prevents others from doing so:

> "What kind of dancer was Phil, Polly? I forget!" Tish lifted her arms as
> though the memory would come up and dance her away to remind her.
> "Firm," said Laurel. She turned her cheek a little further away on the pil-
> low. (p. 125)

However, she has remained faithful for some twenty years to Phil. She
has never married again, apparently has never loved again. Because of
Phil's early death, Laurel "had to believe" that "her life, any life . . .
was nothing but the continuity of its love. . . . just as she believed
that the confluence of the waters was still happening at Cairo" (p. 160).
Central to her life is the continuity of her love for Phil and her parents.

Whereas Laurel has preserved and honored the love she and Phil
shared, her father, she must think, has been unfaithful to the love he
and Becky shared. His marriage to Fay both violates the concept by
which Laurel lives and, because of her love and respect for her father,
seems to challenge the concept itself. Laurel is very disturbed.

And disturbed too by guilt: has she herself not betrayed the love she
and her father shared? As his loving daughter, she should have been
there when he needed her. In her journey into the past on the stormy
night that she flees from the chimney swift into the womb of the house
(her mother's small interior sewing room), Laurel recalls Becky's loving service to her own ill father and Becky's anguish later in life over

having "not been there" when a parent needed her. Laurel also remembers that Becky, shortly before she died a blind invalid, had said to her daughter, " 'You could have saved your mother's life. But you stood by and wouldn't intervene. I despair for you' " (p. 151). This legacy of episodes stressing a child's duty to her parents is revived for Laurel by the present situation. Old friends of Becky's only half-jokingly accuse Laurel of having brought Fay on them by not coming home to be with her father after her mother's death, and even Fay implies that Laurel neglected her father: " 'After Papa died, we all gave up everything for Mama, of course. Now that she's gone, I'm glad we did. Oh, I wouldn't have run off and left anybody that needed me. Just to call myself an artist and make a lot of money' " (pp. 27–28). Now Laurel recalls that her father only two years ago had urged her to take some time off and go abroad with him; she had not done so. The next time she heard from him, he was planning to get married. Her father was a lonely man calling out to his daughter, and she was not there for him.

So, when Laurel comes home to bury her last parent, she is suddenly burdened with guilt. The guilt drives her to blame Fay rather than herself but also to try to make up for what she sees as her past neglect of her father by now repossessing him: she will protect him from both those who would falsify his past and those who would soil his dignity.

But when Laurel, huddled in the sewing room, delves into the past, she makes discoveries that force her to alter her image of her parents' marriage and reassess her own marriage to Phil. And in doing so she frees herself from guilt and from the past.

Naturally, with her father's death, she recalls the death of her mother. Whereas her father was hospitalized briefly before he died, her mother had lingered a bed-ridden invalid for five years. It was a hard time, for unlike her father in his recuperation, her mother was no patient, passive sufferer. She fought back; she cried out against the injustices of life—against the tragedy of blindness and the certainty of approaching death. Remembering her mother's last years, Laurel has to correct the blissful image of her parents' marriage that she has held onto. Their last years together were full of tumult and torment. Early in the novel, Laurel tells Nate Courtland that her parents differed from one another, but only now, as she stirs up the past, does she realize the degree and significance of their different personalities.[10] During Becky's ill health,

Clinton McKelva had begun calling himself an optimist, implying that
he had faith in Becky's recovery. Rather than optimism, Clint actually
had an emotional blindness as acute as Becky's physical blindness. Much
like characters in some other Welty works, he refused to see the dark
side of things, in particular the tragedy of Becky's position. Not a storyteller, he did not romanticize away suffering, evil, and death in tales,
but neither did he look at these openly. Becky, suffering debilitating
blindness and anticipating death, was horrified by what was happening
to her and wanted Clint to be horrified too. But Clint would not, could
not, join her in her sense of desperation. Instead, he, as always, pam-
pered her—just as he later would his second wife.

Now recognizing these personality differences that led to the dishar-
mony of her parents' later years, Laurel can understand her father's
marriage to Fay. She had made the mistake of expecting of her father
feelings and actions inconsistent with his personality. Clinton Mc-
Kelva was not Becky, not Laurel. They three were one as a family,
but individually they were different, influenced by different pasts, and
they would lead different lives. Clint's life revolved around two things:
serving his region through his work and doting on those he loved. After
his daughter left home and then his wife died, he no longer had anyone to dote on daily, but he still had his work. Then he retired. He
was saved from loneliness by Fay. She gave him " 'something to live
for,' " according to Adele Courtland (p. 116); someone to spoil, according to the maid Missouri (p. 59). And Clint would have been too
blind to see her flaws—and oblivious to the possibility of a better match
closer to home.

In coming to terms with her father's marriage to Fay, Laurel has
evoked her own marriage to Phil, first as judgment against her father
and then, unavoidably, as possible parallel to her parents' marriage.
For she has to acknowledge that she and Phil were as different from
one another as were her parents. And if her parents' differences could
cause their marriage to go bad at the end—if her parents could cause
each other great pain even while continuing to love one another—then
what might have happened to her relation to Phil, had he lived? This
question is excruciating for Laurel, but being her mother's daughter
she faces it. As her father's daughter—the optimist's daughter—she
had until now been blind in regard to her marriage; had assumed that,
had they lived forever, she and Phil would always have been as happy
as they were in the few days they had together. (In the hospital, she

had again proved herself her father's daughter by pretending in her father's presence that everything was normal: "He never asked about his eye. He never mentioned his eye. Laurel followed his lead," p. 18.) Now, however, Laurel reexamines her marriage and what she has made of it.

The reader comes to realize—and Laurel does too, to a large degree—that with Phil's death the marriage and Laurel's emotional life became suspended in time. "Her father had given [her wedding picture] a silver frame. (So had she. Her marriage had been of magical ease, of *ease*—of brevity and conclusion and all belonging to Chicago and not here)" (p. 121). The brief marriage was idyllic; no flaw, no harsh word ever troubled it. Laurel has frozen it in her memory that way, framed it in silver, and she has continued living in Chicago where the marriage existed, pursuing an active public life (her career) but maintaining her private life as though she were still married to Phil: "She had gone on living with the old perfection undisturbed and undisturbing" (p. 154). But now she sees that the marriage was of "magical ease" *because* it was so short. Had Phil lived, they would have had their arguments, their troubles, and their marriage might have concluded not in ease but in tumult equal to that of her parents' marriage.

Laurel is almost glad that Phil died, leaving her with the beautiful past—until he calls out to her in a dream, " 'I wanted it [life]!' " (p. 155). Laurel weeps. She would not deny Phil life. But, then, the belief that life is only "the continuity of its love" is an unrealistic view of what a long life holds. In living, one must also face pain and misunderstandings and grief and the guilt of outliving loved ones.

In the climactic breadboard scene, which occurs after Laurel has gone through her soul-searching and redemption, she has one last trial. Fay returns to the house from her trip to Texas, and Laurel's resentment is revived. She almost hits Fay with the breadboard—she has again externalized her internal conflict and made Fay the easy villain. But her new insight triumphs: " 'I know you aren't anythiing to the past,' she said. 'You can't do anything to it now.' *And neither am I; and neither can I*, she thought, although it has been everything and done everything to me, everything for me" (p. 179, emphasis added). Laurel has come to terms with her relationship to the past. She has tried to protect the past, preserve it, remain part of it. But now she realizes that all that is impossible and unnecessary.

The past is no more open to help or hurt than was Father in his coffin. The past is like him, impervious, and can never be awakened. It is memory that is the somnambulist. It will come back in its wounds from across the world, like Phil, calling us by our names and demanding its rightful tears. . . . The memory can be hurt, time and again—but in that may lie its final mercy. As long as it's vulnerable to the living moment, it lives for us. . . . (p. 179)

As Phil escapes the idealized past, so is Laurel freed from the past and ready to live a fuller life. "Memory lived not in initial possession but in the freed hands, pardoned and freed, and in the heart that can empty but fill again . . . " (p. 179). In remaining trapped emotionally in the past, Laurel had escaped many of the pains of living in the present, but she had also robbed herself of many of the joys. And in framing Phil and their marriage in silver—as she was about to do her parents and their marriage—she had robbed him of the vulnerability of real life.

Though Laurel's problem is complicated by her "Southern" heritage, it is not defined by that heritage. She has faced, as everyone must face, the death of loved ones, and her problem has been the universal one of having to adjust to that loss. How can one survive the dead and move on to the rest of one's own life yet remain faithful to the dead loved one? Memory, not possession, is the answer Welty offers.

So Laurel leaves Mount Salus to return to Chicago. As she is escorted to the airport by her "bridesmaids," their car passes the school yard where Miss Adele Courtland waves with her pupils. And this scene draws together the two themes about the past. "[Miss Adele] waved. So did the children. The last thing Laurel saw, before they whirled into speed, was the twinkling of their hands, the many small and unknown hands, wishing her goodbye" (p. 180). As Laurel leaves freed from the past, her last glimpse of the community is of Mount Salus at its best: Miss Adele retains an understanding of the old values, not merely an habitual exercise of long-established customs; and she is, as she has been doing for some forty years, imparting her influence on the fresh, unformed minds of Mount Salus's children. Change is coming—the McKelvas are dead or gone, and Fay very well might turn the old McKelva home into a boarding house—yet, we might surmise, as long as there are such people as Miss Adele to instruct the children in the old values, there is hope. But, upon reflection, we find that this apparent sign of hope with which the novel ends is ambiguous. What the novel has led us to fear is not such change as Fay and her kind may bring but the in-breeding changelessness that leads to staleness and slow deterioration. And Miss Adele has not been a successful bulwark against that. Not only is she old, perhaps will be the next to die, but she has the children for only one year of their lives. It is quite likely that some of these fresh, unformed minds will become, years hence, as insipid as those of Laurel's bridesmaids. The many hands waving Laurel goodbye *are* a sign of hope for Laurel—she has left the past behind; but Mount Salus may remain frozen in time.

Set in contemporary times, probably the mid 1960's, *The Optimist's Daughter* suggests that the small Southern community may have less to dread from the "New South" than from itself. Fay is less a threat to Mount Salus than are its long years of in-breeding. And Laurel's discovery might be a lesson to the many characters in Southern fiction who cling to the past and frame it in silver. It is a lesson never learned by such characters as the elderly aunts in *Delta Wedding* who have for sixty years been dressing in mourning for their men killed in the Civil War. In continuing to live in the past, they have themselves become as frozen in time as many of the old traditions followed by Mount Salus—as petrified, for example, as the community's oral tradition, the vitality and viability of which appear nearly exhausted.

9
CONCLUSION: THE OTHER SIDE OF MYTH-MAKING

Everybody talked, as only a Southern family can, talking to each other for the love of all. . . . (Stark Young, *So Red the Rose*, 87)

[T]he typical Southern conversation is not going anywhere, it is not about anything. *It is about the people who are talking*, even if they never refer to themselves, which they usually don't, since conversation is only an expression of manners, the purpose of which is to make everybody happy. (Allen Tate[1])

Several critics have suggested that an increasing decline in the strength of community and myth since the middle of this century has handicapped Southern writers and brought death to the Southern Renaissance.[2] Yet even if we agree with this general thesis, we will not likely find it relevant to Welty's art. For Welty's writing—unlike that of several Southern writers who published their first works between the ends of the two World Wars—has never been predicated primarily on an absorption in community and the past. Rather, her writing seems predicated on a delight in the art of storytelling and has been shaped by her broad interest in traditions of storytelling, and these influences have so far sustained her. Possessing the "historical sense" lauded by T. S. Eliot, Welty draws on narrative traditions from Homer to recent times, including those of her own country and region. In fact, her fiction demonstrates that the Southern Renaissance can itself be a valuable resource for today's writer, its myths, patterns, and themes having entered the contemporary consciousness.

But the Southern community does provide Welty with substance. Indeed, rather than handicapping Welty's writing, the much-discussed decline in community and myth proves part of the inspiration for *The Optimist's Daughter*. Moreover, though *The Optimist's Daughter* shows Welty's awareness that the Southern community may have lost some of its strength and the oral culture some of its vitality, her autobiographical essays and interviews give evidence that the author herself, still living among lifelong friends in her hometown of Jackson, Mississippi, maintains a strong sense of community and a vigorous love of storytelling. Her most recent book, *One Writer's Beginnings*, testifies to the oral culture's continuing influence on her writing. In this book, not only does Welty describe her childhood fascination with hearing neighbors and family tell tales, and not only does she draw on the family tales her mother told her as she reconstructs her family's history, but also her long immersion in the oral culture is reflected in the method of the book itself. For although *One Writer's Beginnings* is an expansion of three lectures Welty delivered in the History of American Civilization program at Harvard University in 1983, her writing here (and, presumably, that of the papers she read at Harvard) does not belong to the genre of the academic lecture but to the genre of storytelling. Her purpose is to discuss influences on her development as a writer, yet her method is basically narrative rather than analytical. Preferring concrete example to abstractions about her development, she tells tales about her childhood, letting these suggest, or portray, various influences on her. Like her storytelling mother and her talkative neighbors, and like the Fairchilds of *Delta Wedding*, Welty "[tells] happenings like narrations, chronological and careful" (*DW*, 19).

One Writer's Beginnings is a warm and affectionate book; the author obviously cherishes her family and community. But appreciating her heritage does not blind her to flaws in her South. In her fiction, she exposes the doubleness of many conventional virtues and revered Southern traditions. Most particularly, she demonstrates that family love and the parallel sense of community may promote self-centeredness and narrowness as easily as they purvey warmth and security. Describing her family in her diary, Shelley Fairchild writes, "All together we have a wall, we are self-sufficient against those who come up knocking, we are solid to the outside" (*DW*, 84). The families and communities in Welty's novels all erect walls against those who come up knocking, all are solid to the outside. In some cases, Welty emphasizes a group's narrowness by contrasting it with the all-embracing love of an individual. Jack Renfro can even love his family's enemy Julia Mortimer: " 'I reckon I even love her,' said Jack. 'I heard her story' " (*LB*, 361).

For most of Welty's characters, however, hearing a story about someone perceived as an outsider does not lead to love of the person. Like Stark Young, Welty depicts the Southern family's talking as an expression of love for one another, but she also shows the oral tradition to abet not only the group's cohesiveness but also its exclusion of those on its fringes. In their small worlds, the characters talk about hardly anything except people and events within their own circles, thus reinforcing local values and customs. Moreover, whenever outsiders are the subjects of tales, rejection of them and their ways is explicit.

More subtly, the community's narrowness infects the myth-making about heroes. Humorous and harmless as the myth-making appears, it has its disturbing side. On the positive side, tales about heroes provide entertainment. For the community, they offer vicarious adventures and subjects for daydreams. For the family, they develop in members a sense of identity and pride, and they nourish ideals. But a close look at the family's and community's tale-telling will discover that the groups discriminate not only against persons they deem outsiders but also against some they claim as their own—as much through what they overlook as through what they deliberately exclude and include.

' Welty shows the Southern society to have a very definite but selective notion of heroism. Ironically, despite its conservative character, it glorifies self-sacrificing, Christian-like behavior rarely, self-centered, assertive behavior often. In *The Optimist's Daughter*, as we have seen, Judge McKelva is not eulogized by his friends for his devotion to his invalid wife through her lengthy illness nor for his service to his community but instead for a much-embellished episode which could be straight out of a typical Western movie or tale. Similarly, in *The Golden Apples* Virgie Rainey's long and self-denying devotion to her widowed mother is taken for granted by Morgana, Mississippi, while the town makes a glamorous legend of a man who deserts his wife and children. These communities have a conventionally romantic notion of heroism.

Not all conventionally heroic acts win approval, however; the characters' sense of the heroic is indeed selective. George Fairchild separates two fighting Negro boys and catches a thrown knife in midair—behavior reminiscent of the heroism of men in cowboy movies and

American folklore. Yet in witnessing George's action as a child, Dabney is offended rather than thrilled, for to her the scene means only that George has violated a family standard in caring about people outside the family. The Fairchilds make an amusing tale of the incident but do not much repeat it. A comparable conventionally heroic action of Troy Flavin, the Shellmound overseer, is neither praised nor preserved in a tale by the romanticizing Fairchilds. Also like a hero of cowboy legend, Troy breaks up a fight by shooting an ice pick out of a Negro's hand, without injuring the assailant. Yet Shelley, who witnesses Troy's apparently heroic action, just as Dabney did George's, can only see Troy's behavior as vulgar. In this case, a performance exhibiting the usual characteristics of heroism is not viewed as heroic because the person who has performed it has no chance of being a hero in the family's eyes or, therefore, in their tales.

The society's values preclude not only overseers but also females from being the objects of its hero-worship. Though individual females are subjects of single, scattered tales, none of these inspires a general mythology, as do Don McInnis, Denis Fairchild, George Fairchild, King MacLain, Daniel Ponder, Sam Dale Beecham, and Jack Renfro. On the contrary, females who become frequent subjects of tales are likely to be presented by the narrators as villains or unpopular strangers: Miss Sabina ("Asphodel"), Miss Eckhart (*GA*), Miss Julia Mortimer (*LB*). Not even pretty females of the family who die young become legendary heroines. Like her brother Denis, Annie Laurie (*DW*) was much loved, died young, and left a young daughter behind, yet unlike Denis, Annie Laurie seems rarely to appear in her family's thoughts, except as her death serves as a marking point in time: "[T]hey could say so easily, 'Before—or after—Annie Laurie died . . . ,' to count the time of a dress being made or a fruit tree planted" (p. 134). And another dead relative, Miss Rowena, "the quiet old maid," was "*forgotten*, if a Fairchild could be," Robbie believes. "She let all her brothers take from her so, she *let* them! Robbie shivered for Miss Rowena" (*DW*, 145).

The basis for the absence of mythicized females is traceable to the double standard, which is an accepted fact of life in the South of Welty's fiction. As their heroes the people select individuals whom they interpret as sensuous nonconformists or as strong, capable protectors of the family, and these roles, in the conventional society, are generally reserved for men.

The women "rule the roost" in Welty's South—as Robbie observes of the Fairchild women (*DW*, 144)—but "the roost" means, of course, the home and domestic-related activities. They take charge of funeral, reunion, and wedding activities. But it is always from the males that the stars are drawn, even when the males and females differ little in personality and character: "The boys were only like all the Fairchilds, but it was the boys and the men that defined that family always. All the girls knew it" (*DW*, 14). And all the Fairchild girls accept and encourage it, for the double standard is the way of the world, so far as they have experienced the world. So young nieces and sisters flit around the male favorites of their families, and they and their elders narrate the exploits of these favorites.

In fact, the women themselves become defensive whenever a fellow female singles herself from the rest. In *The Golden Apples*, Jinny Love Stark MacLain is jealous of sensuous Virgie Rainey for remaining un-married while she herself has accepted the conventional female role and thus has lost her identity as an individual. She advises Virgie, now middle-aged, to get married: " 'Listen. You should marry now, Vir-gie. Don't put it off any longer.' . . . She was grimacing out of the iron mask of the married lady. It appeared urgent with her to drive everybody, even Virgie for whom she cared nothing, into the state of marriage along with her. Only then could she resume as Jinny Love Stark, her true self" (p. 225). As young, unmarried Jinny Love Stark, daughter of one of Morgana's leading families, Jinny Love had been a darling of the community and was granted considerable freedom. As Jinny Love Stark MacLain, her identity is as wife to Ran MacLain and mother of their children.

Whereas sensuousness, independence, and defiance in a male will be overlooked, forgiven, or admired and made the subject of legend, these same qualities are feared and condemned when they appear in a female. Welty exposes this prejudice by using Virgie Rainey with her responsible free-spiritedness as a foil to the legendary King MacLain with his hedonistic Dionysianism. Virgie enjoys bathing in the river in the nude, a practice conventionally condoned only for males, such as the young boys who watch her (and George and Denis Fairchild in *Delta Wedding*). She further defies the Morgana social code for women and earns the scorn of the town by remaining unmarried and having dis-creet affairs. Yet Virgie's free-spiritedness, unlike King's, appears not to have harmed others. Whereas she quelled her desire to roam in staying home to support and be a companion to her widowed mother, King deserted his wife, who longed for his return, and his sons, who in adulthood longed for their father's advice and companionship. Another of Morgana's free spirits, Loch Morrison, could leave home to pursue the life he desired without neglecting moral responsibilities since his unmarried sister Cassie remained at home to comfort and care for their father after their mother's suicide (just as Virgie as an unmarried daughter stayed home with her mother after her father's death). But Virgie and King had to choose not only between independence and Morgana's conformity but also between home duties and personal pleasure. And they made opposite choices. King returns home to stay only after he becomes an old man who needs someone to look after him; Virgie feels free to pursue more fully her gusto for life only after her mother is dead and her obligations fulfilled.

The weight of the double standard can be seen particularly in the contrast between Virgie's popularity in her childhood and her unpopularity later. Because children only gradually and unconsciously adopt community attitudes (young children are the only ones who see King MacLain without the mythic enlargement), and, moreover, as childhood behavior is not judged by the same code as adult behavior, Virgie's status can change while her character remains the same.

In their childhood years, Virgie's classmates view her as a heroine. Just as in "Moon Lake" Easter's defiance and daring behavior make her fascinating to Morgana youngsters, so in "June Recital" do Virgie's vitality and her defiance of good-girl behavior make her heroic to her classmates. In the children's view, Virgie is "full of the airs of wildness" and "as exciting as a gypsy would be." The children imagine that she will "go somewhere, somewhere away off." Even older Morgana can find her leadership and charisma appealing as long as she is a child: "Miss Lizzie Stark's mother, old Mrs. Sad-Talking Morgan, and Virgie would be the first lady governor of Mississippi . . ." (p. 38).

But Morgana interprets such independence in a sixteen-year-old young lady as improper and finds Virgie's behavior now shocking. By high school age, Virgie's classmates are in step with Morgana standards, and Virgie, who plays the piano at the picture show every night, is "not popular any more" (p. 32). Along with older Morganans, they scorn Virgie for her exuberance and sexual freedom, which began with an affair with a sailor when she was sixteen (the approximate age that the male MacLain twins are introduced to sex in the Morgana woods). Some years later, Virgie is an outcast in the community. Though she has lived in her childhood home all her life, Morgana treats her at her mother's funeral as if she is a stranger to both Morgana and her own house. Ironically, had Virgie been born male, her uninhibited actions, even her promiscuity, would have titillated but not scandalized Morgana. And had she been born a MacLain and male, these actions would have assured her of legendary glory.

We can be sure that it is not Virgie's low social class (she is the daughter of a milkman and produce saleswoman) but her sex that accounts for the lesser liberties which Morgana will grant her when we realize that Jinny Love Stark MacLain, though part of upper-crust Morgana, suffers similar restrictions. In a society which places people according to who their parents are ("Then Morgana could hold them, and at last they were this and they were that," "June Recital," p. 79), the MacLains, Morgans, and Starks are fortunate, for the old established families occupy the top places and are allowed more latitude than the rest. In fact, the MacLains are expected to be mystifying aberrations—it is their assigned place or role in the community. However, the freedom which the MacLains enjoy stems not only from the fact that they are MacLains but also from the fact that they are men. Jinny Love Stark MacLain, as a daughter of Morgans and Starks and wife of a MacLain, is awarded high status and some concessions, yet as a woman she is still bound by the double standard. Her affair with Woody Spright is never elevated above the level of gossip, whereas her husband's reactions to the affair become a glamorous legend. In "The Whole World Knows," Snowdie MacLain spells out the double standard in speaking to her son Ran, Jinny's husband: "Mother said, *If I thought you'd ever go back to that Jinny Stark, I couldn't stand it.*—No, Mother, I'm not going back.—*The whole world knows what she did to you. It's different from when it's the man*" (GA, 157). Actions that are admired and made subject of legend in King and Ran MacLain and Don McInnis will not be condoned for Virgie Rainey or even Jinny Love Stark MacLain.

By elevating a chosen few males to legendary glory, the oral tradition passes over not only females but also other males. Battle Fairchild was the brother left out in his generation. First his older brother Denis and then his younger brother George were singled out as favorites. In like fashion, the position of honor in the Beecham-Renfro family descended from Sam Dale Beecham to his young nephew Jack Renfro, passing over several uncles and cousins. In accepting the double standard, women presumably do not expect to become favorites, but we might wonder if there is any resentment from male relatives, brothers in particular, when they see their siblings given much more honor and attention than are they.

While there is no evidence that Battle harbors resentment, his thoughts never being revealed, at one point his wife realizes that he may have suffered silently from the preference given his brothers, a preference which she implies is irrational. In a moment of tenderness toward her husband, Ellen thinks that "there's no reason in the world why he should have been cowed in his life by Denis and George" (*DW*, 190). Yet even perceptive Ellen seldom sees the brothers as equal. Earlier, she had remarked to Robbie on a similarity among the three brothers, but she emphasized the quality in Denis and George: " 'George loves a great many people, just about everybody in the Delta, if you would count them. Don't you know that's the mark of a fine man, Robbie? Battle's like that. Denis was even more, even more well loved' " (p. 164). Ellen's last remark is a significant slip-of-tongue. Though she began by comparing the brothers' generous love for others, she ends by remarking on the large love of others for Denis. If it was indeed this latter love—the love others have for the brothers—that Ellen was thinking of all along, then it is not surprising that Battle gets slighted in her remark since his two brothers are obviously more intensely and widely loved than is he.

Losing Battles presents less ambiguously the sense of rejection that an unhonored brother might feel. All the action of the novel is external—except for a half-dozen-page section rendered, significantly, from the point of view of Jack's twelve-year-old brother Vaughn. And Vaughn clearly resents his brother's higher status.

With Jack away in prison for almost two years, Vaughn has been awarded all Jack's responsibilities but none of his honor or glory. He is aware that the family's dependency on him will soon shift again to Jack, now that Jack has returned: "For a year and a half it had been 'Vaughn! Vaughn!' every minute, though it would turn before he knew it back into 'Jack!' again" (p. 363). Vaughn's resentment of his family's preference for his older brother is expressed in earlier passages as well. While the rest of the reunion is telling tales about Jack in happy anticipation of his return, Vaughn, perhaps in an effort to get attention, says, " 'I don't care if he don't get here till tomorrow' " and " 'I don't care if he don't get here till the *next* reunion' " (p. 11).

Vaughn's bitterness is no doubt partially attributable to the family's inconsistency. Jack receives praise for anything he does, or tries to do, while Vaughn receives none. Even on this day, as Vaughn fulfills thankless chores, Jack is being cheered for his efforts to scare a car into a ditch and being acclaimed one who will redeem the family from poverty. Moreover, Vaughn is criticized and derogatorily compared to Jack over and over. In front of the reunion guests, his mother says, " 'He'll never be Jack. . . . Says the wrong thing, does the wrong thing, doesn't do what I tell him. And perfectly satisfied to have you say so!' " (p. 12). He is blamed for the school bus's ending up in the ditch, though his sister and Jack are responsible for that, and is scolded also for the loss of the hay crop—a crop that he had cut and then been forced to neglect because his mother required his help with the reunion preparations. At another point, his mother says, " 'Vaughn can't rob a hen's nest without Jack to tell him. Vaughn is not Jack and never will be' " (p. 402).

The events of the novel indicate that only the last part of Beulah's comparison of the two brothers is correct; Vaughn is not Jack and never will be. Vaughn approaches life carefully and practically, whereas Jack plunges head-first into any activity. In his impulsive, charming enthusiasm, Jack creates as much trouble for the family as he solves, though the family in their love for him never realize this. While the others sleep, Vaughn manages alone to get the school bus out of the ditch, whereas Jack, who had badly needed a vehicle with which to pull Judge Moody's car off Banner Top, had considered the bus useless once his little sister ran it into the ditch in an attempt to help him. " 'Without Jack, nothing would be no trouble at all,' " Vaughn says to himself in his soliloquy (p. 364). To add insult to injury, when Vaughn, the official school bus driver, starts on his route after milking the cows the next morning, big brother Jack commandeers the bus to tow the judge's car to town, and Vaughn is relegated to the back of the long towing procession which Jack puts together; he must ride a mule and serve as the tow line's brakes. Thus does Vaughn once again take a back seat, both literally and symbolically, to his brother, for their roles in the procession are representative of their positions in the family: Jack, driving the towing vehicle, is seen as the leader and gets credit for the success of the venture, while Vaughn as brakesman quietly assumes the responsibility for keeping the ride safe.

Ironically, the family's praise of Jack had begun when, at about Vaughn's present age, he had had to take over most of the farm operations—he was applauded for doing the very things that Vaughn does now without praise. Thus the family unconsciously discriminates against even its own, thereby frustrating and creating resentment in such characters as Vaughn. The exaltation of selected males through the hero-worship and tale-telling becomes, in effect, a rejection of others.

These and other negative implications about the society are apparent in Welty's fiction without defining that fiction. They emerge through the author's carefully crafted portraits of a place and a people, portraits in which comedy reigns as Southern talkers come alive. Allen Tate is quoted at the beginning of this chapter as saying that Southern conversation isn't about anything except the "people who are talking." At the heart of much of Welty's comedy is the truth of this statement. Tate also says that the purpose of Southern conversation "is to make everybody happy." Welty might agree. As a comic-realist, however, she knows that not everybody *is* made happy by Southern conversation. In her fiction, the listeners are affected in many different ways, depending on their individual dispositions and their positions within, or outside of, the group, while the person made happiest by Southern talk is usually the person doing the talking. But Welty would probably suggest that this characteristic is true of oral traditions in general, not just of Southern ones. In her short story "Circe" (*BI*), about another time and another storytelling people, Circe listens for hours to the fantastic tales of adventure told by Odysseus and his men, anticipates a tale to be told of Odysseus's death, and then ponders the question, "For whom is a story enough?" And her answer? For those "who will tell it—it's where they must find their strange felicity" (p. 111).

In reading Welty's fiction, Cleanth Brooks is reminded that "Homer, the father of the poetry of Western civilization, was himself a poet of the oral tradition, even though he was to become the very cornerstone of the written tradition." Welty, Brooks observes, is another who achieves "a true wedding" of the oral and written traditions, successfully incorporating the oral into the written and thus "giv[ing] it an enduring life."[3] I would add that not only has Welty preserved the oral tradition; she has built much of her fiction on a recognition of connections between the oral and the written—and between Southern storytelling and other story or storytelling traditions. She reminds us that the oral and written traditions have been intertwined since the time of Homer and perhaps nowhere more so, in the twentieth century, than in the American South.

NOTES

PREFACE

1. Charles E. Davis, "The South in Eudora Welty's Fiction: A Changing World," *Studies in American Fiction*, 3 (Autumn 1975), 200.

2. M. E. Bradford has previously observed this defensiveness. He points out that scholars (John Edward Hardy, Alfred Appel, Jr., Ruth M. Vande Kieft) have attempted to protect *Delta Wedding* "from guilt by association" by arguing that the novel "is not about the South" ["Fairchild as Composite Protagonist in *Delta Wedding*," in Peggy Whitman Prenshaw, ed., *Eudora Welty: Critical Essays* (Jackson: University Press of Mississippi, 1979), p. 202]. In a recent study of Welty's universality, *Eudora Welty's Achievement of Order*, Michael Kreyling also briefly sounds the defensive note in his introduction. His aim, he says, is "to show that Welty's fiction truly encompasses 'the general consciousness,' that it is not primarily regional writing, but is the vision of a certain artist" whose peers are "Woolf, Bowen, and Forster, among others—who have never been called regional" (Baton Rouge: Louisiana State University Press, 1980, p. xx).

3. "Eudora Welty's Mississippi," in Prenshaw, ed., *Eudora Welty: Critical Essays*, p. 158.

4. See Albert J. Devlin, *Eudora Welty's Chronicle: A Story of Mississippi Life* (Jackson: University Press of Mississippi, 1983); and Jennifer Lynn Randisi, *A Tissue of Lies: Eudora Welty and the Southern Romance* (Washington, D.C.: University Press of America, 1982). Elizabeth Evans also allots substantial space to the Southern interest in her general study, *Eudora Welty*, Modern Literature Series (New York: Frederick Ungar, 1981).

CHAPTER 1

1. "The Corner Store," *Esquire*, December 1975, p. 212.

2. Linda Kuehl, "The Art of Fiction XLVII: Eudora Welty," *Paris Review*, 55 (Fall 1972), 79.

3. "Introduction," *A Curtain of Green* (1941), rpt. in *Selected Stories of Eudora Welty*, p. xiv.

4. "A Sweet Devouring" (1957), in *The Eye of the Story: Selected Essays and Reviews* (New York: Random House, 1978), pp. 281, 285.

5. Jean Todd Freeman, "Eudora Welty," in *Conversations with Writers II*, A Bruccoli Clark Book (Detroit: Gale Research Co., 1978), p. 287.

6. John Griffin Jones, "Eudora Welty," in *Mississippi Writers Talking* (Jackson: University Press of Mississippi, 1982), p. 22.

7. Don Lee Keith, "Eudora Welty: 'I Worry Over My Stories,' " *The Times-Picayune*, September 16, 1973, rpt. in Peggy Whitman Prenshaw, ed., *Conversations with Eudora Welty* (Jackson: University Press of Mississippi, 1984), p. 142.

8. Freeman, p. 290.

9. "New Writer," *Time*, November 24, 1941, p. 111; Warren, "Love and Separateness in Eudora Welty" (1944), rpt. in Warren, *Selected Essays* (New York: Vintage Books, 1958), p. 157.

10. Warren, p. 156; Van Gelder, "An Interview with Eudora Welty" (1942), rpt. in Van Gelder, *Writers and Writing* (New York: Scribner's, 1946), p. 289.

11. The tone of "Clytie" suggests that Welty may be parodying the typical Southern Gothic story. Parody in her works is discussed later in this study.

12. Van Gelder, pp. 288, 299.

13. Welty, "Looking Back at the First Story," *Georgia Review*, 33 (Winter 1979), 752.

14. Welty, "Looking Back at the First Story," p. 752; Van Gelder, p. 289.

15. Welty, " 'Is Phoenix Jackson's Grandson Really Dead?' " *Critical Inquiry*, 1 (September 1974), rpt. in *The Eye of the Story*, p. 161.

16. Welty in the Kuehl interview, p. 88.

17. An early story only recently published, *South Carolina Review*, 11 (November 1978), 26–33.

18. Kuehl, p. 89. Welty quotes the sentence about Monsieur Boule in the Van Gelder and Kuehl interviews and in *One Writer's Beginnings*.

19. Warren, pp. 160–61; Appel, *A Season of Dreams: The Fiction of Eudora Welty* (Baton Rouge: Louisiana State University Press, 1965), p. xiii.

20. Warren, p. 157.

21. Welty, "Place in Fiction," *South Atlantic Quarterly*, 55 (January 1956), 58.

22. Ruth M. Vande Kieft, *Eudora Welty*, Twayne's United States Authors Series (New Haven: College and University Press, 1962), p. 164.

23. Welty, *Short Stories* (New York: Harcourt, Brace, 1950), p. 13.

24. She speaks about the two stories in separate interviews: Charles T. Bunting, " 'The Interior World': An Interview with Eudora Welty," *Southern Review*, 8 (October 1972), 735; and Freeman, p. 303.

25. "New Writer," p. 111.

26. Lytle, "Foreword," *A Novel, a Novella and Four Stories* (New York: McDowell, Obolensky, 1958), p. xvii.

27. See Freeman, pp. 308, 295–96.

28. Kuehl, p. 79.

29. Welty, "The Radiance of Jane Austen," in *The Eye of the Story*, pp. 3–4. Rev. and enl. from "A Note on Jane Austen," *Shenandoah*, 20 (Spring 1969).

30. *One Time, One Place* (New York: Random House, 1971), p. 6.

31. Quotations from the Bunting interview, p. 716; and Welty, "The Radiance of Jane Austen," p. 6. See Seymour Gross's description of Welty's comic vision in "A Long Day's Living: The Angelic Ingenuities of *Losing Battles*," in Prenshaw, ed., *Eudora Welty: Critical Essays*, pp. 325–29.

32. Tom Royals and John Little, "A Conversation with Eudora Welty," *Bloodroot* (Spring 1979), rpt. in Prenshaw, ed., *Conversations with Eudora Welty*, p. 255.

33. Griffith, "Henny Penny, Eudora Welty, and the Aggregation of Friends," in Prenshaw, ed., *Eudora Welty: Critical Essays*, p. 86.

34. Alfred J. Griffith summarizes early criticisms of Welty's style in "The Poetics of Prose: Eudora Welty's Literary Theory," in John F. Desmond, ed., *A Still Moment: Essays on the Art of Eudora Welty* (Metuchen, N.J.: Scarecrow Press, 1978), pp. 51–52. Also see John F. Fleischauer, "The Focus of Mystery: Eudora Welty's Prose Style," *Southern Literary Journal*, 5 (Spring 1973), 64–79.

35. Welty's adjectives are typically words of color, size, or number. She occasionally uses a more descriptive style, with a freer flow of adjectives. Chapter 7 includes discussion of a special use of the latter style in *Losing Battles*.

36. Thomas Daniel Young argues that the bigamy is the character's fantasy. See Young's review of *Eudora Welty's Achievement of Order* by Michael Kreyling, *Sewanee Review*, 90 (Spring 1982), xiv.

37. Kuehl, p. 80.

CHAPTER 2

1. Willie Morris, "A Sense of Place and the Americanization of Mississippi," *The Southern Quarterly*, 17 (Spring-Summer 1979), 8–9.

2. Roy Reed, "Revisiting the Southern Mind," *New York Times Magazine*, December 5, 1976, p. 99.

3. "Humor of the Old Southwest" (1937), rpt. in M. Thomas Inge, ed., *The Frontier Humorists* (Hamden, Conn.: Archon Books, 1975), p. 51. In separate essays in *The Frontier Humorists*, Inge, Franklin J. Meine, and John Donald Wade also link the written tradition of frontier humor to an oral tradition.

4. For more detailed discussion of characteristics of the folk humor tale, see Richard M. Dorson, *American Folklore* (Chicago: University of Chicago Press, 1959), pp. 200 ff.; and M. Thomas Inge, ed., *The Frontier Humorists*.

5. Rubin, "Two in Richmond: Ellen Glasgow and James Branch Cabell," *The Curious Death of the Novel* (Baton Rouge: Louisiana State University Press, 1967), pp. 172–73.

6. Cabell, *Let Me Lie* (New York: Farrar, Straus, 1947), p. 145.

7. An excellent record of such a versatile family-community saga tradition is *All God's Dangers: The Life of Nate Shaw* (New York: Alfred A. Knopf, 1975), which Theodore Rosengarten compiled from many hours of taped conversation with an elderly Alabaman and his family. What Rosengarten heard were tales the family had previously exchanged only among themselves and with friends. Covering family history over several generations, the tales vary greatly in tone and content, from the heroic and tragic to the merely anecdotal, and from criticism to admiration to ridicule of their major figures.

8. Page's stories are among the earliest in this literary pattern. Ironically, the structure of these early examples may have been borrowed from the Southwest frontier humorists, or from the humorists by way of Joel Chandler Harris. For his Uncle Remus stories, Harris adopted a frame tale format, a structure then widely familiar in tales of the frontier humorists. In presenting Southern characters reminiscing nostalgically about the war and pre–war days, Page also chose the frame tale format. He even adopted the humorists' use of an educated gentleman-narrator as the recorder of tales supposedly told to the gentleman during his travels through the South. The tales themselves were presented, however, in the illiterate diction of their original narrators—not bragging and brash frontiersmen this time but garrulous and brash ex-slaves.

9. Kennedy, *Swallow Barn* (1832), rpt. in American Authors Series, ed. Jay B. Hubbell (New York: Harcourt, Brace, 1929), p. 56.

10. *Sartoris* (1929; rpt. New York: Random House, 1956), p. 9. Pages for citations from *Sartoris* will hereafter be given in the text.

11. *The Moviegoer* (New York: Alfred A. Knopf, 1962), p. 49. Pages for citations from *The Moviegoer* will hereafter be given in the text.

12. *So Red the Rose* (New York: Charles Scribner's Sons, 1934), pp. 76, 150–51. Pages for citations from *So Red* will hereafter be given in the text.

13. William Humphrey, *The Ordways* (New York: Alfred A. Knopf, 1965), p. 36.

14. Emerson, in manuscript of speech prepared for meeting of National Council of Teachers of English, 1974, p. 1.

15. "The Old Order," in *The Leaning Tower and Other Stories* (New York: Harcourt, Brace, 1944), p. 35.

16. Ransom, "Delta Fiction," *Kenyon Review*, 8 (Summer 1946), 507. Some scholars argue that *Delta Wedding* is not about the South. See note 2 of the preceding chapter.

17. Kuehl, p. 79.

18. Buckley, "The Southern Imagination: An Interview with Eudora Welty and Walker Percy," *Mississippi Quarterly*, 26 (Fall 1973), 495–96. Transcript of "Firing Line," Public Broadcasting Service, December 24, 1972.

19. "Old Mortality," in *Pale Horse, Pale Rider* (New York: Harcourt, Brace, 1939), p. 17.

20. Bunting, p. 718.

CHAPTER 3

1. John Crowe Ransom, "Reconstructed But Unregenerate," in Twelve Southerners, *I'll Take My Stand* (1930; rpt. New York: Harper and Brothers, 1962), p. 12.

2. "An Interview with Eudora Welty," *Comment: University of Alabama Review* (Winter 1965), rpt. in Prenshaw, ed., *Conversations with Eudora Welty*, p. 21.

3. Welty discusses criticism of her alleged lack of a social consciousness in Freeman, pp. 296–97. Also see Victor H. Thompson, "Introduction," *Eudora Welty: A Reference Guide* (Boston: G. K. Hall and Co., 1976), pp. ix–xv.

4. *Weeds* (1923; rpt. Carbondale: Southern Illinois University Press, 1972), pp. 4–5.

5. Louis D. Rubin, Jr., "Introduction to the Torchbook Edition," *I'll Take My Stand*, p. xxv.

6. In *Delta Wedding*: "They drove up and down the street three times and had Coca Colas, speaking to people over and over, with all the men's hats going up and down" (p. 127).

7. "An Interview with Eudora Welty," pp. 19–20.

8. For these descriptions of Sister, see Katherine Anne Porter's "Introduction" to Welty's *A Curtain of Green*, rpt. in *Selected Stories of Eudora Welty*, p. xx; and Charles E. May, "Why Sister Lives at the P. O.," *Southern Humanities Review*, 12 (Summer 1978), 243–49.

9. Examples include Quentin Compson of *The Sound and the Fury* and *Absalom, Absalom!*, young Bayard Sartoris of *Sartoris*, Ike McCaslin of "The Bear," Jack Burden of *All the King's Men*, Miranda of "Old Mortality," Binx Bolling of *The Moviegoer*, Lacy Buchan of Allen Tate's *The Fathers*, the narrator of William Humphrey's *The Ordways*.

10. Ransom, "Forms and Citizens," in *The World's Body* (1938; rpt. Baton Rouge: Louisiana State University Press, 1968), p. 35.

CHAPTER 4

1. Kuehl, p. 80.

2. King, *A Southern Renaissance: The Cultural Awakening of the American South, 1930–1955* (New York: Oxford University Press, 1980), pp. 8–9. King regards several major female writers of the South this way.

3. Katherine Anne Porter describes the family in "Old Mortality" as "lov[ing] to tell stories, romantic and poetic, or comic with a romantic humor" (p. 6). The Fairchilds' tales also fall into these categories.

4. Exceptions occur in grotesque fiction or scenes, where revolting wounds and deaths in tales about the past are part of the comic horror of the works. Through his narrator's reminiscence in *The Ordways*, Humphrey focuses in on, and magnifies, an injury: the legs of a man hit by shrapnel at Shiloh had been "so shredded they had looked like boiled soup shanks." The foul-smelling, "suppurating legs" attracted flies (pp. 27–28).

5. W. J. Cash sees Southerners' love of play as a manifestation of their romantic proclivities. *The Mind of the South* (1941; rpt. New York: Vintage Books, n.d.), pp. 46–55.

6. Although subsequent tale-telling during the reunion indirectly provides some substance for Granny's explanation, that explanation could, even in the most generous view, hardly justify Nathan's murder of a man, his letting a Negro hang for his crime, and his self-mutilation.

CHAPTER 5

1. *Eudora Welty*, p. 187.

2. See discussions of Welty's use of these contrasting character types in Warren, "Love and Separateness in Eudora Welty," pp. 165–66; Vande Kieft, *Eudora Welty*, pp. 58–63; and Appel, *A Season of Dreams*, pp. 86–92, 188–89.

3. *A Season of Dreams*, pp. 91, 85–86.

4. See Vande Kieft, p. 59.

5. See Vande Kieft, p. 113. Also see Thomas L. McHaney's discussion of mythic allusions in *The Golden Apples*, in "Eudora Welty and the Multitudinous Golden Apples," *Mississippi Quarterly*, 26 (Fall 1973), 589–624.

6. The allusions, Robert L. Phillips says, "make the reader's experience richer, for the reader can sense that King and Snowdie have transcended the limitations of . . . Morgana to experience freely the primal joys of a fertile marriage" ("A Structural Approach to Myth," in Prenshaw, ed., *Eudora Welty:*

Critical Essays, pp. 59–60). Phillips interprets the allusions related to King in the same way he interprets those related to Phoenix in "A Worn Path." Yet King, unlike Phoenix, is a mock hero, and the role of the allusions seems consistent with the comic portrayal of him.

7. Indeed, there is a somewhat similar situation in the myth of Danae and Zeus, involving Danae's son Perseus and Perseus's grandfather.

8. *Eudora Welty*, p. 87.

9. See Edith Hamilton, *Mythology: Timeless Tales of Gods and Heroes* (1942; rpt. New York: New American Library, n.d.), pp. 59–60.

10. *Eudora Welty*, p. 112.

11. From Katie Rainey's tale about King: "Children known and unknown, scattered-like" ("Shower of Gold," *GA*, 4). The assumption that Loch and Easter are King's actual children, however, may indicate that critics are giving in to, and contributing to, the myth-making about King.

CHAPTER 6

1. At one point in *One Writer's Beginnings*, she delightfully satirizes her own college-girl romanticizing. Having read a poem about the persona's " 'need of silence and stars,' " she was sure she needed the same, despite the silence and stars all around her: "This did not impinge upon my longing. In the beautiful spring night, I was dedicated to *wanting* a beautiful spring night. To be *transported* to it was what I wanted" (p. 79).

2. This pattern or motif in Southern literature is discussed in the first section of Chapter 2.

3. John A. Allen discusses heroes in Welty's fiction informatively in "Eudora Welty: The Three Moments," in Desmond, ed., *A Still Moment*, pp. 12–34.

CHAPTER 7

1. From an interview: Bill Ferris, "A Visit with Eudora Welty," *Images of the South*, Southern Folklore Reports, No. 1 (Memphis: Center for Southern Folklore, 1977), p. 21.

2. A locally famous old tree at Newburgh, New York, is alleged to have sprung from a riding crop discarded by George Washington. See Richard Severo, "A 17th Century Tree in Newburgh May Be 20th Century Traffic Victim," *New York Times*, June 25, 1974, p. 33.

3. "Old Mortality," p. 4.

4. Yardley, "The Last Good One?" *New Republic*, May 9, 1970, p. 36; and Bradford, "Looking Down from a High Place: The Serenity of Miss Wel-

ty's *Losing Battles*," *RANAM*, 4 (1971), rpt. in Desmond, ed., *A Still Moment*, pp. 103, 194.

5. This parodic inclination is displayed undisguisedly in a little-known early essay, "*Women!! Make Turban in Own Home!*," first published in 1941 in *Junior League Magazine* (rev. and rpt., Palaemon Press Limited, 1979). Here, Welty pokes fun at both her own youthful efforts to make a "Hedy Lamarr turban" and—as the title of the essay suggests—the genre of "Make-It-Yourself" essays which tempted her to try, a genre she discovered as a child through her enthusiastic and undiscriminating reading of *Popular Mechanics* magazine.

6. Arnold, "Eudora Welty's Parody," *Notes on Mississippi Writers*, 11 (Spring 1978), 15–22.

7. Bradford, "Looking Down from a High Place," p. 104.

8. A shorter version of this discussion appeared as a paper I delivered at the annual NEMLA conference in Pittsburg in 1977. For a different discussion of *Losing Battles* as a comic epic, see Mary Anne Ferguson, "*Losing Battles* as a Comic Epic in Prose," in Prenshaw, ed., *Eudora Welty: Critical Essays*, pp. 305–24. Robert B. Heilman has also pointed out some of the novel's mock-heroic effects. See "*Losing Battles* and Winning the War," in Prenshaw, pp. 269–304.

9. See Christopher Ricks's review of *Losing Battles*, in *New York Review of Books*, July 23, 1970, p. 10; also Carol A. Moore, "The Insulation of Illusion and *Losing Battles*," *Mississippi Quarterly*, 26 (Fall 1973), 657.

10. From Book Two, *The Odyssey*, trans. Robert Fitzgerald, Riverside Literature Series (Boston: Houghton Mifflin, 1965), p. 16.

11. Quotes from "Author's Preface," *Joseph Andrews* (1742), rpt. *Joseph Andrews/Shamela*, ed. Martin C. Battestin, Riverside (Boston: Houghton Mifflin, 1961), pp. 7–8.

12. A frequent description of Odysseus in *The Odyssey*, Fitzgerald translation.

13. A mock-romantic description of Gloria on page 73 of the novel recalls the mock-romantic descriptions of Eula Varner and Ike Snopes's beloved cow in *The Hamlet*.

CHAPTER 8

1. In Rubin's *The Curious Death of the Novel*, p. 283.

2. Kuehl, p. 82.

3. Buckley, p. 498.

4. The theme of the changing South and the character contrasts appear, with varying emphases, in many works, including *The Sound and the Fury, So Red the Rose, All the King's Men*, and Tom Wicker's *Facing the Lions*.

5. See, for example, *The Sound and the Fury, All the King's Men*, and William Styron's *Lie Down in Darkness*. In the first two, as in *The Optimist's Daughter*, the clock in the house of an old established family no longer operates properly. See also Carson McCullers, *Clock Without Hands*.

6. *Ellen Glasgow* (New Haven: College and University Press, 1962), p. 113.

7. Robert Penn Warren, *All the King's Men* (1946; rpt. New York: Bantam Books, 1971), p. 121.

8. Thomas Daniel Young has previously shown that through subtle handling of point of view Welty determines how we react to Fay and Laurel. He also discusses helpfully the "pageant of grief" which Mount Salus stages. See Chapter 5 in his *The Past in the Present: A Thematic Study of Modern Southern Fiction* (Baton Rouge: Louisiana State University Press, 1981), pp. 87–116.

9. For discussions of Laurel's character, see John F. Desmond, "Pattern and Vision in *The Optimist's Daughter*," in *A Still Moment*, pp. 118–38; and Thomas Daniel Young, Chapter 5, *The Past in the Present*, pp. 87–116.

10. See Desmond's discussion of these differences in "Pattern and Vision in *The Optimist's Daughter*."

CHAPTER 9

1. "A Southern Mode of the Imagination," in Tate's *Collected Essays* (Denver: Alan Swallow, 1959), p. 560. His emphasis.

2. See, for example, Walter Sullivan, *A Requiem for the Renascence: The State of Fiction in the Modern South* (Athens: University of Georgia Press, 1976). Sullivan finds that *The Optimist's Daughter* demonstrates that "the postmodern world with its loss of community and myth will no longer support Welty" (p. 57).

3. Brooks, "Eudora Welty and the Southern Idiom," in Louis Dollarhide and Ann J. Abadie, eds., *Eudora Welty: A Form of Thanks* (Jackson: University Press of Mississippi, 1979), p. 24.

SELECTED BIBLIOGRAPHY

FICTION BY WELTY

"Acrobats in a Park." *South Carolina Review* 11 (November 1978), 26–33.
The Bride of the Innisfallen and Other Stories. Harvest Book. New York: Harcourt Brace Jovanovich, 1955.
A Curtain of Green and Other Stories. 1941; rpt. in *Selected Stories of Eudora Welty*. New York: Modern Library, 1954.
Delta Wedding. New York: Harcourt, Brace, 1946.
"The Demonstrators." *The New Yorker*, November 26, 1966, pp. 56–63.
The Golden Apples. New York: Harcourt, Brace, 1949.
Losing Battles. New York: Random House, 1970.
The Optimist's Daughter. *The New Yorker*, March 15, 1969. Rev. and enl. New York: Random House, 1972.
The Ponder Heart. New York: Harcourt, Brace, 1954.
The Robber Bridegroom. 1942; rpt. New York: Atheneum, 1963.
The Shoe Bird. New York: Harcourt, Brace and World, 1964.
"Where Is the Voice Coming From?" *The New Yorker*, July 6, 1963, pp. 24–25.
The Wide Net and Other Stories. 1943; rpt. in *Selected Stories of Eudora Welty*. New York: Modern Library, 1954.

NONFICTION BY WELTY

"The Corner Store." *Esquire* 84 (December 1975), 161ff.
The Eye of the Story: Selected Essays and Reviews. New York: Random House, 1978.
"How I Write." *Virginia Quarterly Review* 31 (Spring 1955), 240–51.

Ida M'Toy. Urbana: University of Illinois Press, 1979.

"In Yoknapatawpha." *Hudson Review* 1 (Winter 1949), 596–98.

"Looking Back at the First Story." *Georgia Review* 33 (Winter 1979), 751–55.

One Time, One Place. New York: Random House, 1971.

One Writer's Beginnings. Cambridge: Harvard University Press, 1984.

"Place in Fiction." *South Atlantic Quarterly* 55 (January 1956), 57–72.

Review of *Pilgrim at Tinker Creek* by Annie Dillard. *New York Times Book Review*, March 24, 1974, pp. 4–5.

Short Stories. New York: Harcourt, Brace, 1950.

"*Women!!* Make Turban in Own Home!" 1941; rev. and rpt., Palaemon Press Limited, 1979.

INTERVIEWS

Buckley, William F., Jr. "The Southern Imagination: An Interview with Eudora Welty and Walker Percy." Transcript of "Firing Line," Public Broadcasting Service, December 24, 1972. *Mississippi Quarterly* 26 (Fall 1973), 493–516.

Bunting, Charles T. " 'The Interior World': An Interview with Eudora Welty." *Southern Review* 8 (October 1972), 711–35.

Clemons, Walter. "Meeting Miss Welty." *New York Times Book Review*, April 12, 1970, pp. 2, 46.

Ferris, Bill. "A Visit with Eudora Welty," in *Images of the South*. Southern Folklore Reports, No. 1. Memphis: Center for Southern Folklore, 1977, pp. 12–26.

Freeman, Jean Todd. "Eudora Welty." *Conversations with Writers II*. A Bruccoli Clark Book. Detroit: Gale Research Co., 1978, pp. 284–316.

Jones, John Griffin. "Eudora Welty." *Mississippi Writers Talking*. Jackson: University Press of Mississippi, 1982, pp. 3–35.

Kuehl, Linda. "The Art of Fiction XLVII: Eudora Welty." *Paris Review* 55 (Fall 1972), 72–97.

Prenshaw, Peggy Whitman, ed. *Conversations with Eudora Welty*. Jackson: University Press of Mississippi, 1984.

Van Gelder, Robert. "An Interview with Eudora Welty." 1942; rpt. in *Writers and Writing*. New York: Scribner's, 1946.

WORKS ABOUT WELTY: BOOKS, MONOGRAPHS, ESSAY COLLECTIONS

Appel, Alfred, Jr. *A Season of Dreams: The Fiction of Eudora Welty*. Baton Rouge: Louisiana State University Press, 1965.

Boatwright, James, ed. Special issue on Eudora Welty. *Shenandoah* 20 (Spring 1969).

Bryant, J. A., Jr. *Eudora Welty*. Minnesota American Writers Series. Minneapolis: University of Minnesota Press, 1968.

Desmond, John F., ed. *A Still Moment: Essays on the Art of Eudora Welty*. Metuchen, N.J.: Scarecrow Press, 1978.

Devlin, Albert J. *Eudora Welty's Chronicle: A Story of Mississippi Life*. Jackson: University Press of Mississippi, 1983.

Dollarhide, Louis and Ann J. Abadie, eds. *Eudora Welty: A Form of Thanks*. Jackson: University Press of Mississippi, 1979.

Evans, Elizabeth. *Eudora Welty*. Modern Literature Series. New York: Frederick Ungar, 1981.

Howard, Zelma Turner. *The Rhetoric of Eudora Welty's Short Stories*. Jackson: University and College Press of Mississippi, 1973.

Issacs, N. D. *Eudora Welty*. Steck-Vaughn Southern Writers Series. Austin, Tex.: Steck-Vaughn, 1969.

Kreyling, Michael. *Eudora Welty's Achievement of Order*. Baton Rouge: Louisiana State University Press, 1980.

Prenshaw, Peggy Whitman, ed. *Eudora Welty: Critical Essays*. Jackson: University Press of Mississippi, 1979.

Randisi, Jennifer Lynn. *A Tissue of Lies: Eudora Welty and the Southern Romance*. Washington, D.C.: University Press of America, 1982.

Simpson, Lewis P., ed. Special issue on Eudora Welty. *Mississippi Quarterly* 26 (Fall 1973).

Thompson, Victor H. *Eudora Welty: A Reference Guide*. Reference Guides in Literature. Boston: G. K. Hall and Co., 1976.

Vande Kieft, Ruth M. *Eudora Welty*. Twayne's United States Authors Series. New Haven: College and University Press, 1962.

WORKS ABOUT WELTY: ARTICLES AND REVIEWS

Aldridge, J. W. "Eudora Welty: Metamorphosis of a Southern Lady Writer." *Saturday Review*, April 11, 1970, pp. 21ff.

Arnold, Marilyn. "Eudora Welty's Parody." *Notes on Mississippi Writers* 11 (Spring 1978), 15–22.

Boatwright, James. "Speech and Silence in *Losing Battles*." *Shenandoah* 25 (Spring 1974), 3–14.

Bryant, J. A., Jr. "Seeing Double in *The Golden Apples*." *Sewanee Review* 82 (Spring 1974), 300–315.

Carson, F. D. " 'The Song of the Wandering Aengus': Allusion in *The Golden Apples*." Notes on Mississippi Writers 6 (Spring 1973), 14–17.

Carson, Gary. "The Romantic Tradition in Eudora Welty's *A Curtain of Green*." *Notes on Mississippi Writers* 9 (Fall 1976), 97–100.

Davis, Charles E. "The South in Eudora Welty's Fiction: A Changing World." *Studies in American Fiction* 3 (Autumn 1975), 199–209.

Eisinger, Chester E. "Eudora Welty and the Triumph of the Imagination." *Fiction of the Forties*. Chicago: University of Chicago Press, 1963, pp. 258–83.

Emerson, O. B. Manuscript of speech prepared for meeting of National Council of Teachers of English, 1974.

Fleischauer, John F. "The Focus of Mystery: Eudora Welty's Prose Style." *Southern Literary Journal* 5 (Spring 1973), 64–79.

Glenn, Eunice. "Fantasy in the Fiction of Eudora Welty." *A Southern Vanguard*, ed. Allen Tate. New York: Prentice-Hall, 1947, pp. 78–91.

Gossett, Louise Y. "Eudora Welty's New Novel: The Comedy of Loss." *Southern Literary Journal* 3 (Fall 1970), 122–37.

―――. "Violence as Revelation: Eudora Welty." *Violence in Recent Southern Fiction*. Durham, N.C.: Duke University Press, 1965, pp. 98–117.

Hardy, John E. "*Delta Wedding* as Region and Symbol." *Sewanee Review* 60 (Summer 1952), 397–417.

Haupt, Christopher Lehmann. Review of *Losing Battles*. *New York Times*, April 10, 1970, p. 37.

Holland, Robert B. "Dialogue as a Reflection of Place in *The Ponder Heart*." *American Literature* 35 (November 1963), 352–58.

Howell, Elmo. "Eudora Welty and the City of Man." *Georgia Review* 33 (Winter 1979), 770–82.

―――. "Eudora Welty and the Use of Place in Southern Fiction." *Arizona Quarterly* 28 (Autumn 1972), 248–56.

Jones, Alun R. "The World of Love: The Fiction of Eudora Welty." In *The Creative Present*, ed. Nona Balakian and Charles Simmons. Garden City, N.Y.: Doubleday, 1963, pp. 175–92.

Jones, William M. "Name and Symbol in the Prose of Eudora Welty." *Southern Folklore Quarterly* 22 (December 1958), 173–85.

Landess, Thomas H. "More Trouble in Mississippi: Family vs. Antifamily in Miss Welty's *Losing Battles*." *Sewanee Review* 79 (Autumn 1971), 626–34.

McHaney, Thomas L. "Eudora Welty and the Multitudinous Golden Apples." *Mississippi Quarterly* 26 (Fall 1973), 589–624.

MacKethan, Lucinda H. "To See Things in Their Time: The Art of Focus in Eudora Welty's Fiction." *American Literature* 50 (1978), 258–75.

McMillen, William E. "Conflict and Resolution in Welty's *Losing Battles*." *Critique* (Summer 1973), 110–24.

Marshall, Margaret. "Notes by the Way." *Nation*, September 10, 1949, p. 256.

Masserand, Anne. "Eudora Welty's Travellers." *Southern Literary Journal* 3 (Spring 1971), 39–48.

May, Charles E. "Why Sister Lives at the P. O." *Southern Humanities Review* 12 (Summer 1978), 243–49.

Moore, Carol A. "The Insulation of Illusion and *Losing Battles*." *Mississippi Quarterly* 26 (Fall 1973), 651–58.

Myers, Susan L. "Dialogues in Eudora Welty's Short Stories." *Notes on Mississippi Writers* 8 (Fall 1975), 51–57.

"New Writer." *Time*, November 24, 1941, p. 111.

Phillips, Robert L. "Patterns of Vision in Welty's *The Optimist's Daughter*." *Southern Literary Journal* 14 (Fall 1981), 10–23.

Porter, Katherine Anne. "Introduction." *A Curtain of Green and Other Stories* by Eudora Welty. 1941; rpt. in Welty's *Selected Stories of Eudora Welty*, pp. xi–xxiii.

Ransom, John Crowe. "Delta Fiction." *Kenyon Review* 8 (Summer 1946), 503–7.

Ricks, Christopher. "Females and Other Impersonators." Review of *Losing Battles. New York Review of Books*, July 23, 1970, pp. 8–13.

Rubin, Louis D., Jr. "Everything Brought Out in the Open: Eudora Welty's *Losing Battles*." *Hollins Critic* 7 (June 1970), 1–12.

Stroup, Sheila. " 'We're All Part of It Together': Eudora Welty's Hopeful Vision in *Losing Battles*." *Southern Literary Journal* 15 (Spring 1983), 42–58.

Trilling, Diana. "Fiction in Review." Review of *The Wide Net. Nation*, October 2, 1943, pp. 386–87.

Warren, Robert Penn. "Love and Separateness in Eudora Welty." *Kenyon Review* 6 (Spring 1944); rpt. in *Selected Essays*. New York: Vintage Books, 1958, pp. 156–69.

Wood, Michael. "Cunning Time." Review of *The Optimist's Daughter. New York Review of Books*, June 29, 1972, pp. 8–9.

Yardley, Jonathan. "The Last Good One?" *New Republic*, May 9, 1970, pp. 33–36.

———. "The New Old Southern Novel." *The Partisan Review* 40, no. 2 (1973), 286–93.

Young, Thomas Daniel. "Miss Welty and the Art of Fiction." Review of *Eudora Welty's Achievement of Order*, by Michael Kreyling. *Sewanee Review* 90 (Spring 1982), xiii–xiv.

OTHER SOURCES (FICTION INCLUDED IS LIMITED TO WORKS QUOTED)

Benjamin, Walter. "The Storyteller." In *Illuminations*, ed. Hannah Arendt, trans. Harry Zohn. New York: Harcourt, Brace and World, Inc., 1968, pp. 83–109.

Bradbury, John M. *Renaissance in the South*. Chapel Hill: University of North
    Carolina Press, 1963.
Cabell, James Branch. *Let Me Lie*. New York: Farrar, Straus, 1947.
Calhoun, Richard James. "Southern Writing: The Unifying Strand." *Missis-
    sippi Quarterly* 27 (Winter 1973–74), 101–8.
Cash, W. J. *The Mind of the South*. 1941; rpt. New York: Vintage Books,
    n.d.
Dorson, Richard M. *American Folklore*. Chicago: University of Chicago Press,
    1959.
————. *American Folklore and the Historian*. Chicago: University of Chi-
    cago Press, 1971.
Faulkner, William. *Sartoris*. 1929; rpt. New York: Random House, 1956.
Fielding, Henry. "Author's Preface." *Joseph Andrews*. 1742; rpt. in *Joseph
    Andrews/Shamela*, ed. Martin C. Battestin. Riverside edn. Boston:
    Houghton Mifflin, 1961, pp. 7–12.
Frazer, James George. *The Golden Bough*. Abridged edn. 1922; rpt. New York:
    Macmillan, 1963.
Gayley, Charles Mills. *The Classic Myths in English Literature and in Art*.
    1893; rev. and enl., 1911; rpt. Boston: Ginn, 1939.
Gray, Richard. *The Literature of Memory: Modern Writers of the American
    South*. Baltimore: Johns Hopkins University Press, 1977.
Hamilton, Edith. *Mythology: Timeless Tales of Gods and Heroes*. 1942; rpt.
    New York: New American Library, n.d.
Hoffman, Frederick J. *The Art of Southern Fiction*. Carbondale: Southern Il-
    linois Press, 1967.
Holman, Hugh C. *The Roots of Southern Writing: Essays on the Literature of
    the South*. Athens: University of Georgia Press, 1972.
Humphrey, William. *The Ordways*. New York: Alfred A. Knopf, 1965.
Inge, M. Thomas, ed. *The Frontier Humorists*. Hamden, Conn.: Archon Books,
    1975.
Kelley, Edith Summers. *Weeds*. 1923; rpt. Carbondale: Southern Illinois Uni-
    versity Press, 1972.
Kennedy, John Pendleton. *Swallow Barn*. 1832; rpt. and ed. Jay B. Hubbell,
    American Authors Series. New York: Harcourt, Brace, 1929.
King, Richard H. *A Southern Renaissance: The Cultural Awakening of the
    American South, 1930–1955*. New York: Oxford University Press, 1980.
Lytle, Andrew. "Foreword." *A Novel, a Novella and Four Stories*. New York:
    McDowell, Obolensky, 1958.
Morris, Willie. "A Sense of Place and the Americanization of Mississippi."
    The Southern Quarterly 17 (Spring-Summer 1979), 3–13.
Percy, Walker. *The Moviegoer*. New York: Alfred A. Knopf, 1962.
Porter, Katherine Anne. "Old Mortality." *Pale Horse, Pale Rider*. New York:
    Harcourt, Brace, 1939.

————. "The Old Order." *The Leaning Tower and Other Stories*. New York: Harcourt, Brace, 1944.

Ransom, John Crowe. *The World's Body*. 1938; rpt. Baton Rouge: Louisiana State University Press, 1968.

Reed, Roy. "Revisiting the Southern Mind." *New York Times Magazine*, December 5, 1976, pp. 42–43ff.

Rosengarten, Theodore. *All God's Dangers: The Life of Nate Shaw*. New York: Alfred A. Knopf, 1975.

Rouse, Blair. *Ellen Glasgow*. Twayne's United States Authors Series. New Haven: College and University Press, 1962.

Rubin, Louis D., Jr. *The Curious Death of the Novel*. Baton Rouge: Louisiana State University Press, 1967.

————. *Writers of the Modern South: The Faraway Country*. Seattle: University of Washington Press, 1966.

Rubin, Louis D., Jr. and C. Hugh Holman, eds. *Southern Literary Study: Problems and Possiblities*. Chapel Hill: University of North Carolina Press, 1975.

Severo, Richard. "A 17th Century Tree in Newburgh May Be 20th Century Traffic Victim." *New York Times*, June 25, 1974, p. 33.

Simonini, R. C., Jr., ed. *Southern Writers: Appraisals in Our Time*. Charlottesville: University Press of Virginia, 1961.

Skaggs, Merrill M. *The Folk of Southern Fiction: A Study in Local Color Traditions*. Athens: University of Georgia Press, 1972.

Sullivan, Walter. *A Requiem for the Renascence: The State of Fiction in the Modern South*. Mercer University Lamar Memorial Lectures, No. 18. Athens: University of Georgia Press, 1976.

Tate, Allen. *Collected Essays*. Denver: Alan Swallow, 1959.

Twelve Southerners. *I'll Take My Stand*. 1930; rpt. Harper Torchbook edn. New York: Harper and Brothers, 1962.

Warren, Robert Penn. *All the King's Men*. 1946; rpt. New York: Bantam Books, 1971.

Young, Stark. *So Red the Rose*. New York: Charles Scribner's Sons, 1934.

Young, Thomas Daniel. *The Past in the Present: A Thematic Study of Modern Southern Fiction*. Baton Rouge: Louisiana State University Press, 1981.

INDEX

About the Author

CAROL S. MANNING is Assistant Professor of English at Mary Washington College, Fredericksburg, Virginia.